# Critical Essays on Henry James: The Early Novels

HENRY JAMES
(1843–1916)
From the *Century*, November 1882

# Critical Essays on Henry James: The Early Novels

## James W. Gargano

G.K. Hall & Co. • Boston, Massachusetts

Library of Congress Cataloging in Publication Data

Critical Essays on Henry James: The Early Novels.

(Critical essays on American literature)

Includes index.                                    ·
1. James, Henry, 1843–1916—Criticism and
interpretation. I. Gargano, James W. II. Series.
PS2117.C75    1987         813'.4        87-226
ISBN 0-8161-8876-9 (alk. paper)
    0-8161-8882-3 (set)

*This publication is printed on permanent/durable acid-free paper*
*MANUFACTURED IN THE UNITED STATES OF AMERICA*

# CRITICAL ESSAYS ON AMERICAN LITERATURE

This series seeks to anthologize the most important criticism on a wide variety of topics and writers in American literature. Our readers will find in various volumes not only a generous selection of reprinted articles and reviews but original essays, bibliographies, manuscript sections, and other materials brought to public attention for the first time. This volume on Henry James, the first of two, contains a selection of reprinted reviews and comments by many of James's contemporaries, including Edgar Fawcett and William Dean Howells. There are also reprinted articles by Richard Poirier, James Tuttleton, William H. Gass, Leon Edel, Irving Howe, and many others. In addition to an extensive introduction by James W. Gargano, there is an original essay by Adeline Tintner written especially for publication in this volume. We are confident that this volume will make a permanent and significant contribution to American literary study.

JAMES NAGEL, GENERAL EDITOR

*Northeastern University*

# CONTENTS

# INTRODUCTION

More than sixty years ago, Van Wyck Brooks pictured Henry James as an anemic virtuoso who preferred European drawing rooms to the vitality of his native land.[1] Today, with the approach of the 150th anniversary of his birth, James ranks with Hawthorne, Melville, and Twain as one of the supreme American novelists of the nineteenth century. In addition, his assured reputation as critic, travel writer, autobiographer, and appraiser of the American scene has established him as perhaps the most versatile man of letters his country has produced. Uniquely among his American peers, moreover, he may be regarded as a major British writer and as a seminal force in the development of modern experimental fiction.

Since his death in 1916, James has grown from a cult figure treasured by the fastidious few to a writer whose novels and tales continue to win readers and to turn up in various guises on television, in films, and on the stage. Academic critics pore over even his minor works for new nuances, and novels like *What Maisie Knew, The Awkward Age,* and *The Sacred Fount* threaten to attract a satellite critical literature as *The American, The Portrait of a Lady, The Turn of the Screw,* and *The Ambassadors* have already done. Credit for the phenomenon once called the James revival must go to discerning admirers like Percy Lubbock, Joseph Warren Beach, F. O. Matthiessen, Philip Rahv, F. R. Leavis, T. S. Eliot, Constance Rourke, Lionel Trilling, and R. P. Blackmur. The publication of *The Notebooks of Henry James* gave a further impetus to research by affording an intimate view of James's passionate engagement with his art.[2] Perhaps the greatest stimulus to a reevaluation of James, however, has been given by Leon Edel in his roles as editor, bibliographer, and critic. Professor Edel's five-volume biography has divested James of the magisterial remoteness of his later years and revealed him in his vulnerable, many-faceted, and appealing humanity. Equally valuable, Edel's edition of the *Letters* shows James as he saw himself, as he wanted others to see him, and for all his precautions, as he never meant to be seen.

A survey of recent bibliographical essays in the *Henry James Review* will reveal that James's life and work are being analyzed from every conceivable perspective by a growing number of scholars. Apparently, Arthur

1

L. Scott's "A Protest Against the James Vogue" (1952) and Maxwell Geismar's attack in *Henry James and the Jacobites* (1963) have not availed against the tidal wave of interest in James.[3]

# I

Henry James, Jr., was born in New York City on 15 April 1843 into a family notable for its financial and intellectual achievements. The novelist's grandfather emigrated to the United States from Ireland in 1789 and prospered in his new homeland, becoming a director of banks and the kind of earnest civic leader who helped to set his adopted country on the materialistic course from which the author of *The Ambassadors* carefully distanced himself. Yet, the three million dollars he left his children enabled them to live in relative prosperity and made possible the milieu into which Henry James, Jr., was born.

Henry James Sr. did not share his father's fundamentalist Presbyterian faith or his passion for profit and public affairs. Instead, after graduation from Union College, he floundered through years of religious uncertainty before arriving at the solace of Swedenborgianism. The elder Henry's early inadequacy and troubled quest for spiritual fulfillment may have had their mixed origins in the crippling amputation of a leg and in antipathy to the Calvinist deity who, he confessed, filled his childhood with "insane terror." In any case, his psychological unrest reached a terrible climax when, in a hallucinatory moment, he was tormented by a "damned shape" exuding "from his fetid personality influences fatal to life."[4] Fortunately, Swedenborgianism taught him to accept this "vastation" as the first phase in the process of regeneration; then, like a good convert, he preached, through lectures, magazine articles, and books, a philosophy of emancipation from oppressive ecclesiasticism and a brand of Fourierism that would free mankind from economic competition and materialistic obsessions.

Henry James, Sr.,'s writing, characteristic examples of which can be found in F. O. Matthiessen's *The James Family*, is more notable for its stylistic verve and spirit of inquiry than for its resolutions. Rich in metaphor and humorous quirkiness of phrase, its message was largely ignored by a secular and technological age. To an individualistic America, he inveighed against "selfhood" as an instrument of human corruption and social degeneracy; to a laissez-faire nation he prescribed love, brotherhood, and spirituality in terms as elusive but less inspirational than those of his friend Emerson.

The children of such a philosophic Quixote were bound to be innocent victims of his zeal. His educational ideals kept them moving from one less than perfect school to another, and he jealously shielded them from influences that might compromise their morals or afflict them with provincial, vocational, or utilitarian biases. In the United States, the nomadic Jameses lived between New York, Albany, and Cambridge; in Europe, Henry Sr.'s shortlived enthusiasms took them to England, France, Switzerland, and Germany. By promoting such exclusions and uprootings, the well-intentioned father, who wished to spare his children growing pains similar to his own, perhaps contrived new problems for them.

Of Henry Sr.'s five children, the youngest, Alice (1848–92) is generally remembered as a chronic invalid who confessed two years before her death: "I am working away as hard as I can to get dead as soon as possible."[5] Yet, her *Diary* reveals a witty and compassionate intelligence that places even her illnesses in healthy perspective. Alternately gossipy and searchingly analytical, she speaks through a persona that saw "the jocose humbuggery called Life" as a "contest between my body and my will."[6] In a spirit not unworthy of her famous brothers, she sustained herself with the belief "that the only thing which survives is the resistance we bring to life and not the strain life brings to us."[7]

The short life of Garth Wilkinson James (1845–83), known as Wilky to his family, had a moment of glory and an aftermath of bad luck and poor health. The least literary of the James children, he fought with distinction in the Union Army in the Civil War and was severely wounded in the famous assault on Fort Wagner. His postwar career began inauspiciously, however, when he and his brother Robertson failed in their attempt to operate a plantation in Florida with the help of paid Negro laborers. Abandoning his scheme, he plunged into other unfortunate ventures that strained his father's resources.

Like Wilky, Robertson (1846–1910) served gallantly in the war but broke down before the quieter rigors of civilian life. He failed in business, destroyed his marriage by compulsive philandering, and struggled against alcoholism. Even brotherly loyalty could not restrain Henry from referring to "Bob's" "brutalities" and "terrible personality" and describing his death as a "painless, enviable end to a stormy career."[8]

In contrast to Wilky and Robertson, William James (1842–1910) attained eminence in his profession, fame as a thinker and writer, and happiness in marriage. Yet, for all his youthful charm and precocity, his success came only after painful misdirections and an almost maddening crisis that resembled his father's vastation. Although he overcame his psychological traumas, poor health and the search for cures became obstinate facts of life for him. Finally, after "false" starts in painting and the practice of medicine, he joined the Harvard faculty and settled into a career as a popular teacher and the author of enduring works of psychology and philosophy.

In a letter to T. S. Perry, Henry James described the effect that William's death had upon him: "he had been my ideal Elder brother, and I still, through all the years, saw in him, even as a small timorous boy yet, my protector, my backer, my authority and my pride. His extinction changes the face of life for me—besides the mere missing of his inexhaustible company, personality, originality, the whole unspeakably vivid and beautiful presence of him."[9] Touching as it is, Henry's cri de coeur does not tell the whole story about a relationship that may have been a source of anxiety as well as strength. To the younger brother William displayed from youth what must have seemed an enviable genius for living, a talent for painting, and an ability to cope with those elements of education that intimidated Henry.

Of course, all the members of the family helped to form Henry James's complex inner life. Although he never adopted his father's religious notions, he never renounced his distrust of materialism and his goal of converting the flux of life into the stuff of consciousness. It may be, also, that Henry Sr.'s disability and impracticality turned the sensitive boy toward his protective mother whose favorite he became. Some critics suggest that the strong maternal presence during his youth accounts for the recurrence of dominant women and pallid male figures in much of James's fiction. It may be, too, that William's boyhood precocity and the younger brother's assumption of manhood in the Civil War may have confirmed Henry in his developing spectatorial engagement with life.

Although autobiography when written by a novelist often resembles fiction, it may be profitable to see James's beginnings as he preferred to chronicle them. In A Small Boy and Others, he recalls, in a new century and with the charm and perversities of his later style, the innocence and "naturalness" of the Old New York in which he, his brothers, and his sister grew up as "hotel children." Stressing that the United States was "young with its own juvenility," he records with epicurean delight a feast of theater-going, visits to Barnum's "halls of humbug," forays into bookstores, visits to churches of various denominations, and treats in ice-cream parlors. He describes the freedom with which he, his brothers, and cousins, explored their immediate world in a manner "worthy of the golden age," but his rhapsodies fasten on particularities remembered with sharpness and detail.[10]

James's "re-created" childhood resembles that of the heroine of What Maisie Knew in his gaping, amassing of memories, and divining of answers. He summons up pleasures in Albany as well as urban joys in New York as elements in a life of observation that seizes upon and infuses meaning into cities, houses, and the humanity peopling them. He wonders, more darkly than a child of the golden age, about aunts and uncles who make up a "chronicle of early deaths, arrested careers, broken promises, orphaned children"; the "radiant and rare" Minny Temple, doomed to early extinction but reincarnated in two of James's greatest heroines; and extraordinary relatives who loom as willing accomplices to unjust fates. In reliving his past, James calls it "an education like another," but the pupil emerges as an avid one who merely wishes "to be somewhere—almost anywhere would do—and somehow receive an impression or an accession, feel a relation or a vibration."[11]

Accidental education taught the young Henry more than he would glean from the series of schools he attended in New York or in Europe.

Home taught him a distrust of business, a relish for inconsistency and paradox, and an easy tolerance of every species of religious opinion. In contrast,
the classroom represented confinement and intellectual apathy. At home,
he experimented with playwriting and tried his hand at drawing in emula-
tion of his brother; in his street adventures, he considered Broadway "one
of the alleys of Eden"; but he remains amazed that "my association with
my 'studies,' . . . should be with almost anything but the fact of learning."[12]

James's first fully experienced stay in Europe, lasting from 1855 to
1858, furnished richer material than New York for the form of education he
called "taking in," "appropriating," and "possessing." With the probing
eyes and imagination of a destined novelist, the adolescent American saw
Cruikshank types in London, Thackerayan originals in Boulogne-sur-mer,
and a real Empress in Paris. His powers of assimilation, so negligible when
challenged by arithmetic, increased to voracity at exhibits at the National
Gallery and among the treasures of the Louvre. Contact with Europe accel-
erated the education of the impressionistic youth who maturely decided
that "one way of taking life was to go in for everything and everyone, which
kept you abundantly occupied, and the other way was to be as occupied
. . . with the sense and the image of it all, and on only a fifth of the actual
immersion."[13]

Well before Henry James reached his majority he felt more alive in
Europe than in his Edenic America. As his autobiography attests, he consoled himself when exiled to Newport and Cambridge by reading the *Re-
vue des Deux Mondes*. For all his subsequent tergiversations and divided
loyalties, he had perhaps as early as the 1860s been too fundamentally
drawn to Europe to renounce it. Even his friends in Newport took on importance because of their connection with art and Europe: William Hunt,
under whom William studied painting, had been taught by French masters, and it was under the tutelage of John La Farge, an "embodiment of
the gospel of aesthetics" and the type of the "European," that he read Balzac and Browning, writers who were to influence him profoundly.

The Civil War deferred James's hopes for settling in Europe and complicated his relations with his native land at a time of crisis. In his autobiography, he ascribes his failure to enlist to a back injury that became a "less
and less bearable affliction," but which "a great surgeon" treated with a
"comparative pooh-pooh."[14] Attempts to explain this mysterious injury have
taxed the ingenuity of biographers and critics who have variously interpreted it as a real or figurative castration, a psychosomatic response to the demands of a painful duty, or a rationalization for avoiding the perils of the
battlefield. Nevertheless, although James saw the conflict from the safety
of the Harvard Law School, his recollections in *Notes of a Son and Brother*
betray a large emotional investment in its events.

At Harvard, James dutifully sat through lectures and, according to a
later confession, broke down in an attempt to argue a case "in the fierce
light of a 'moot court.'" Soon after his inevitable withdrawal from law

school, he launched his literary career with the anonymous publication of a short story, "A Tragedy of Errors," in the *Continental Monthly* for February 1864. Thirteen months later, "The Story of a Year," significantly about the war, inaugurated a long association with the *Atlantic Monthly*. Proof that self-education had progressed in the midst of academic ineptitude is evident in James's reviews for the *Nation* and the *North American Review*, during the 1860s, of novels, poems and critical essays by prominent and not so prominent French, British, and American writers. With characteristic urbanity and a mastery of a style always copious and sometimes dazzling, James solidified his position among the best magazine critics in America. He took most pride, however, in the more than dozen short stories printed between 1865 and 1870 in the *Atlantic* and the *Galaxy*. As late as 1914, he could still savor the "blest violence" experienced upon receiving Howells's acceptance of his first submission to the *Atlantic*.[15]

James's literary successes in America did not lessen the attractions of Europe. Indeed, renewed visits to England after the war and the discovery of Italy in 1869–70 were followed by another European venture (1872–74) spent partly in Paris and in Rome. After a brief repatriation, he was again in Paris (1875–76) enjoying the society and literary talk of Ivan Turgenev and the members of Flaubert's *cénacle:* a note of cosmopolite self-satisfaction rings through his confession to Howells in 1876 that "I am turning into an old and very contented Parisian."[16] Six months later, he tells his father of his decision to emigrate to London, and once established in Bolton Street at the end of 1876, he assures his sister Alice that, despite the "darkness, dirt, and poverty and general unaesthetic *cachet*" of the English capital, he is extremely glad to have settled there.[17]

James's expatriation came after many withdrawals from and retreats to the United States, many high hopes indulged and frustrated and a sense of estrangement overcome. In Florence, in 1869, he admits his awareness of "the bitterness of exile," and, at the same time, he responds rapturously to the allure of Italy. Amidst Rome's many appeals, he confides to William that he is "perpetually and deliciously preoccupied with home." Feeling himself outside the vital stream of Italian and French society, he asks Howells: "What is the meaning of this destiny of desolate exile?"[18] At the beginning of 1874, James laments that Americans can never have any but an "artificial" relation to Europe; in March, he tells his parents that he likes Europe more and more; and by May he closes a letter to William with "I could howl with homesickness." It was hard for James to be an American in Europe, but it was harder for him to be "European" in Cambridge or New York. When at the age of thirty he proclaimed that "I take possession of the old world—I inhale it—I appropriate it!"[19]—he chose not to repudiate the United States but to live in the midst of visual richness and social complexity that, he felt, most fully fed his art.

James's inability to immerse himself in the many streams of American life prevented him from writing novels like Howells's *A Modern Instance* or *The Rise of Silas Lapham,* but with rejections came compensatory accumulations. Living in and between two worlds, he had the luck to be present at a major historical event, the American post-war irruption into Europe. He knew the old families who with their inherited wealth bought or rented villas and acquired Italian and French art and bibelots; he knew the aesthetes, the pleasure-seekers, and the merely curious; and he met overworked businessmen and girls, not at all like Minny Temple, on their old-world romps. Detached, ironic, and fascinated by nuances of manners, he was uniquely prepared to ring as many changes on the "international theme" as the variety of his compatriots warranted.

## II

Before freeing himself to "international" fiction, James had limited some of his apprentice work to American scenes and subjects. Still, the American setting of his first novel, *Watch and Ward,* has little visual richness or depth. Serialized in the *Atlantic* from August to December 1871, it includes among its characters a ruined and desperate adventurer from the American west whose suicide intimates James's early aversion to financial speculators; his daughter, Nora Lambert, who becomes the ward of the unromantic hero, Roger Lawrence; the Reverend Hubert Lawrence, the hero's handsome cousin and a genteel philanderer among his flock; and George Fenton, the heroine's shifty, fortune-hunting cousin. These characters, except for Fenton, can be detached from their milieu, and his predatoriness betrays James's bias against the crude young apostles of American enterprise and opportunism.

The author of *Watch and Ward* demonstrates less promise as a painter of American character and environment than as a student of the inner tremors and sudden insights that accompany growth in consciousness. Notably, too, Roger's design of educating his ward as a model wife for himself shows the young novelist's concern with one character's attempt, in this case surprisingly benign, to mould another to his needs. Mrs. Keith's role as the hero's counsellor looks forward to James's more sophisticated use of the confidante or *ficelle,* and the opposition between the two Lawrences foreshadows what S. Gorley Putt calls "a tendency to distribute over two or more contrasting characters . . . the split personality of the geminian author."[20] In addition, despite the artifice of its central situation, the novel has the stylistic finish, the symmetrically balanced incidents, and the poised irony of a writer steeped in the best Gallic fiction.

Because James postponed the book publication of *Watch and Ward* till 1878, many reviewers compared it to *Roderick Hudson* and *The American,* and, in most cases found it inferior to both. In its highly favorable notice, *Appleton's Journal* declared it much "less ambitious in scope than Mr. James's later and more famous novels," and the *New York Times* qualified its good opinion by stating that comparisons with "the later works . . . attest the progress he has made." In contrast to the *Boston Evening Transcript*, which pronounced it "infinitely more pleasant" though less artistic than the *American*, the *New York World* patronized it as of "slight interest," and the *Nation* evinced little enthusiasm. The *Chicago Tribune* and the *Philadelphia North American* considered it admirable, and the English *Athenaeum* commended it as "bright and full of interest."

With rare prescience, the *Times* asserted that James should "now . . . be classed with the very few leading romance writers of England and America." *Appleton's* went farther in forecasting that *Watch and Ward* would take its place "beside those other volumes which may sometime be cited as evidence that that long-prophesied American novelist has at length appeared." In its appreciation, the *Literary World* distinguished *Watch and Ward* from the mass of contemporary novels as a "story which just misses being perfect."[21]

Twentieth-century critics have disagreed more about the sophistication and conscious art of *Watch and Ward* than about its merits. Leon Edel points out examples in it of "innocent erotic statement" and imagery, while Oscar Cargill and Putt insist on James's fully conscious use of sexual symbolism, and Richard Poirier admits to being uncertain "in these earlier efforts that James is aware of the psychological peculiarities of his heroes." However, even Cargill, who cites the novel's bold and "free inquiry into the nature" of love as its chief value and Putt, who accepts it as a "charming and underrated story," concede *Watch and Ward* to be distinctly minor.[22]

Of course, James's own decision to exclude it from the New York Edition of his fiction indicates no lasting regard for it: indeed, he could rate it in a letter to his father as "very thin, and as 'cold' as an icicle."[23]

With *Roderick Hudson*, published in 1875 as it neared its year-long run in the *Atlantic*, James achieved stature as a leading American writer. Whatever its faults, the novel dramatizes the international theme with complexity, creates a convincing Roman ambiance, and portrays a gallery of American characters who reveal their natures in the chiaroscuro of the European scene. Although James's center of consciousness, Rowland Mallet, resembles Roger Lawrence of *Watch and Ward* in attempting to mould Roderick's life, he moves in a denser medium and contends with a volatile, perhaps suicidal personality. Moreover, the psychological keenness of James's novel clearly derives from its larger conception and its surer craftsmanship; whereas in *Watch and Ward*, Europe functions as a finishing school for the ladylike heroine, in *Roderick* it takes on symbolic dimensions and bristles with seductions that lure Hudson to self-destruction. In addition, the secondary figures in *Watch and Ward* exist to enhance Roger's modest perfections while Mallet and his protege emphasize each other's incompleteness and are further defined by a congeries of acquaintances. Clearly, too, Nora and Mrs. Keith pale before Roderick's anxious mother and the sympathetic antiheroine, Christina, whose Cleopatra-like histrionics contrast with the general control of the half-developed New England nun, Mary Garland. Finally, by making Rowland his central observer, James began his career-long preoccupation with the analysis of an intense consciousness in the act of perceiving and interpreting himself and other characters as parts of his life.

British reviewers generally lavished encomiums on the novel's art and regretted its unpleasantness and tragic denouement. The British *Quarterly Review*, for instance, granted James an "almost supreme ability" in the exercise of a "rare faculty of moral analysis," but shrank from the pessimism that reduces his novel to the dark wisdom of Ecclesiastes. Although pleased by a "realism as vivid as that of a Dutch painter," the reviewer asked whether the author aspired to be "the Schopenhauer of modern fiction." In a notice that James dismissed as "with all respect inane," the *Spectator* applied the word "dismal" to most aspects of *Roderick*. More tolerantly, the *Academy* noted that James's wit and liveliness modify the influence of Turgenev and make his book "only pleasantly discomfortable." Obviously preferring James's more agreeable stories, the *Westminster Review* feared that *Roderick*, like so many "inferior" productions of good writers, will be more popular than his "better works."[24]

Praise predominates in the American reviews though the *New York Times* criticized James for his fastidiousness and the *Nation* objected to the indirect presentation of Roderick from Mallet's point of view. The *Nation* also singled out "the anomalous relation" of the two main characters as so "strange a flaw as to damage" the whole novel. James's friend, Sarah Wister, in the *North American Review* complained of the characters' interminable talk and inaction, James's lack of human warmth, and the failure of Roderick as a convincing hero. Still, the review accords the work distinction, and the *Times,* for all its strictures, hails *Roderick* as "one of the best novels produced in America of late years."[25]

Perhaps the most discriminating and thorough analyses appeared in the *Atlantic* and the *New York World*. The former, which James referred to as a "charming notice," remarks on a "certain chilliness" in *Roderick's* "aesthetic perfection" but dwells on its salient virtues—the portraits of Christina Light and the young sculptor, the subtle movement of the plot from one surprise to another, and the vivacity and variety of style which lend a "certain indestructibleness" to the "texture of Mr. James's language." More measured in its commendation, the *World* spoke for those "patriotic critics" who will celebrate *Roderick* as "the best romance we have produced . . . since the 'Marble Faun' was written." The reviewer further applauds the effectiveness with which James's scenic descriptions advance his narrative, and he found Mallet as fine a creation as Thackeray's Dobbin. Indeed, his principal demur is that, though the main characters are brilliantly presented, the minor figures remain shadowy.[26]

James thought well enough of his first long novel to submit it to intensive revision and to include it in the New York Edition. Much admired by Robert Louis Stevenson, who preferred it to *The Portrait of a Lady, Roder-*

*ick* has been perhaps exorbitantly praised by F. R. Leavis as a book that can be "read at the adult level of demand in a way that no novel of Thackeray's will bear." Leavis's authority, however, has not forstalled controversy about the book. Some critics have been repelled by its melodramatic ending and others have assumed that James weakened his narrative by making Mallet a reflector of his own ideas. Attacking the view of Mallet as a priggish stand-in for his creator, Oscar Cargill maintains that James preserved his authorial objectivity by lodging his point of view in a character whose interference in Roderick's life precipitates disaster. In a recent article, Peter J. Conn argues that Rowland, instead of acting as a "surrogate for James's moral imagination," is an egotist whose "arrogated divinity" cruelly sacrifices his artist-victim. This is a far cry from Richard Poirier's contention that Mallet and Christina "represent, in humanly fallible form, the absolute standard of full consciousness" and the "willingness to be selfless in the interest of an ideal." As the reviewers of James's novel could not help seeing, Rowland and Roderick are strangely linked and curiously polar. Not surprisingly, modern critics have interpreted them as disparate parts of James himself or, in Edward Engleberg's terms, as conscience and consciousness, mirroring and perhaps reevaluating the Arnoldean dichotomies of Hebraism and Hellenism. The question that persists, however, is whether James has so polarized his characters as to make any resolution impossible.[27]

Appeal to James's preface to the New York Edition will not resolve the problems raised by his fiction. In acting as his own critic, James apologizes for the improbable motivation of Rowland's passion for Mary Garland, the too rapid collapse of Hudson's genius, and the mismanagement of the antithesis between the highly "coloured" Christina and the "plain" Mary Garland. James does, however, clarify his aesthetic intention in terms of the character he regards as *his* hero: "The centre of interest throughout 'Roderick' is in Rowland Mallet's consciousness, and the drama is the very drama of that consciousness."[28]

Since its appearance from June 1876 to May 1877 in the *Atlantic, The American* has held its position as a favorite among James's international novels. With patent similarities to *Roderick,* it excels its predecessor in its wit and ironic dialogue, the complex interrelationships of its characters, and its sharp delineation of minor figures like Babcock, the fussy Unitarian minister, Urbain de Bellegarde's inanely audacious wife, the pathetically genteel M. Nioche, and the bonvivant drifter, Tom Tristram. While looking backward, however, *The American* refines upon the patterns, techniques, and ideas that would remain, in various transformations, constants in much of James's later fiction. For Newman, Europe archetypically functions as the theater which captivates the American imagination and dashes the aspirations it inspires. The novel's action moves from a phase in which the innocent Newman, like Roderick and some protagonists of James's twentieth-century novels, commands opportunity to another phase in which he must face personal limitations and social realities that frustrate his desires. The confidante becomes a staple of James fiction in *The American*, but Mrs. Tristram's feline sophistication lends a new individuality to that role. Valentin de Bellegarde acts as the hero's geminian counterpart, and Mme. de Bellegarde, her son Urbain, and Noémie Nioche resemble other Jamesian exploiters who use their talents, status, or sexual magnetism to wreck lives. Notably, too, *The American* abounds in recurring imagery, motifs drawn from art, analogous and parallel situations, and other symmetries that signify the author's endemic passion for the precise, perhaps finicky ordering of structure. Finally, Newman's involvement in events that cross the bounds of realism into melodrama and even a fairy-tale ambiance gives him a kinship with the mythic princesses and ambassadors of James's later works.

Reviews of *The American* are too numerous and diverse to be categorized, but as James W. Tuttleton has shown many of them disapproved of the novel's ending as reflecting James's chronic tendency to leave tensions and antinomies unresolved.[29] In addition, a number of the English reviewers, like the critic for the *Spectator*, objected to the subject matter of *The American* as "scarcely agreeable." In one notice for the *Academy*, George Saintsbury took James to task for emulating Balzac's habit of analyzing unpleasant people; in a second notice, he repeated his charge that the novelist expended "immense pains on characters . . . not worth the trouble." *Blackwood's* vacillated between praise of James's narrative skill and wonder at the improbability of his incidents, and concluded that he designedly makes his Europeans disagreeable in order to "elevate his countrymen in the eyes of the world."[30]

Among the favorable reviews, that of the *Athenaeum* accepted Newman's unconventional behavior as an "amusing" element in a "humorous" novel enlivened by "unusually spirited" dialogue. Even the Nioches, who are "amusing in a wretched way," fit into the comic pattern, and the novel's "sombre termination" does not distress the reviewer. The *British Quarterly* related the ending to a "relentless realism" which rejects the tidy resolutions of art, and emphasized the novel's prosaic qualities—the "clear cut and incisive" Dutch pictures—rather than its sprightliness. As if to compound critical confusion, the *Westminster Review* commended James for making "everything plain" and establishing a warm Thackerayan rapport with his readers.[31]

Edward Burlingame, in the *North American Review*, focused discussion on the analytical detachment that he and other American reviewers took to be the most limiting quality of James's genius. Burlingame maintained that the "purely intellectual enjoyment" to be derived from *The American* reduced its characters to unsympathetic "specimens." The *Chicago Tribune* pettishly denounced James's book as a "pale and passionless composition," the staid *New York Times* lost patience with the "cool consideration" that exults in its own clever detachment, and the *Nation* admitted that "the element of passion is wanting" in Newman's supine surrender to fate. While the *Boston Evening Transcript* ascribed James's tepidness to his scientific, dissecting technique, the *New York Tribune* lamented that James writes like a man who has never known an enthusiasm and the *Independent* pronounced him "cold blooded."[32]

Yet, for all their reservations, most journalistic critics treated *The American* with the deference due the work of a rising luminary. The *New York World* ranked James as "our best American novelist," and the *Galaxy* affirmed that his latest book "will richly repay reading." The *Catholic World* certainly stood with the minority in its well-nigh total condemnation: "There is nothing in *The American* to improve anybody's morals or manners; and the style, as an illustration of American progress in literary art, is not likely to bring us credit."[33]

Professor Tuttleton's centennial essay (printed in this volume) deals comprehensively with James's contradictory opinions about the realism and romanticism of *The American,* the nature and value of his much discussed revisions, and twentieth-century attitudes toward James's early masterpiece. Tuttleton's insightful study probes the novel's weaknesses and merits and proves that after more than one hundred years it still encourages critical discoveries.

In *The Europeans,* serialized in the *Atlantic* from July to October 1878, James varied his treatment of the international theme in two ways: by recreating New England as it was in the 1840s and by transporting two Europeans, Felix Young and his sister Eugenia, the Baroness Munster, to a country estate outside of Boston. There on a fortune-hunting visit to the Wentworths, their American relatives, Felix and Eugenia exhibit almost opposing sides of the European sensibility: as a happy Bohemian and artist, he represents an old world subordination of moral scruples to facile contentment with being, seeing, and enjoying; on the other hand, the Baroness possesses the reserve, cultivated tastes, and the manipulative talents of a *femme du monde.* If the brother and sister are "ambassadors" from an early nineteenth-century Europe, the Americans seem like children of nature living in a golden age clouded by a vestigial Calvinism. As social historian, James depicts Mr. Wentworth and his elder daughter as pristine Americans in their congenital distrust of pleasure and artifice, their adherence to truth, plain living and church going, and their want of humor and vivacity. In Gertrude Wentworth's moody discontents, however, James envisions a new American type yearning for ampler opportunities for self-fulfillment and ready to seek salvation in Europe. Unlike the impulsive Gertrude, Robert Acton exemplifies the prudential New Englander who sees beyond provincial pieties and aesthetic simplicities but who cannot commit himself to Eugenia's equivocal and perhaps slightly tainted brand of civilization.

With ironic impartiality and sparkling dialogue, James carries out his intention of making *The Europeans* a "joyous little romance," and though he does not keep his promise to convert "a dusky, dreary domestic circle to epicureanism,"[34] his Europeans bring vivid personalities, new visions, and not too much shadow into the green garden world they invade. Although the Baroness is not above duplicity, she has none of Madame de Bellegarde's forbidding hauteur; Felix's amiability, moreover, awakens Gertrude and brings about the fairy-tale rescue that Newman could not effect. Even the blank and downright Mr. Wentworth listens for an "echo" of her laughter after she and Felix have departed. The marriages that James arranged as a concession to Howells have a comic rightness and enhance the novel's aesthetic symmetries. For once, polarities appear largely illusory and modify themselves into harmonies. Never just to *The Europeans,* James remained cool to its fresh luster, belittling it as a "sketch" and keeping it out of his New York Edition.

*The Europeans* appealed to many American critics, the *Christian Union* extolling the sketch of Gertrude and the *Detroit Free Press* and the *Eclectic* preferring it to *The American.* After an invective against *The American,* the *Chicago Tribune* predicted that " 'The Europeans' will go far to establish Henry James's rank among the first American writers of fiction." Despite minor fault-finding Harriet W. Preston in the *Atlantic* cited James's style and the portrait of Eugenia as reasons why "Mr. James's *The Europeans* is, to me, his best work." The *Boston Evening Transcript, Appleton's,* and the *Literary World* were perhaps disarmed by its sunny depiction of the American scene. In a spirited display of chauvinism, the *New York Tribune's* London correspondent assailed the *Athenaeum* for its cavils against James's use of Americanisms in a work meant to be full of "local color" and "racy New-England colloquialisms." The correspondent boasted that James had "done no work which reveals more power than this" and that he no longer depended on English reviewers for his reputation. Deriding the *Athenaeum's* "fatuity" as untypical of the British press, he mentions appreciations of James in the *Daily News* and the *World.*[35]

The *Athenaeum's* cursory notice was less adverse than *Blackwood's* disparagement of Eugenia and Felix as "very shabby representatives of the Old World in the New" and its indictment of James's confused dramatization of his foreigners' mission in New England. The same bewilderment over the novel's structure was only one of the cirticisms leveled against *The Europeans* by some lukewarm American reviewers. The *Philadelphia North American,* for one, could see no reason for James's shifting of his focus from Eugenia to "personages in whom the reader has no interest." *Harper's* felt that the "sketch" lacked "the intimate fusion of parts essential . . . to dramatic unity," and the *New York Times* paradoxically pronounced James's book "superior to his other works" and "unsatisfactory" in its inconclusive treatment of Eugenia. A second *Atlantic* critic, betraying little tolerance for James's "methodical minuteness and ecstatic patience [as] a microscopist," made the invidious distinction that the reader "hears" James's eloquent and witty characters but never really "sees" them. Finally, the *North American Review* repeated its earlier charge that James's analysis is a kind of scientific experiment that divests his dramatis personae of real life.[36]

A sampling of twentieth-century critics indicates that they have arrived at no consensus about even fundamental aspects of *The Europeans*. Defining James's "essential purpose" as "a study of the New England ethos," F. R. Leavis observes that James's little "masterpiece of major quality" examines manners and morals from an ideal vision of social order and uses his Europeans as "a foil" for the Americans. Poirier stresses Eugenia's centrality in clariyfing the novel's "conflict between people who believe in manners and artfulness . . . and those suspicious of them." The candid Bohemian, Felix, thus, symbolizes as much of Europe as a humorless, duty-bound New England can endure while Eugenia's richer nature inspires provincial resistance. From Acton's marriage to a "nice girl" in preference to Eugenia, Poirier extrapolates American "rejection of at least a kind of sophisticated art and manner." Cargill among others imputes less importance to Eugenia, and Ronald Wallace insists that "Felix is the prime mover of the plot." Edward Geary takes a middle position in maintaining that the Felix-Gertrude and Acton-Eugenia "plot lines are admirably balanced in developing the novel's major theme." Informed and perceptive, Geary's article in the *Henry James Review* sums up past and present critical perspectives on James's genial dramatization of a young America throwing open its doors to a pair of Europeans who introduce surprise and trouble into its sleepy hollow.[37]

Before the serialization of *Confidence* in *Scribner's Monthly* from August 1879 to January 1880, Henry James had reached the height of his popularity with the publication of *Daisy Miller,* a curiously poetic and yet dispassionate study of an American girl whose innocence, untutored charm, and free spirit outraged many readers and alarmed the convention-ridden characters of James's little novella into social persecutions that drive Daisy into temerities resulting in her death. In *The Conquest of London: 1870–1881,* Leon Edel recounts the story of *Daisy's* rejection by *Lippincott's,* its appearance in Leslie Stephen's *Cornhill* in 1879, its pirated American editions, and its substantial sale of 20,000 copies in a few weeks after its inclusion in *Harper's* Half-Hour Series. In Edel's words, "James had discovered nothing less than 'the American girl'—as a social phenomenon, a fact, a type."[38]

With *Confidence,* James sought relief from the international theme and wrote what has been consistently nominated his worst novel. *Confidence* marches in disciplined episodes that take place at Siena, Baden-Baden, New York, the Norman coast, and Paris. Its antithetical characters balance too neatly into a rationalist, Gordon Wright, who cannot understand emotions, and an artist, Bernard Longueville, who accepts life with nonchalance. The contrasting women are Angela Vivien, an enigma with an ability to plumb others' feelings and act on her intuitions, and Blanche Evers, a shallow prattler with conspicuous beauty and an appetite for social distractions. In love with Angela, who has once refused him, Wright invites Bernard to "study" her in order to determine whether he should pursue his courtship. Aware of her predicament, she contrives to displease Bernard, who reports his negative impression to his friend. In his next "move," James shows Wright purchasing misery by marrying Blanche and Bernard discovering, with surprise, that he loves Angela. When she accepts his proposal, and he communicates this to his friend, the rationalist denounces Bernard, threatens to divorce Blanche, and demands another chance to woo Angela. The last move comes when the resourceful girl persuades Gordon and Blanche that they love each other. James imposes his happy ending with such transparent artifice that only the over-ebullient Blanche survives as a living character, and he gives the impression of being at the mercy of psychological undercurrents he cannot contend with. Authorial contrivance, conspicuous in all the earlier novels, keeps the characters in *Confidence* under such firm control that they appear to do what they are programmed to do. Even authorial wit and irony function as means of maintaining a relatively cool emotional temperature.

The success of *Daisy* did not guarantee approval from James's reviewers. Granting *Confidence* both taste and literary qualities, the *Spectator* was chilled by its determined evasion of passionate scenes. The *Academy* informed its readers that the novel was "brisk," "stirring," but ultimately "flimsy." The *Athenaeum* credited James with writing "in his more cheerful mood" and delighted in nearly every aspect of *Confidence*. A brief survey of the American responses may begin with the *New York Sun*, which coupled its enthusiasm for James's heroine with "contempt" for the hero for not knowing his mind; it praised James's "originality" while deprecating his constructive powers; and it joined the critical chorus that belittled both author and characters for their affected drawing-room English. Revolted by the novel's patched-up denouement, Susan Coolidge in the *Literary World* declared, with shrewdness mixed with peeve, that in real life the "imbroglio" presented in *Confidence* "would have terminated in murder or the madhouse." *Harper's* responded coolly to James's dissection of characters who harden into abstractions, and the *Nation*, the *Boston Evening Journal*, the *New York Post*, the *Eclectic*, and *Scribner's* couched their favorable comments in a context of reservations. Even the *Atlantic* seemed to hint faults and hesitate dislike in its cautious commendations of James's painterly skills.[39]

In revealing that James originally planned his novel as a tragedy in which the rationalist's murder of his wife makes the marriage of the hero and the heroine impossible, the *Notebooks* may have disclosed the comedy's inherent problems. Still, Putt believes that despite its "preposterous" plot, James's witty masquerade has the qualities of "an Elizabethan tragicomedy of errors." Reading the novel in psychological terms, Edel points out the correspondence between the heroine's name and "Angel," as young

Henry was called by his family. Noting Angela's further resemblance to her creator in being "all insight and perception," Edel suggests that James may have projected an "intricate series of fantasies" having their source in his troubled relations with his brother William. More concerned with the comic elements, Poirier locates the weakness of *Confidence* in James's failure to endow his protagonist with a public as well as a private identity, but he acknowledges that the novel makes "unconscious motivation a . . . consistently effective part of the action." Daniel Schneider's fresh view of *Confidence* in a very recent article contends that James's bland resolution reveals his inability or unwillingness to confront, at this stage of his development, the evil implicit in the complications he has allowed to evolve.[40]

James often expressed dissatisfaction with his next novel, *Washington Square*, a nostalgic fictional return to Old New York that transmutes what his autobiography pictures as a golden age into a closed, father-dominated world. In a letter to Howells, James linked the thinness of its local color to America's lack of those established forms, class distinction, and institutions that he had angered many Americans by enumerating in his study of Hawthorne (1879). Tagging his "poorish story," which first appeared in the *Cornhill* and *Harper's* in 1880, as "purely American," he admits that it made him "feel acutely the want of 'paraphernalia' " in his native land.[41] *Washington Square*'s assured place in the James canon belies his estimate of it and even proves that he created a brilliant American tableau out of a purely English story told to him by the actress Fanny Kemble.

*Washington Square* describes the clash of wills between the "rational" Dr. Sloper and his dull, dutiful daughter Catherine. James makes Sloper incontestably right in his clinical dissection of those who oppose him: Catherine *is* naively romantic in trusting her suitor, Morris Townsend, a genteel version of a long line of Jamesian predators; Townsend *has* an unreliable, sybaritic nature; and Mrs. Penniman, Catherine's aunt and abettor of her love, *has* an innate passion for harebrained, romantic escapades. Still, the doctor acts with a ruthless strategy that not only drives Townsend from the field but alienates his daughter. The internecine warfare, unexpectedly, eventuates in Catherine's growing awareness of her father's inhumanity and in Sloper's inability, for all his rationalist pride, to fathom her motives and intentions. In the end, the girl, once the butt of paternal merriment and sarcasm has arrived at spinsterhood and an accurate assessment of her caustic father, her Dickensian aunt, and the mercenary Townsend.

James's little masterpiece generated as much ridicule as tribute among reviewers. A glance at three English notices reveals that only the *Academy* credits James with striking a "new chord" in choosing a plain girl for his center of consciousness and in artfully managing his narrative strategies. In contrast, the *London Times* lumped the novel with a species of stories "now very common" and criticized James for making "his people as unpleasant as he often does." The *Athenaeum* devoted most of its notice to soothing those Americans who may have felt offended by the animus behind James's satires of the American girl in Europe: Catherine is even seen as the sort of girl "we expect to meet with in an English country parsonage."[42]

On the whole, American reviewers brought as little acuity as their British confreres to the examination of *Washington Square*. One of them expressed disappointment with James's artificial world and the unsympathetic people in it; another, after offering to publish any explanation that a "penetrating" reader might submit to his journal, deflated James as not even "an eminent trifler"; and still another complained that "Fiction used to be creative, now it is anatomical." The *Chicago Tribune* was cocksure in its belligerency while the *Dial* remained lukewarm in its praise and the *New York Times* hoped that James would "put some of his intensely realistic men and women through a few complicated situations and experiences." The *New York Tribune* speculated that *Washington Square* owed its genesis to James's "over indulgence in the prolix perplexities of . . . Trollope's heroines." It deplored the "sluggish" plot, the "cold-blooded" anatomizing of characters, and the "lofty and tolerant" tone that mars this novel as well as *The American* and *The Europeans*.[43]

A twentieth-century favorite, *Washington Square* has been adapted for the stage and films and has earned high praise from Leavis, Dupee, Putt, Poirier, and Millicent Bell. Professor Edel's treatment succinctly touches on its chief merits: the psychological "realism" that achieves "a considerable degree of intensity and pathos"; the memorable ending in which Catherine takes up her embroidery "for life, as it were"; the economical evocation of the atmosphere of Old New York; and the assault on "the destructive power of a materialism untouched by imagination." Poirier's subtle assessment of *Washington Square* as comedy dwells on Sloper as a "fixed" personality who, inflexibly refusing to see any principle of growth in his daughter, grows more and more melodramatic in his language, action, and outlook: "Melodrama is the voice of the scientific mind when its theories have been defied by facts." Darshan Singh Maini's essay in the first issue of the *Henry James Review* sums up previous readings of the novel and proposes as its "major theme" James's concern with "the morality of irony" as practiced by Sloper.[44]

With the serialization of *The Portrait of a Lady* in 1880–81 in *Macmillan's* and the *Atlantic,* James climaxed the first period of his creative career with an international novel on the grand scale. Its dramatis personae include English, Italianate-American, and true-blue American characters; and the English country house where the action begins is only the first of the fateful houses in Florence, Rome, and Albany in which America and Europe meet in a drama of universal significance. European forms embody themselves in American lives, and Europe's monuments and ruins enforce history's lesson of limitation, blight, and mortality. At the center of this large drama, Isabel Archer figures as the Jamesian innocent compelled to test her nebulous aspirations for total freedom and the noble life in an arena not benevolently organized. Ralph Touchett, her cousin, is a complex evolution of characters like Roger Lawrence and Rowland Mallet who empower their proteges to develop latent selves; and Madame Merle and Gilbert Osmond are impressive and less theatrical examples of people who, like the Bellegardes and Dr. Sloper, use other human beings as means to attain their own ends. Isabel may hark back to Newman, but James touches deeper chords of her nature and enters more harrowingly into her psyche. The minor characters, too, take on richer personalities because of their involvement in the destiny of a character whose greatness is inseparable from her tragic flaws. Once again, also, polarities cannot be reconciled, but in *The Portrait* the opposed characters are locked in a loveless marriage.

With few exceptions, the British reviews of *The Portrait* were full of quibble and misunderstanding, the *Spectator* deducing that Isabel finally takes a " 'straight path' to a liaison" with Caspar Goodwood. The *Pall Mall Gazette* indulged in pleasantries about James's flattering portrayal of the English characters and the harsh depiction of Americans, and then noted as the novel's "great, if not unmixed" merits the "extraordinary pains" spent on all the characters, and the cleverness and interest of the narrative; the chief fault it reprobates is James's fondness for "marivaudage," the artificial word-coinages associated with Marivaux. The *Athenaeum* censures James for leaving his "so-called portrait . . . unfinished" and for having "contrived to write a dull book" in "tertiary tints." The *British Quarterly* was oppressed by James's "languid pessimism," and the *London Times* was offended by the novel's "disagreeable people," characterizing Isabel as "one of those . . . cold-blooded animals who may be operated upon without appreciable discomfort." *Blackwood's* made its obligatory obeisance to James's art, but declared that "nothing so elaborate could ever be real." For a change, the *Academy*, despite dissatisfaction with the end of the novel, called the portrait of Isabel "masterly" and praised "the impalpable radiations of character" and James's "passion for perfection in the technique of craftsmanship."[45]

By 1881, American critics had adopted fixed positions about James. They expected his novels to be full of analyses that deadened human feeling, to be well made except for irresolute denouements, and to present life with a disturbing moral neutrality. A survey of a few reviews will show that the scope and richness of *The Portrait* did not, on the whole, change these attitudes. Elizabeth Stuart Phelps in the *Penn Monthly* made a number of conventional strictures: the characters are automatons, the book is tedious, and "ending there is none." *Lippincott's* review sounded like an echo of the others: James's felicities of style cannot compensate for the lack of a "regular dénouement," the absence of a religious motive, and characters who have no "weight." The *Critic* multiplied commonplaces in a jaunty manner: the offensive characters "bite, and snap, and criticise each other," and they in turn are annihilated by "protracted analysis." The *Chicago Tribune* and the *New York Times* agreed with the *Dial* that the ending is lame, and the *American* and the *Catholic World* stigmatized the novel as "morbid and unwholesome." Even the *Atlantic,* which had serialized the novel, scored it for presenting an artificial world with little relation to actuality. A hint of the same attitude inheres in the *Atlanta Constitution's* assertion that the only thing absent from James's work is "rage."[46]

Yet, the reviewers for the *New York Tribune, Harper's,* and the *Nation* celebrated *The Portrait* as a novel that "will remain one of the notable books of the time," as an extraordinary adaptation of the painter's art in fiction, and as "the most eminent example we have thus far had of realistic art in fiction." These perceptive reviewers compared James's masterpiece to the works of the great English novelists, the *Nation* praising the delineation of Warburton as excelling Trollope's depiction of Englishmen. From the West coast, the *San Francisco Chronicle* also eulogized James's book as so good in its dialogue and characterization as to be the best novel of the year.[47]

F. R. Leavis's description of *The Portrait* as one of the "two most brilliant novels in the language" testifies to its staying power. Joseph Warren Beach finds in its freshness, clarity, and leisurely development the perfection of James's early manner. Itself a richly organized experience, Dorothy Van Ghent's analysis of *The Portrait* shows the abundance of felt life in its texture. For Cornelia Pulsifer Kelley, James's fiction has as much "life" as the works of George Eliot and Turgenev and "more art." Eminent critics such as Matthiessen, Rahv, Blackmur, Edel, Tony Tanner, and Laurence B. Holland have explored the novel's theme, symbolism, and psychological substructure without exhausting it. In envisioning a "second hundred years" for *The Portrait,* William Stafford goes to the heart of its continuing appeal: "I am struck, as I think more and more readers will be, with the *wholeness* of this book, the loving care and wit and grace that went into the rendering of every character, every scene, and every setting."[48]

Howells saluted James's fictional achievement up to 1882 with a generous essay in the *Century* that ironically rallied hostile critics against both novelists. In designating James the leader of a new school of fiction, which "derives from Hawthorne and George Eliot," Howells looked askance at the "confidential attitude" of Thackeray and Dickens, the "prolixity of Richardson [and] the coarseness of Fielding." He then consigned these "great men," along with Trollope and Reade, to the "past," hailing James as shaping American fiction according to the principles of Daudet. The British press reacted indignantly, *Blackwood's* upbraiding Howells for his arrogance and boasting that "even in America, the old gods will outlive the temporary dazzling of Mr. Henry James's fine style, and delicate power of analysis." In the United States, the *Boston Evening Transcript* doubted that James's passionless novels represent the wave of the future. The *Literary News* reprinted a denigration from the *Boston Traveller* of James and Howells as "made" rather than "born" novelists who will never attain "that inimitable touch of spontaneity, of vitality, of inherent power, that charac-

terizes Dickens and Thackeray."[49] The transatlantic flurry caused by Howells lasted well into 1883, and enlivened the literary pages of the *Nation*,
*Harper's*, and the *New York Tribune* as well as those of British periodicals.

## III

The initial work of James's second period represented another return,
as if he could not abandon it, to the United States. *The Bostonians* opened
its ill-fated, year-long run in the *Century* in February 1885 and was almost
immediately lampooned by newspaper critics. A thoroughly American
novel that James once called "the best fiction I have written," the book may
have dealt his reputation a blow from which he never fully recovered. In
addition, its satirical portrait of Miss Birdseye was construed as an ungra-
cious caricature of Hawthorne's sister-in-law, Elizabeth Peabody. Moreover, James narrates the love story of Basil Ransom and Verena Tarant, his
Southern hero and New England heroine, with a dispassionate irony and a
minute attention to emotional fluctuations that must have estranged
readers of racier postwar romances. It may be, too, that the unspectacular
Ransom, who fails in his law practice, the malleable Verena, and the tragi-
cally incomplete Olive seeking to feed on Verena's vitality, were better
subjects for analysis than popular fiction. Becoming defensive about his
failed venture into American social history, James offered as an apology to
his older brother that he "had the sense of knowing terribly little about the
kind of life I had attempted to describe."[50] Whatever it may lack as a fictional scrutiny of early feminist activities, however, *The Bostonians* possesses scintillations of phrase, a probing psychological study of Olive Chancellor's passionately possessive nature, a crowded canvas of singular
American reformers and cranks, and some Balzacian notation of New York
and Boston neighborhoods.

Although it represented a new departure for James, *The Bostonians*
did not jolt reviewers out of their habitual stances toward him. To begin
with, many critics protested against the novel's length, admitting to boredom or to having turned pages with listlessness or irritation: "*The Bostonians* is ponderous" (the *New York Tribune*); the "story drags" (the *Nation*);
James talks to himself in "ecstatic subjectivity" (the *Chicago Tribune*); interest will "flag" for most readers (the *Pall Mall Gazette*); and nobody has
finished the book (the *Catholic World*). A host of periodicals expressed the
old impatience with James's analytical habits: "long analyses of feelings, or
minute descriptions . . . produce . . . irritation" (the *Athenaeum*); there is
a "lamentable misuse of . . . keen analytical powers in reporting Olive's
states of feeling" (the *Literary World*); and the author is "wearisomely minute in his own analysis" (the *Dial*). Strident objections to James's preoccupation with unpleasantness continue to reverberate: *The Bostonians* contains a "disagreeable subject" and "vulgar characters" (the *New York
Tribune*); "The author's realism is becoming sordid" (the *Chicago Tribune*);

and the relationship between Olive and Verena is neither "natural or reasonable" (the *Atlantic*). Ransom's melodramatic rescue of Verena and James's unmelodramatic last sentence draw their quota of recriminations: there is no preparation for the concluding histrionics (the *New York Tribune*); the novel should have suggested more about Olive's and Verena's future lives (the *Academy*); and there is no need for the "disagreeable sort of snap in [James's] last sentence" (the *Spectator*).[51]

In a number of reviews the critics appear to struggle between serious reservations and sensitive approbation. The *Nation*, for example, granted the slow motion of the narrative while predicting that James's social canvases, like those of Howells, "must ever remain a constituent portion of American literature." Horace Scudder in the *Atlantic,* although unable to stomach the portraits of Verena and Ransom, "stands in amazement before the delicacy of workmanship." The *Spectator* called the novel brilliant and tedious, powerful and disagreeable, and the *New York Times* was attracted by James's interiors and landscapes and repelled by his "hot-house" effects. Nearly all of the critics who took *The Bostonians* seriously, however, concurred in their relish for the portraits of Miss Birdseye, Mrs. Farrinder, and Dr. Prance; in fact, James's epigrammatic diminution of Mrs. Farrinder's husband as an appendage to his wife, so admired today, was recognized as a stroke of genius. The *New York Sun's* reviewer instanced the sketch of Miss Birdseye as "one of the most veracious, impressive, and memorable in contemporary fiction, and commended James for abandoning the drawingroom and addressing himself to a serious subject.[52]

In the twentieth century, F. R. Leavis has ranked *The Bostonians* one of the greatest novels in English, but even favorable critics like Rahv, Lionel Trilling, Marius Bewley, Irving Howe, and Peter Buitenhaus have done little to establish a critical consensus about it. For instance, the major influence upon James's novel has been traced by Bewley to Hawthorne's *Blithedale Romance* and by Buitenhaus to Daudet's *Evangeliste* while Marcia Jacobson has argued persuasively that James found some of his inspiration in the popular fiction of his day. Disagreement about James's attitude toward his male protagonist, Basil Ransom, has been acute, some readers accepting him as his author's mouthpiece while others consider him a flawed hero or a cruelly possessive antihero. The Olive-Verena intimacy, viewed as abnormal by some nineteenth-century reviewers, has led to controversy over James's awareness of the sexual basis of Olive's "love" for Verena. In fact, *The Bostonians*, despite its exclusion from the New York Edition, grows more topical as "the woman question" James set out to explore precipitates intenser politcal debate and action: not surprisingly, as Richard A. Hocks and John S. Hardt report, "more articles on this novel appeared in 1978 and 1979 than on any Jamesian work except *The Turn of the Screw.*"[53]

*The Princess Casamassima's* appearance in the *Atlantic* from September 1885 to October 1886 marked another stage in James's decline in the popularity he coveted and briefly tasted with *Daisy Miller* and *The Portrait of a Lady*. Indeed, he pours into Howells's "most private ear" a tale of "the mysterious and . . . inexplicable injury wrought . . . upon my situation by my two last novels, the *Bostonians* and the *Princess*. . . . They have reduced the desire, and the demand, for my productions to zero."[54]

With *The Princess*, James's long residence in London fructified in a novel based on the economic discontent and revolutionary activity of the English laboring classes. The narrative, however, is distinguished for the documentation of the protagonist's accruing social vision and search for identity and lacks the turbulent action and suspenseful pace that might have given it popularity. The hero, Hyacinth Robinson, contains within himself the irreconcilable polarities James so often embodies in two characters: he is the son of a working-class French woman who murders her aristocratic lover, Hyacinth's presumed father; he works as a wage-earning bookbinder but, almost as a gift of nature, excels in artistic bindings; and though he admires the health and vitality of Millicent Henning, one of James's most striking characters, he immediately recognizes the superior refinement and attractions of the Princess, a later, world-weary version of Christina Light from *Roderick Hudson*. Two flawed worlds blunder toward vague ends and, unable to realize himself in either world, the betrayed Hyacinth kills himself instead of the aristocratic victim the revolutionary leader had assigned him to assassinate.

Reviews of *The Princess* ranged from *Harper's* panegyric ("it is a great novel") to the *New York Times*'s obituary tone (The "decadence of a great art, once most distinguished, we think is appreciable in 'The Princess Casamassima' "). For the *Dial* and the *Boston Evening Transcript*, James had made a promising "new departure"; for the *Critic*, he is still a psychological casuist specializing in "hairs radiantly split," and for *Lippincott's*, James preserves throughout his novel the "superior air of one who has outgrown emotion and enthusiasm." The *New York Tribune* downplayed its strictures for praise of James as "a rare and brilliant master" with an unusual command of his material. The *Nation* apologetically noted James's psychological niceties and finicky style, but strongly approved of his daring subject matter, his tenderness and even intensity of emotion, and his great gallery of international characters. As if divided against itself, the *Catholic World* ranked *The Princess* above any other of James's novels, but observed its tone of doubt is so "settled that it does not care to ask even Pilate's question." The only concession to the novel made by the Atlanta *Constitution* is that it is better than *The Bostonians*: otherwise it resorts to a kind of irony that compromises every compliment.[55]

A sampling of British opinion reveals that *The Princess* was on the whole greeted as a flimsy social document. The *Westminster Review*'s commendation was polite while the *Academy* wasted no urbanity in declaring that James's novels "are admirable examples of style, and devoid of the faintest glimmer of interest." Some of the old complaints continued to surface: *The Princess* is mere "speculation and imagination" (the *London Quarterly Review*); the novel does not give off a "glimmer of conviction or moral standard" (the *Contemporary Review*); the "minute stippling" makes the book too verbose (the *Scottish Review*); and the book is "remarkable both in its perceptions and its mistakes" (*Blackwood's*).[56]

Nineteenth-century criticism, however, anticipated twentieth-century views in its fondness for Millicent Henning and for James's stylistic elegance. A few reviewers guessed that the Russian novelists and Flaubert may have served James as sources, but none of them guessed the full extent of his indebtedness to Turgenev and other influences. Early twentieth-century students of James tended to go along with assumptions that the events of *The Princess* were concocted by James's fertile fancy. However, Trilling's multifaceted essay in *The Liberal Imagination* showed, among other things, the solidity of James's documentation. Trilling relates Hyacinth to the tradition of the Young Man from the Provinces who figures as the center of interest in such novels as *The Red and the Black, Père Goriot, Great Expectations,* and *The Sentimental Education;* moreover, he maintains that there is not a single detail of the revolutionists' activities "which is not confirmed by multitudinous records"; and, going beyond the discussion of sources, he celebrates Hyacinth's suicide as "an act of heroism" in defense of civilization and the noblest creations of man. More recently, W. H. Tilley, Cargill, Mark Seltzer, and Marcia Jacobson have expanded on Trilling's views. It is wise to remember, nevertheless, that James himself traced the germ of the novel to his own London ramblings: "The simplest account of the origin of *The Princess Casamassima* is . . . that this fiction proceeded quite directly, during the first year of a long residence in London, from the habit of walking the streets."[57]

*The Reverberator* (1888) and *A London Life* (1889) are short novels illustrative of James's ability to look at life from alternating moods of gayety and gravity. In both novels, Americans bring havoc to the European social scene. The sprightly comedy of the former results from the indiscreet revelations made by Francie Dosson to George Flack, an American journalist who contributes international gossip to the *Reverberator:* an ingenuous American beauty about to marry into an old American-Parisian family, Francie innocently divulges details about the private lives of the Proberts to Flack, who shares his "scandal" with his readers and shocks the sensibilities of the French family. A more serious work, *A London Life,* is unusual for the candor with which it presents the promiscuities of genteel English society and the strains on an international marriage. Living in an English country house as a guest of her sister Selina, whose marriage to Lionel Berrington has turned into a fiasco, Laura Wing cannot overcome her American horror at Selina's sexual license, Lionel's eagerness to drag his wife into the notoriety of a divorce court, and the readiness with which Lady Ringrose and other British worthies abet Selina's escapades. Clutching at straws to escape her situation, the neurotic Laura "invites" an astonished American named Wendover to propose to her and then, shrinking from her audacity, flees in panic to her native land.

The *Chicago Tribune*'s protest against the theme and characters of *The Reverberator,* in sharp contrast to Howells's glowing reception of the novel, may serve as an exaggerated example of the chauvinistic animus aimed at James in the late 1880s. Stung by the novel's witty acerbity, the reviewer reproved James for having "grown more and more alien," for having become "obtuse in things American," and for catering "to the taste of American-despising London." James was charged with taking revenge on American journalists for their criticism of his "peculiar fiction." James's malice, moreover, was seen in the skill he expended on making his heroine and her family as deficient in manners as in good sense: "James shows what a man can do when he sets out to group a number of Americans and render them all detestable." In his castigation of his fellow Americans, the critic concluded, the author of *The Reverberator* has himself emulated the methods of the "odious" Flack and will be praised by supercilious foreigners. Ironically the *Quarterly Review* (London) while relishing James's satire thought the Dossons' talk "too idiotic" even for "empty young American provincials."[58]

Many English reviewers were as unkind to *A London Life* as American critics were to *The Reverberator.* Writing for the *Academy,* Saintsbury judged the quarrels between Selina and her husband to "have a dull disagreeableness" and tolerated Laura as "not a disagreeable young woman." With a flourish of invidious adjectives, the *Spectator* called James's subject "intensely disagreeable," two of his characters, "very disagreeable," Lady Davenant "particularly odious," and the picture of Lionel, once again, "odious." James, the critic continued, throws out "disagreeable hints" about Lionel's life, and the characters are "for the most part repellent, and certainly unloveable." Back in the United States, the *Literary World* intoned that James's "works . . . have the effect of regarding the world through the cold transparency of a club window."[59]

The new year, 1889, began auspiciously for James with the first installment of *The Tragic Muse,* another purely English novel, in the *Atlantic.* A sprawling narrative that dramatizes the conflicts faced by artists in their pursuit of aesthetic expression, it shifts its focus from Miriam Rooth, who subordinates all personal relations to her life as an actress, to Nick Dormer, who vacillates between a devotion to painting and a seat in Parliament that will be crowned with a respectable marriage, and to Peter Sherringham, who resists giving up a diplomatic career for Miriam and the stage. Untouched by conflict and free to wander where beauty summons, Gabriel Nash acts as a mocking spirit whose aesthetic self-sufficiency makes light of human struggle and the passions it generates.

The reviews of *The Tragic Muse* can be conveniently classified into three groups: those that scoff at James for his so-called inveterate faults; those that hope he may be emerging from a sphere of artificial lights and social puppets into a thicker, denser reality; and those who hail an accomplished master at the height of his genius. Typical of the first group, the *Chicago Tribune* categorized *The Muse* as a "sofa novel" whose style is faultless, but whose "matter . . . is fairly fit for gun wads." With more sophistication, Saintsbury jeered at James's language and characters as deriving from "thrice and thirty times redistilled literary decoctions of life." Representative of the second group, the *New York Tribune* trusted that James is emancipating himself from "a method which . . . has hitherto dulled the point and weakened the effect of his work." As proof of James's partial success, it points to the study of Miriam—"the finest and most perfect and coherent work Mr. James has yet achieved." The third group, almost unequivocal in its praise, included Howells in *Harper's*, and the critics for the *Nation*, the *New York Times*, and the *Atlantic*. The *Boston Advertiser's* reference to *The Muse* as a "real event" seems tame in comparison to the *Nation's* claim that, in Miriam, James drew the "most brilliant and faithful representation of the successful modern actress that has ever been achieved in English fiction." The *Times* complimented James's presentation of all his major characters, even Nash whom the *New York Sun* had called a "bore" and the *New York Tribune* had ridiculed as a creature of the "dim inane"; indeed, the *Times* viewed James's "former work" as a mere "schooling for his latest book." Howells wasted no quibbles and perhaps intended to send his friend a message of ardent encouragement: "The whole picture of life is a vision of London aspects such as no Englishman has yet been able to give; so fine, so broad, so absolute, so freed from all necessities of reserve or falsity."[60]

Twentieth-century critics, while not endorsing Howell's generous appraisal of *The Muse*, have done justice to its breadth and color and its significance in James's literary development. Leon Edel, for example, has clearly demonstrated that, in the drama of Nick Dormer and Sherringham's divided nature, James "wrote out, on a large scale, the duality which existed within himself" between the claims of art and of life. Lyall Powers has argued that the novel represents a transition from such relatively naturalistic works as *The Bostonians* and *The Princess* and the "dramatic experiment of the first half of the nineties." He defends the novel against the charge that, in its frequent change of focus, it forfeits unity and remains essentially episodic. He also gives the book an unorthodox "sanguine reading," which holds that Nick Dormer does not end by sacrificing his art for marriage with his public-spirited, philistine fiancée.[61] Expectedly, however, interest continues to focus on Gabriel Nash, the wit and aesthete whose paradoxes have led critics to interpret him as an Ariel-like sprite, a Jamesian mouthpiece, or an irresponsible trifler. In an unusual interpretation of Nash, Ronald Wallace sees him as a cousin to Felix Young of *The Europeans* and a "close fictional representation of Meredith's Comic Spirit" who laughs at the absurdities of the struggling, compromising characters.[62]

As the 1890s approached, James, feeling that he had lost his audience, turned to playwriting as a means for gaining the fame and financial rewards that fiction had not brought him. His dramatic version of *The American* was well enough received when acted in Southport, near Liverpool, on 3 January 1891, to justify the raptures James communicated in a telegram to his sister: "Unqualified triumphant magnificent success universal congratulations great ovation for author great future for play."[63] Although he apologetically tells Robert Louis Stevenson that "chastening necessity" has driven him to write for the stage,[64] he confides in a more optimistic spirit to his brother William that he has at last discovered in the drama "my real form." In fact, he patronizes "the pale little art of fiction, as I have practised it" and disparages it as "but a limited and restricted substitute" for the new art that seized his imagination.[65] Like one of his own characters, he marched to disaster with unimpaired confidence.

I take this opportunity to express my debt to all the James scholars—most of them known to me only by their works—who have deepened my knowledge and informed my taste. I am grateful to David Kraueter, Assistant Librarian at Washington and Jefferson College, for his cheerful efficiency in helping me obtain rare books and even rarer periodicals, and to my daughters, Carolyn and Elizabeth, for their practical support. Above all, I thank my wife, Margaret Bilyeu Gargano, for her sensitive encouragement and creative involvement in my work.

*James W. Gargano*

## Notes

1. Van Wyck Brooks, *The Pilgrimage of Henry James* (New York: Dutton, 1925).

2. F. O. Matthiessen and Kenneth Murdock, *The Notebooks of Henry James* (New York: Oxford Unviersity Press, 1947).

3. Arthur L. Scott, "A Protest Against the James Vogue," *College English* 13 (1952):194–201; Maxwell Geismar, *Henry James and the Jacobites* (Boston: Houghton Mifflin, 1963).

4. F. O. Matthiessen, *The James Family: A Group Biography* (New York: Alfred A. Knopf, 1947), 161.

5. *The Death and Letters of Alice James,* ed. Ruth Bernard Yeazell (Berkley: University of California Press, 1981), 185.

6. Ibid., 149.

7. Ibid., 96.

8. *Letters of Henry James*, Vol. 4, ed. Leon Edel (Cambridge, Mass.: Harvard University Press, 1984), 557. Hereafter referred to as *Letters* 4.

9. Ibid., 561.

10. *Autobiography*, ed. Frederick W. Dupee (Princeton: Princeton University-Press, 1983), 89 ff. This volume contains *A Small Boy and Others, Notes of a Son and Brother,* and *The Middle Years.*

11. Ibid., 17.

12. Ibid., 120.

13. Ibid., 164.

14. Ibid., 416.

15. Ibid., 494.

16. *Letters of Henry James*, vol. 2, ed. Leon Edel (Cambridge, Mass.: Harvard University Press, 1975), 51. Hereafter referred to as *Letters* 2.

17. Ibid., 82.

18. *Letters of Henry James*, vol. 1, ed. Leon Edel (Cambridge, Mass.: Harvard University Press, 1974), 396. Hereafter referred to as *Letters* 1.

19. Ibid., 484.

20. S. Gorley Putt, *Henry James: A Reader's Guide* (Ithaca: Cornell University Press, 1966), 27–28.

21. *Appleton's Journal*, n.s. 5 (August 1878): 189; *New York Times*, 12 July 1878, 3; *Boston Evening Transcript*, 27 May 1878, 6; *New York World*, 10 June 1878, 2; *Nation* 27 (22 August 1878); 117–18; *Chicago Tribune*, 22 June 1878, 9; *Philadelphia North American*, 31 May 1878, 4; *Athenaeum*, 10 August 1878, 177; *Literary World* 9 (August 1878):47.

22. Leon Edel, introduction to *Watch and Ward* (New York: Grove Press, 1979), 7–8; Oscar Cargill, *The Novels of Henry James* (New York: Macmillan, 1961), 12; Putt, *Henry James: A Reader's Guide*, 33; Richard Poirier, *The Comic Sense of Henry James: A Study of the Early Novels* (New York: Oxford University Press, 1967), 16.

23. *Letters* 2:167.

24. *British Quarterly Review* 70 (October 1879):529–30; *Spectator* 5 (5 July 1879):854–55; *Academy* 16 (9 August 1879):99; *Westminster Review* 113 (January 1880):619.

25. *New York Times*, 10 December 1875, 2; *Nation* 22 (9 May 1876):164–65; *North American Review* 122 (April 1876):420–25.

26. *Atlantic Monthly* 37 (February 1876):237–38; *New York World*, 29 November 1885, 2.

27. F. R. Leavis, *The Great Tradition* (New York: New York University Press, 1960), 130; Cargill, *The Novels of Henry James*, 29–30; Peter J. Conn, *Nineteenth-Century Fiction* 26 (June 1971):65–82; Poirier, *The Comic Sense of Henry James*, 39; Edward Engelberg, "James and Arnold: Conscience and Consciousness in a Victorian *Künstlerroman*," in *Henry James's Major Novels: Essays in Criticism*, ed. Lyall H. Powers (East Lansing: Michigan State University Press, 1973), 3–24.

28. *Roderick Hudson*, New York edition (New York: Charles Scribner's, 1907), xvii.

29. Tuttleton, "Rereading *The American*: A Century Since," *Henry James Review* 1 (Winter, 1980):139–53.

30. *Spectator*, 50 (21 July 1877):925; *Academy* 12 (14 July 1877):33; *Blackwood's* 125 (July 1879):100–5.

31. *Athenaeum*, 7 July 1877, 14–15; *British Quarterly Review* 70 (July 1879):268–69; *Westminster Review* 57 (January 1880):285–86.

32. *North American Review* 125 (September 1877):309–15; *Chicago Tribune*, 26 May 1877, 12; *New York Times*, 21 May 1877, 3; *Nation* 24 (31 May 1877):325–26; *Boston Evening Transcript*, 6 June 1877, 6; *New York Tribune*, 8 May 1877, 6; *Independent*, 29 (17 May 1877):9.

33. *New York World*, 14 May 1877, 2; *Galaxy* 24 (July 1877):135–38; *Catholic World* 28 (December 1878):331–34.

34. *Letters* 2:106.

35. *Christina Union* 18 (30 October 1878):361; *Detroit Free Press*, 15 November 1875,

8; *Eclectic*, n.s. 29 (January 1879):123; *Chicago Tribune*, 2 November 1878, 9; *Atlantic* 43 (January 1879):106–8; *Boston Evening Transcript*, 4 December 1878, 6; *Appleton's*, n.s. 6 (January 1879):94–95; *Literary World* 10 (18 January 1879):28; George Smalley, "London Literary Topics: Mr. James Jr., and His Reviewers," *New York Tribune*, 2 November 1878, 8.

36. *Athenaeum*, 5 October 1878, 430; *Blackwood's* 125 (July 1879):107; *Philadelphia North American*, 31 October 1878, 4; *Harper's* 58 (January 1879):309; *New York Times*, 4 November 1878, 3; *Atlantic* 43 (February 1879):167–69; *North American Review* 128 (January 1879):101–6.

37. F. R. Leavis, *The Great Tradition*, 139–41; Poirier, *The Comic Sense of Henry James*, 115–41; Cargill, *The Novels of Henry James*, 62–72; Ronald Wallace, *Henry James and the Comic Form* (Ann Arbor: University of Michigan Press, 1975), 54; Edward A. Geary, "The Europeans: A Centennial Essay," *Henry James Review* (Fall 1982), 36.

38. Leon Edel, *The Conquest of London: 1870–1881* (New York: J. B. Lippincott, 1962), 309.

39. *Spectator* 53 (10 January 1880):48–49; *Academy* 17 (7 February 1880):101; *Athenaeum*, 3 January 1880, 16; *New York Sun*, 23 May 1880, 2; *Literary World* 2 (10 April 1880):119–20; *Harper's* 60 (May 1880):945–46; *Nation* 30 (25 March 1880):289–90; *Boston Evening Journal*, 9 March 1880, 1; *New York Post*, 29 March 1880, 1; *Eclectic*, n.s. 31 (May 1880):634–35; *Scribner's* 20 (June 1880):311; *Atlantic* 46 (July 1880):140–41.

40. Matthiessen and Murdock, *The Notebooks of Henry James*, 3–6; Putt, *Henry James: A Reader's Guide*, 101, 104; Edel, *The Conquest of London*, 385–86; Poirier, *The Comic Sense of Henry James*, 160; Daniel Schneider, "The Figure in the Carpet of James's Confidence," *Henry James Review* 4 (Winter 1983):127.

41. *Letters* 2:268.

42. *Academy* 19 (12 March 1881):185; *Times* (London), 19 April 1881, 9; *Athenaeum*, 12 February 1881, 228.

43. *Philadelphia North American*, 17 December 1880, 4; *Literary World* 12 (1 January 1881):10; *Boston Evening Transcript*, 2 December 1880, 6; *Chicago Tribune*, 8 December 1880, 10; *Dial* 1 (January 1881):195–96; *New York Times*, 28 December 1880, 10; *New York Tribune*, 6 February 1881, 8.

44. Edel, *The Conquest of London*, 399, 400; Poirier, *The Comic Sense of Henry James*, 181; Darshan Singh Maini, "Washington Square: A Centennial Essay," *Henry James Review* 1 (November 1979):81–101.

45. *Spectator* 54 (26 November 1881):1504–6; *Pall Mall Gazette*, 3 December 1881, 20–21; *Athenaeum*, 26 November 1881, 699; *British Quarterly Review* 75 (January 1882):227; *Times* (London), 14 December 1881, 3; *Blackwood's* 131 (March 1882):374–83; *Academy* 20 (26 November 1881):397–98.

46. *Penn Monthly* 13 (March 1882):233–34; *Lippincott's* 29 (February 1882):213–15; *Critic* 3 (27 January 1883):333; *Chicago Tribune*, 10 December 1881, 10; *New York Times*, 27 November 1881, 5; *Dial* 2 (18 January 1882):214, 216; *American* 3 (31 December 1881):186–87; *Catholic World* 34 (February 1882):716–17; *Atlantic* 49 (January 1882):126–30; *Atlanta Constitution*, 16 April 1882, 4.

47. *New York Tribune*, 25 December 1881, 8; *Harper's* 64 (February 1882):474. *Nation* 34 (2 February 1882):102–3; *San Francisco Chronicle*, 4 December 1881, 6.

48. F. R. Leavis, *The Great Tradition*, 153; Joseph Warren Beach, *The Method of Henry James* (New Haven: Yale University Press, 1918), 205–11; Dorothy Van Ghent, *The English Novel: Form and Function* (New York: Holt, Rinehart and Winston, 1953), 211–28; Cornelia Pulsifer Kelley, *The Early Development of Henry James* (Urbana: University of Illinois Press, 1965), 300; William T. Stafford, "*The Portrait of a Lady:* The Second Hundred Years," *Henry James Review* 2 (Winter 1981):100.

49. W. D. Howells, "Henry James Jr.," *Century* 25 (November 1882):25–29; *Black-*

*woods's* 133 (January 1883):144–48; *Boston Evening Transcript*, 7 November 1882, 6; *Literary News*, n.s. 4 (April 1883):36–37.

50. *Letters* 3:121.

51. *New York Tribune*, 28 March 1886, 6; *Nation* 42 (13 May 1886):407–8; *Chicago Tribune*, 3 April 1886, 13; *Pall Mall Gazette*, 15 March 1886, 5; *Catholic World* 43 (July 1886):560–61; *Athenaeum* (6 March 1886), 323; *Literary World* 17 (12 June 1886):198; *Dial* 7 (May 1886):15; *Atlantic* 57 (June 1886):850–57; *Academy* 29 (6 March 1886):162; *Spectator* 59 (20 March 1886):388–89.

52. *New York Sun*, 4 April 1886, 4.

53. Marius Bewley, *The Complex Fate* (London: Chatto and Windus, 1952), 11–30; Peter Buitenhaus, *The Grasping Imagination* (Toronto and Buffalo: University of Toronto Press, 1970), 141–59; Marcia Jacobson, *Henry James and The Mass Market* (University, Ala.: University of Alabama Press, 1983), 20–40; Richard A. Hocks and John S. Hardt, "James Studies, 1978–1979: An Analytical Bibliographical Essay," *Henry James Review* 2 (Winter 1981):141.

54. *Letters* 2:209.

55. *Harper's* 74 (April 1887):829; *New York Times*, 21 November 1886, 12; *Dial* 7 (December 1886):189; *Boston Evening Transcript*, 3 November 1886, 6; *Critic*, n.s. 7 (29 January 1887):252–53; *Lippincott's* 39 (February 1887):359; *New York Tribune*, 14 November 1886, 10; *Nation* 44 (10 February 1887):123–24; *Catholic World* 44 (January 1887):554–59; *Atlanta Constitution*, 21 November 1886, 13.

56. *Westminster Review* 71 (January 1887):264–65; *Academy* 30 (13 November 1886):323; *London Quarterly Review* 67 (January 1887):383; *Contemporary Review* 50 (December 1886):899–901; *Scottish Review* 9 (January 1887):202; *Blackwood's* 140 (December 1886):786–92.

57. Lionel Trilling, *The Liberal Imagination* (New York: Viking Press, 1950), 58–92; W. H. Tilley, *The Background of The Princess Casamassima* (Gainsville, Fla.: University of Florida Press, 1961)); Cargill, *The Novels of Henry James*, 146–73; Mark Seltzer, "The Princess Casamassima: Realism and the Fantasy of Surveillance," *Nineteenth-Century Fiction* 35 (March 1981):506–34; Marcia Jacobson, *Henry James and the Mass Market*, 41–61: *The Princess Casamassima*, New York edition (New York: Charles Scribner's, 1908), v.

58. *Chicago Tribune*, 7 July 1888, 10; *London Quarterly Review* 71 (October 1888):190–91.

59. *Academy* 35 (1 June 1889):374; *Spectator* 63 (17 August 1889):211–13; *Literary World* 20 (25 May 1889):25.

60. *Chicago Tribune*, 22 June 1890, 14; *New York Tribune*, 22 June 1890, 14; *Harper's* 81 (November 1890):639–41; *Nation* 51 (25 December 1890:505–6; *New York Times*, 29 June 1890, 2; *Atlantic* 66 (September 1890):419–22; *Boston Advertizer*, 14 June 1890, 5; *New York Sun*, 12 July 1890, 5.

61. Edel, *The Middle Years: 1882–1895*, 256; Lyall Powers, ed., *Major Novels of Henry James: Essays in Criticism*, 149–68.

62. Ronald Wallace, "Gabriel Nash: Henry James's Comic Spirit," *Nineteenth-Century Fiction* 28 (September 1973):221.

63. *Letters* 3:320.

64. Ibid., 326.

65. Ibid., 329.

# Reviews and Contemporary Commentary

## [Review of *Watch and Ward*]   Anonymous*

The many admirers of the most distinguished of all our American novelists will read with pleasure *Watch and Ward*, an early romance of Mr. James', which appeared in the *Atlantic Monthly* some seven years ago. The book itself is interesting as it may by comparison with the later works of Mr. James attest the progress he has made. In the present form it has been minutely revised, receiving quite a number of verbal alterations. A more troublesome topic, or one more cleverly handled, it is difficult to imagine. Roger Lawrence, a rather prosaic man in action, with a tender heart, and a genius for common sense, takes for ward a young girl, the daughter of a suicide, and brings her up. Nora Lambert is a wonderfully natural heroine, and as sweet a character as Mr. James has ever drawn. Roger has been unfortunate in a former love *rencontre* and early bestows his affection on his ward. The perilous experiment of a man taking a child and bringing her up to be his wife is admirably depicted. That keen analysis Mr. James possesses permits him to show how in Roger the feeling of paternity and the affection of the lover may go on together. Fenton, the rascal, the low-bred man of the book, is well described, and so is the selfish Hubert Lawrence. Mr. James' skill in handling his subject is shown in many ways. As charming a bit as can be found in *Watch and Ward* is when Roger, in his travels, goes to South America, and in Lima falls in love with the plump little Teresita. Roger might have married her, but "her nails were not fastidiously clean." The ungodly, selfish minister, Hubert Lawrence, half a French abbé of the times of the Regency, with an ugly varnish of American egotism, is a very perfect study. It is the sharp crystalline method which Mr. James possesses which makes him so distinguished. What is tawdry, flashy, or even sensational, he utterly disregards as foreign to his nature. He may not always be impassioned, yet *Watch and Ward* contains some really true bits of warm color, especially where Nora leaves her protector and is thrown on the world. What position Mr. James may take in the future of

*Reprinted from the *New York Times*, 12 July 1878, 3. The last sentence of the review, dealing with "The Passionate Pilgrim," has been omitted.

general English literature we do not attempt to prophesy. We are quite satisfied that now he should be classed with the very few leading romance writers of England and America.


# Watch and Ward    Anonymous*

Mr. HENRY JAMES, jun., is already well known to English readers. *Watch and Ward* should widen his reputation. It is a novel of a class which unfortunately has not much chance of flourishing while the novel-reading public is content to follow a formal fashion. The fact that, as a rule, novels to have a chance of success, must be in three volumes, remains a mystery of fate. *Watch and Ward* is in one volume, clearly printed, and of a very handy size. That is its recommendation on the face. Its inner merits are in an inverse proportion to its size. The story is bright and full of interest; and readers who, instead of plucking at the plot, like to read the book, will be rewarded. A prefatory note says that the story originally appeared in the *Atlantic Monthly* in 1871, and has since been minutely revised. It displays plenty of well-spent care. Mr. James's style is, if anything, rather too fancifully polished. In his descriptions of his characters every sentence is a composition. At times one is reminded of Nathaniel Hawthorne, not in the matter, but in the diction. Hawthorne's fancy is more ethereal and melancholy; when Mr. James recalls him, whether by conscious imitation or not we cannot say, it is in some strained simile or over-subtle reflection. We shall, perhaps derogate from our own grant of praise if we say that the only fault we find with the story is its rather sudden end. It seems too much as if the heroine had come to return the hero's love because she had miserably failed in her other ventures.

*Reprinted from the *Athenaeum*, 10 August 1878, 177.


# [*Roderick Hudson:* A Surprising Exhibition of Power]    Anonymous*

Mr. Henry James, Jr., in a recently published essay on Honore De Balzac [*sic*], sums up the characteristics of that author's work in saying that it lacks charm, but possesses incomparable power. Precisely the converse statement has hitherto seemed applicable to Mr. Henry James's own writings. And if we still qualify the word power with the adjective incompara-

*Reprinted from the *New York World*, 29 November 1875, 2. A long summary of the plot and some unessential material have been omitted.

ble, it is doubtless applicable to this, his last and most pretentious production. Nevertheless, to persons familiar with the former work of Mr. James, it is the power of *Roderick Hudson* rather than any other of its admirable qualities which will seem surprising. For Mr. James has made the reputation—and a very excellent reputation it is—of a graceful and cultivated essayist and charming narrator of short stories, rather than of a great author, in any sense of the term. There is probably not a writer on this side of the water whose pen is more facile, whose style is purer, and, at the same time, so warm—who uses words with a nicer sense of their meaning than Mr. James. . . . Mr. James has held a much higher position in our opinion than Mr. Howells, and his writings have furnished quite a satirical commentary upon the "efforts" of "Colonel" Higginson, which have been exerted, so to speak, in the same line. All this has been so unquestionably true that it has seemed a great pity that Mr. James should have contented himself with the work of a litterateur, a charming prattler about books and pictures, with a bit of artistic storytelling now and then, instead of attempting something in creative authorship; and at the same time it has raised the presumption that Mr. James had, after all, found his level, and that the distinction between criticism and creation was likely to be as marked in his case as it has been in so many others. But *Roderick Hudson* has quite disposed of that inference. It is the best romance we have produced, as the patriotic critics might say, since the *Marble Faun* was written. It is at once more gracefully written and more powerful in portraiture than the somewhat slender novels of Mr. Howells. It is to the romance of Mr. Julian Hawthorne what ripe fruit is to green, and to the last novel of Mr. Frank Lee Benedict—which so captivated the London *Spectator*—what the production of a trained mind is to that of literary instinct merely. We suppose that the author of *Elsie Venner* and *The Guardian Angel*, and the author of *Katherina* will forgive us for failure to institute comparison between literary artists and themselves.

Artistic is eminently the word by which to characterize *Roderick Hudson*. In objectiveness of form at least, if not of feeling, it could scarce fail to suit, even M. Taine, who has a most sovereign disregard for fiction which is not written by Balzac or by George Sand. Despite the temptation, in a story the scene of which is laid in Italy and Switzerland, to rhapsody in the description of natural scenery . . . Mr. James shows a perfect appreciation of the difference between his figures and his backgrounds. . . . Nature and art in *Roderick Hudson* play the part to which a writer of romance and a portrayer of character ought always to assign them—an illustrative part, namely, only to be considered in its relation to the characters and events which are to be analyzed and described. And yet there is scarcely a recent book with more of both art and nature in it than *Roderick Hudson*, enshrouding character and incident in a fine and luminous haze of charm and fragrance and lending to the narrative a delicate flavor which it is difficult to analyze, but impossible not to detect and enjoy.

The different characters themselves are portrayed (delineated rather than dissected, which, with due respect to the later English novelists, is the more artistic method) with varying skill though with constant and faithful sympathy. . . .

Roderick Hudson himself is described with surprising skill. Mr. James has succeeded better in the portrayal of a man with exquisite sensibilities and without moral sense than the elder Hawthorne in Donatello or the younger Hawthorne in Bressant, and the latter character is in its way very near a masterpiece. There is absolutely no moral side to Roderick Hudson; he never feels a sentiment of generosity, of gratitude or of remorse. . . . Despite all this, Mr. James has made him a "natural" character. Possibly it is an ideal creation, possibly there never was such a person; but as Thackeray once said of one of Dickens's creations, "Lord bless you, how easily there might have been!" How Mr. James has accomplished this it is quite needless to say. Perhaps it would be impossible; at all events it would be difficult. He has done it and has displayed in the doing of it not a little power. It is not dramatic power; there is hardly anything passionate about it; it is simply the power of subtlety. Almost as good an illustration of it as Roderick is Christina Light. And Mr. Mallet—for Mr. James's conceptions constantly recall Thackeray's—seems to us to the full as good in his way as Major Dobbin, and we are not confident that had he lived in that romantic time he would not have been a very fast friend of Colonel Henry Esmond himself.

But here we stop. Beyond these three it would not be well to speak enthusiastically of people who figure in *Roderick Hudson*. . . . It is [the] discrepancy between the way in which subordinate figures are drawn by Mr. James and the way in which they are drawn by the great artists in fiction, which is the blemish of "Roderick Hudson." It is not a great discrepancy, but a discrepancy does nevertheless noticeably exist. . . .

It is not difficult to discover why this is so. Mr. James, in the first place, has too much of what is sometimes called the artistic temperament, and in the second place, he is too distinctively a writer. These traits may be more or less admirable than the qualities which usually go to novel-writing of the highest order; they are, at all events, different to them. In proportion to their predominance over other traits in a novelist they operate generally against his success. In the present instance, as we have indicated, they only prevent to be sure a complete success. But it must be admitted that they have done that much in *Roderick Hudson*. It is exceedingly difficult for any one who represents so thoroughly as Mr. James the product of what Mr. Matthew Arnold might call a ripe culture, to take a deep, wide and human interest in the lesser and more trivial men and things of the world. Nobility, depravity, picturesqueness strike him as forcibly as they did Balzac, for instance, but people and incidents which do not appeal to anything artistic in his nature bore him as they did not bore Balzac. If he were open on more sides, so to speak, it . . . would give him

an insight and a breadth which he does not here display. . . . And it may
be repeated that these criticisms are meant to apply to the support and not
to the stars of Mr. James's company. As for the stars, we shall not expect
to find the equals of Roderick Hudson, Christina and Rowland Mallet in
American literature for many a long day—not at all events, until Mr. James
writes another novel.

## [*Roderick Hudson:* James, the Schopenhauer of Modern Fiction?]    Anonymous*

*Roderick Hudson*, originally published in Boston in 1875, is full of the
subtle but somewhat morbid analysis that is so prominent a characteristic
of Mr. James's genius. He seems very emphatically to dissent from his
hero's theory that ugliness is treason to art, and that if artistic things are
not positively beautiful they are to be set down as failures. Without maintaining what in such an absolute form would be a paradox, we may maintain
that the province of art is to create ideals, and that ideals are necesarily
beautiful, each in its domain. Whereas for ideals Mr. James substitutes
types, which he exaggerates; and as his choice seems instinctively to be of
defect and disorder, the almost uniform impression of his novels is painful.
He does not incite by great examples; he warns by shocking beacons, and
this, we say again, for the hundredth time, is not the true conception of
the poem or the novel any more than of the picture or the statue. Where
processes of development are exhibited almost uniformly the evil element
overcomes the good, not the good the evil. Even in Rowland Mallet, whose
quiet, generous goodness and unselfishness are the latent foil to Roderick
Hudson's egotism and selfishness, the sense of failure is almost unrelieved.
He has no satisfaction in what he so generously does. He only suffers. So
it is with Mary Garland, the pendant of Christina. Admirable as she is, and
admirably drawn, the sense of failure and suffering is supreme. The only
relief is the distant horizon light at the close, that after the dark troubled
night of the story a bright calm day for both Rowland and her may dawn.
We cannot but think that the lurid atmosphere, this predominant painful-
ness, these bitter and tragic issues, are false to epical art. Not a single character throughout the story produces satisfaction. It is as cynical and as pes-
simist as *The American*. . . . Christina and her husband disappear into
infinite possibilities, nay, certainties of misery, if not of shame. Her mother
is left to the bitter reaping of her worldliness, Roderick's mother to the
misery of weak reproaches and senile sorrow. Roderick's own tragic fate is
the great moral of the story. The book is unrelieved in its melancholy fail-

*Reprinted from the *British Quarterly Review* 70 (October 1879):529–30. This review is of
the three-volume edition published in England by Macmillan & Co.

ures, masterly as are the penetration and power with which these are analyzed. It is the pessimism of life. Heraclitus is its presiding genius. It is
Ecclesiastes in a story. The chief conception is the character of the hero—
full of genius and generous sentiment. He is not incapable of the greatest
achievements in art, some of which he as a sculptor actually realizes, but
infirm of purpose, the victim of moody passions and of unrelieved selfishness, taking the form of irresponsible domineering and self-conscious genius. Roderick's baseness to Mary Garland, his shameless infatuation for
Christina, his almost insane insensateness to Rowland's generous kindness,
his supercilious egotism among artists, and his mobile yielding to whatever
may be the fascinations of the moment, exhibit the defects of character
which gradually overpower better qualities and work his ruin. All Mr.
James's subtle power will be found in this story—his rare faculty of moral
analysis, his keen penetration of moral causes, his rich sententious wisdom
inlaying his narrative throughout, and his intense realism, as vivid as that
of a Dutch painter. It is a novel carefully wrought out and of almost supreme ability and its moral—that without self-control and patient persever-
ance great abilities will only induce swifter and more utter ruin—is at all
times most momentous. But we think of it as of a bad dream or a night-
mare. We are troubled by evil, not satisfied with the good. Does Mr.
James aspire to be the Schopenhauer of modern fiction?

# [*Roderick Hudson:* Twenty-eight
Years Later]                                          Anonymous*

In 1875 appeared *Roderick Hudson*, [James's] first long novel, characteristic of the work to follow in the fifteen years which we will call for the
sake of definition his middle period, covering the volumes by which he is
generally estimated and best known. But *Roderick Hudson* marks a significant extension of the author's interest across the Atlantic, and it is something in favour of our "periods" that whereas America supplies themes for
the first, the second is essentially European, while the third scarcely wanders from English soil. Also that handling of the supernatural which figures
so prominently in his earlier and later stories finds in the "middle period"
no place at all; and the contrast in national temperament, which so frequently affords a subject in that middle period, disappears in the more subtle scrutiny which marks the last. The story of Roderick Hudson is in fact
immersed in the shadow of such a contrast: a contrast between Massachusetts and Rome, the New World and the Old, the Puritan aloofness of Mary
Garland and the voluptuous Paganism of Christina Light.

*Reprinted from the *Edinburgh Review* 197 (January 1903):59–85. A description of Mrs.
Hudson has been omitted.

Roderick, weak brilliant unhappy Roderick, passes between them, from a tepid satisfaction in the one, to breathless worship of the other. A speedy transit, for Roderick, though sprung from New England, was born to a wider heritage of the past than was Christina. She was beauty but he was its priest. The story of the brief outburst and burning of his genius is admirably told. There is a tragic hint even in his first successes. He leaves port like some flimsy galleon under a great cloud of sail. One holds one's breath at its disastrous loveliness. And the catastrophe comes not from without but of his inherent weakness. Christina arrives in time to complete the wreckage, but she is not the cause of it. She is, on the contrary, responsible for the last leap of his genius. It is the inspiration of her beauty that breathes a final glow into the smouldering ashes of his capacity, and forces him by a final effort to burn himself out. After that only the tragic note is sounded, a note to which Christina unwillingly and unwittingly contributes. Poor Roderick's efforts to raise himself for a flight after losing the counterpoise of his inspiration resemble nothing so much as the pitiful comical winged somersaults of a bee whose body has been bitten off, and death comes to him as the least ruinous ending. The book is wonderfully complete for a writer's first sustained effort; wonderfully balanced and free from crudity, abounding in happy bits of portraiture and observation. Mrs. Hudson is the first of many ordinary middle-aged women whom the author has drawn with such curious appreciation and fidelity. . . . Mary Garland is treated much less definitely; hers is indeed almost one of those portraitures by omission for which Mr. James developed later such a liking. But then her life was so largely made up of omissions that she has a right to the method. Yet she is no less charmingly and more completely presented than magnificent Christina, whose likeness is rendered unavoidably lustrous by the radiation of her beauty.

## [*The American:* An Intellectual Novel]
Edward L. Burlingame*

Mr. Henry James's latest book has had as it deserved to have, a somewhat exceptional reception. Not only has it been the subject of more careful and excellent criticism than has fallen to the lot of any other American novel of recent years, but it has called forth, both in print and elsewhere, much of that earnest discussion which is the best evidence of the impression made by uncommonly strong work; and in this instance the discussion has been of more than ordinary value in itself.

There has been no question—as, indeed, we think there can be

*Reprinted from the *North American Review* 125 (September 1877):309–15. The reviewer's quotations of James's descriptions of characters have been omitted.

none—with regard to Mr. James's novel, looked at from one point of view. The perfection of his literary skill is almost beyond cavil. His style has rare, strong qualities in admirable combination. It is delicate without weakness; there is a peculiar refinement in it, without a touch of pedantry or a moment's sacrifice of idiomatic force; it is rich without being fantastic, and individual without mannerisms. In this Mr. James compels the tribute of a hearty admiration; and we join willingly with those who give it without reservation. Whatever may be in dispute about him, he is, before all things, a master of the technical portion of his art, and so easily first among the men around him that we should look in vain, perhaps, for a comparison. What Mr. Howells wrote of his first book is true of all he has produced; it is "a marvel of delightful workmanship."

But the discussion with regard to *The American* has been upon another point; and one which concerns not only Mr. James's own prospective place in literature, but incidentally involves, in some degree, the dangerously broad question what a great novel really is.

Mr. James has given us a book appealing almost entirely—we are tempted to say wholly—to the reader's intellectual side. The enjoyment we derive from it is purely intellectual enjoyment. It is obvious to the warmest of his admirers (we do not count ourselves the least among the number), that imagination is not the impelling force with him; that he does not write under the pressure of a strong creative power. On the contrary, he is the representative of a class of men to whom, ordinarily, expression does not seem worth while; of Emerson's "great silent crowd" of highly cultured lookers-on, who feel no impulse toward speech. Even those of them who have the power are apt to feed so long upon the lotus-leaves of a certain kind of modern aesthetic culture, and to be so well satisfied with their meal, that they grow indisposed to all production. Often they drift into criticism of an unproductive kind; but even when they find voice and the wish to use it, they very rarely seek expression through the novel. The influence of their intellectual lotus-eating has taken the vivid dramatic interest out of life for them; they are—to borrow a word from the only race that could have coined it—entirely *désillusionné*. It is a rare strength that enables Mr. James to be in this class and yet not of it. But it has not been quite great enough to enable him to shake off the habit of one who is altogether a *spectator ab extra;* the critic and the analyst, rather than the sharer, of strong feeling.

Not that he is not immeasurably far away from that class of writers who make the reader feel as though he were attending merely on a series of experiments,—a kind of psychological clinic; the quality of his art alone would keep him from any error such as this. With him what Leslie Stephen calls "the cool, hard, and steady hand necessary for psychological dissection" is gentle and kindly in its touch. You do not notice it; you are not conscious of its passage, or of the work that it is doing. Only, he is contented with the mere exhibition of his skill and accuracy; consciously he seems to stop there, as though there were no need of going further. It is not necessary that you should feel when the persons of his story feel—only that you should see that *they* are feeling. It is not needful that you should be in *rapport* with them,—that when a bundle of nerves is laid bare you should feel each one tingle, and when a glimpse of a passion is discovered you should be put in keen enough sympathy with it to know the rest. The delicate and subtle analysis is followed throughout with all a student's interest; but it is an interest that attaches almost altogether to the process, very little to its suggestions or results, and least of all to the characters that may have been its subjects.

We do not ask for better bread than can be made with wheat, however; nor appreciate *The American* the less because it seems to us rather an almost perfect study than a piece of completed or in any sense creative work. It is only because Mr. James stands so near the very head of the school in which he has enrolled himself, that what he writes inevitably raises a question as to the limitations of that school. If we doubt whether he and his companions are not confined, by the very conditions of their method to the production of admirable specimens of skillful workmanship instead of real creations, we do not listen the less hopefully to those of his critics who believe that he will prove the doubt a groundless one. In the reaction which is strong just now against all crudity and carelessness there is danger that they may expect of his rare skill some things which skill alone cannot supply; yet he has shown himself so thoroughly a master in all that he has undertaken, that the one step higher may also be within his power.

Nationality and surroundings are the only things *The American* of Mr. James's present story has in common with the heroes of *Roderick Hudson* and the shorter sketches that made up its author's earlier volume. Christopher Newman is a new type with him; a more strongly marked and finished one than any he has touched before, and one so carefully studied that it is impossible to give a fair idea of it without the fine lights and shades of his own admirable picture. There is nothing of its kind in fiction better than the paragraph in which this hero first appears. . . .

Madame de Cintré, who, with her surroundings, makes up that sharp contrast to his leading character without which Mr. James is never quite content, is to our mind the least successful figure in the book. We can well understand that a certain vagueness and haziness about his delineation of her should be a part of Mr. James's plan, for the sharp, decisive lines of Newman are thus most effectively brought out; but we are not prepared to find her so colorless as to seem somewhat inconsistent with the part she has to play. Beside the women of *Roderick Hudson* she is certainly not a successful piece of drawing; and the ability that Mr. James there showed in the depicting of his heroines leads to a little disappointment that Madame de Cintré should be left so mere an outline.

To atone for his, however, Mr. James has devoted more attention to his minor characters than is his habit; in this case possibly because each one of them adds such a vivid touch of color to the contrasted ground against which his leading figure stands, as we have said, in high relief. Madame de Cintré's mother, Madame de Bellegarde, the central stone of that hard wall against which poor Newman strikes, is a masterpiece of skilful drawing. . . . Her son, Urbain de Bellegarde, the head of the house, is scarce behind this picture. . . . Best of all, however, is a less serious figure than Mr. James is wont to draw, Madame de Cintré's younger brother Valentin. A thorough Frenchman, a thorough light-heart through and through,—the only appearance in Mr. James's books of a type that Thackeray himself might have created,—Valentin is as living a personage as Newman himself. . . .

The ending of the novel will disappoint many beside those who look for a conventional *dénouement*. Its inconsistency with all the probabilities of Newman's character has been the chief objection brought against it by the critics; and it is a sound one. But to us there seems to be another fault as well. The close is somewhat blurred and ineffective; the point that Mr. James seeks to make in his last pages is lost in a vagueness which leaves the reader not unsatisfied, as much strong work will do inevitably,—but positively discontented, and searching dimly for some reason why such sharp and tangible purposes and figures should pass so quickly into smoke.

## [*The American:* Strong, Relentless Realism]                    Anonymous*

Mr. James writes with an individuality and a strength that must give him amongst novelists a rank of a high order. It is not easy to say in what his distinctive qualities consist. The plot of his stories is subordinate to his character-drawing, and his delineations of character are subordinate to the keen penetration, originality, and suggestiveness of his remarks on men and things. His stories have sequence and purpose, but he does not care much for the unities, and still less for poetical justice; they come to no completed development. Like the experiences of life, they have no end at which we can rest; things do not get wound up, his heroes and heroines are not "happy ever afterwards," the end that there is is generally the reverse. His strong relentless realism leaves a large amount of failure and continuing unhappiness; life is left going on with many unravelled threads in its warp and woof; the story that is, is a mere vehicle for sentiment. Claire takes the veil in a Carmelite convent; Newman is at the close the solitary American we first find him. Only a passage of his life is narrated,

*Reprinted from the *British Quarterly Review* 70 (July 1879):268–69. The review is of the Macmillan edition of the novel. A short section dealing with the plot has been omitted.

and that is a tragic failure, and he goes forth into the world to find such further experiences of life as he may. Claire's mother and brother, too, live on "unwhipped of justice," left to the consciousness of their unrevealed crime. We are no great sticklers for conventionality in novel writing, but a novel is an ideal work of art, and we cannot help thinking that the art is defective in construction which leaves issues so loose and destinies so vague. A chronicle has essential differences from a story. The great excellences of Mr. James would not be less, but more, if an artistic plot were more completely wrought out. The character-drawing is more effective than the story-telling, but somehow it does not come up to our ideal. Claire, for instance, is a good deal of a lay figure; we do not seem to know her, she fails to engage our sympathies, notwithstanding the fine qualities in her that are hinted at. Newman, we necessarily get to know better; although his self-contained realism, his hard cynical judgments on life, his self-restrained feelings, his *brusque* honesty and business-like way of looking at things and speaking of them interpose a certain distance. Of the old mother and her eldest son we are told enough. They are admirably drawn portraits, just because they so strongly excite our antipathies. Mr. James, that is, does not win our full sympathies for any of his characters; they are too remote from us; we feel no strong enthusiasm for any of them. Perhaps Valentin takes closer hold of us than any one else. Newman's love-making, for instance, never clarifies itself from the practical purpose of a sensible, high-toned, honourable business man. The higher domain of imagination and passion is never entered. He is a noble fellow, and Claire would have been happy as his wife, but the tone through all is prosaic and realistic. The strength of the writer, and it is very great, lies in the kind of keen, sententious remark of which Thackeray is the great English master. Every page is full of pregnant sentences, laying bare the motives and processes of life; not however, as with Thackeray, blended with touches of imagination, pathos, and passion, so as to excite strong sympathy as well as admiration. Mr. James works in a medium of satire, not fierce but subtle, which interposes as a thin mist between his characters and the reader. . . . Nevertheless, in virtue of the qualities we have indicated, the story is a remarkable one, full of sensible remark and intellectual power, the cynical element being, however, predominant. Mr. James does not, as one of his critics has strangely said, present us with ideals, only with types somewhat exaggerated. The word clever is perhaps the most fitting epithet of characterisation. The book is stimulating in the sense in which olives stimulate the palate. We are interested and absorbed from first to last. Every paragraph is weighted with social wisdom, and is clear cut and incisive as a Dutch picture. His characters are by no means ideals, as with a strange misconception they have been designated, they are types, with a certain exaggeration, necessary for impression. To jaded novel-readers the story is a fine tonic.

# [*The American:* Twenty-five Years Later]

Anonymous*

*The American*, which followed two years [after *Roderick Hudson*], is another international novel, but the contrast is social, not artistic, a contrast between the New World with its naked millions and the proud penury of the old nobility of France. Christopher Newman, who had served an apprenticeship to most trades before making his fortune, sets his intentions more than his affections on Claire de Cintré, the daughter of a house that had looked forward to Charlemagne, and regards trade as somewhat more dully incompatible than crime with traditions. The situation has obvious possibilities; obvious pitfalls too, of insistence and exaggeration. The author avoids these till near the finish, for Mrs. Bread and the melodramatic mystery of the Bellegardes must be considered one into which he has fallen. Newman, with his "look of being committed to nothing in particular, of standing in an attitude of general hospitality to the chances of life, of being very much at one's own disposal," is of a delightful type. He stands smiling, with his back very firmly set against his fortune, ready to admit any man, even a French Marquis, to be his equal, yet fully conscious how much of the pleasure and beauty of life lies outside his compass; shrewd, simple, tender and strong, a figure well worth drawing; and the old hotel in the Rue de l'Université throws it into almost violent relief. But the relief is attenuated by Valentin de Bellegarde, and the pert little Marquise, both more modern than America itself, and he, frankly, ardently, gallantly alive, without money, morals, or the fear of death, is, as a type of manhood, no whit less attractive than Christopher Newman. Claire de Cintré is another portrait by omission; indeed, perhaps in no other of his characters has the author left so much in by leaving so much out. Nothing is explained, very little enumerated; we see her only as a vague figure in those forbidding halls, yet her memory remains as an exquisite fragrance when the vigour of the book is almost forgotten. And the book abounds in vigorous portraiture; the canvas is wonderfully well filled. Little M. Nioche and his audacious daughter are as perfectly seen and as excellently placed as Urbain de Bellegarde and his forbidding mother; and though the book may be most commonly esteemed for its sketch of the deadly serious pretension of life in the Faubourg St. Germain, its real value lies rather in its grip and coherent inclusion of a wide and moving scene. The unheralded melodrama of its close is a commentary on the criticism that, whatever may happen in Mr. James's novels, nothing comes of it. The truth being that the author occasionally in his earlier work displays almost a relish for violence in his conclusions.

*Reprinted from the *Edinburgh Review* 197 (January 1903):59–85.

# [*The Europeans*]    Anonymous*

*The Europeans*, Henry James, Jr.'s latest novel, is as original in plan and vigorous in execution as any of his previous books. As the title page indicates, it is "A Sketch," and the limning shows the hand of an artist. The Baroness Munster . . . comes to America in search of adventures and cousins, both of which she meets with. . . . Her brother Felix, an artist, handsome and *debonaire*, is her companion. . . . He loves and wins for bride . . . one of the new-found cousins, to whom he is the "prince" who has come to awaken her to her real self and the splendor of this beautiful world. Her hitherto sombre life has kept her faculties dormant, but under the influence of love, and the liberty for development that Felix opens to her, she blossoms out into a gracious womanhood. . . . The fascinating baroness, disappointed in some of her schemes, decides that America is not the place for really superior women, and that the older world opens a wider field of action to them. So, barely waiting for her brother's marriage, she flits back to Europe, leaving the other characters in this serio-comedy . . . to find their fitting mates, and all ends happily and satisfactorily. It is a delightful book, and the pleasant picture it leaves in the memory is not the least of its many charms.

*Reprinted, with minor omissions, from the *Boston Evening Transcript*, 4 December 1878, 6.

# [*Confidence:* James's Avoidance of the Passionate Situation]    Anonymous*

It cannot be said of any one of Mr. James's stories, "This is his best," or, "This is his worst": because no one of them is all one thing; like human beings, they are partly good, and partly not so good; they have their phases of exceeding strength and veracity, and also phases which are neither strong nor veracious. It does not concern us to give an explanation of this fact; it is to be found, of course, in the character or literary views of the writer himself; but we may observe that it seems to indicate either an actual lack of experience in certain directions, or else a constitutional reserve which prevents Mr. James from writing up to the experience he has. The experience we refer to is not of the ways of the world, with which Mr. James has every sign of being politely familiar; nor of men and women in their every-day aspect; still less of literary ways and means, of which he may be pronounced, in his own line, almost a master. The experience we

*Reprinted from the *Spectator* 53 (10 January 1880):48–49. This review was of the English edition, published in two volumes by Chatto & Windus.

mean is experience of passion. If Mr. James be not incapable of describing passion, at all events he has still to show that he is capable of it. During the last fifteen years, more or less, he has been writing stories of remarkable subtlety, charm, and literary finish; he has introduced us to many characters who seemed to have in them capacities for the highest passion—as witness Christina Light, in the novel called *Roderick Hudson;* and yet he has never allowed them to bring those capacities to the proof. He uniformly evades the situation; but the evasion is managed with so much ingenuity and plausibility, that although we may be disappointed, or even irritated, we are deprived of the right of giving those emotions satisfactory expression. We feel, more or less vaguely, that we have been unfairly dealt with, but we are unable to show exactly how the unfairness comes about.

This defect in Mr. James's novels would be less noticeable, were they in all other respects less excellent. As it is, they may be compared to a beautiful face, full of culture and good-breeding, but wanting that fire in the eye and fashion of the lip that shows a passionate human soul. Thus the beauty and other good attributes, which would have given the passion its fullest effect, are rendered by its absence akin to deformities. They have no business to be there, because their unsupported presence makes them seem incongruous, and therefore untrue. Beyond this complaint—which, to be sure, goes rather deep—we have little to say of Mr. James's novels that is not complimentary. He does not much trouble himself to contrive intricate plots, or to imagine strange situations but he cuts a slice out of life almost at haphazard, and then goes about to reveal and analyse its constituent parts. This method, when well applied, is very telling, though open to some obvious disadvantages. For, while the human element in fiction has ever the stronger interest, few human lives are so completely rounded as to give opportunity for an artistic *dénouement*. The story ends, but it leaves the reader still with something to wish for. Something in the way of incident and circumstance is useful to fill up the gap. However, Mr. James is never dull; his power of felicitous statement, taken by itself, would ensure him against that; and his occasional wit, his frequent touches of arch irony, and his unfailing thoughtfulness and purity of diction, are all so much to the good. He always puts his reader in a good humour, and makes him feel as if he were moving in the most cultivated society. The interest of his stories lies, as we have said, in the characters; we are introduced to them, and we generally see them distinctly enough, but we do not know them till later on, if at all; and we can never be sure what they will do next. This is what happens in real life; it is piquant and stimulating, and if it be not the very best plan to work upon in fiction (as to which point we are not at present prepared to give an opinion), it has, at all events, the authorisation of so eminent a master as Tourguéneff. What is more to the purpose, it evidently suits Mr. James, whose creed, so far as it may be guessed from his writings, seems to be a refined and elevated sort of materialism, insomuch that he objects to believe in anything that he has not objectively seen or known; and although endowed with a strength of superficial imagination which has seldom been surpassed, he shrinks from setting down in black and white anything for which his imagination is his only warrant. This is a most commendable principle, though there are doubtless limits to the extent to which it should be followed; Shakespeare, for example, could hardly have written some scenes of *Lear* from his actual knowledge; but, grasping as he did the very core of human nature, he was able to construct thence any conceivable human situation. We do not want Mr. James to write another *Lear*, but we do wish, in reference to his present book, that he had been pleased, in the *dénouement*, to trust a little more to what imagination would say might have happened, and a little less to what his personal experience of life had to propound on the matter. In *Confidence*, as in nearly all of Mr. James's novels, there is a point at which the reader could lay down the book and say, "This is one of the finest stories ever written." But the reader goes on, and he is disappointed. All the elements of a masterly conclusion are here, but the opportunity is not taken advantage of. The heroine, Angela Vivian, is one of Mr. James's best and largest feminine conceptions, which is saying a great deal, for his women are always better than his men, and his men are far above the ordinary fiction-level. Angela's character is steadily and luminously developed, without one false note or insufficient phrase, up to the 197th page of the second volume. Thenceforward she, and all the rest of the *dramatis personae* with her, become—to our comprehension, at least—incomprehensible. Gordon Wright, the last person in the world to do such a thing, abruptly puts on the mask of a scoundrel and a "cad." Bernard Longueville, the accomplished and clever man of the world, assumes the guise of a poltroon and an ass. And Angela, the noble, proud, and tender woman, whose mixture of simple honesty and inscrutable reserve has rendered her thus far a heroine for every reader to fall in love with,—Angela lapses into a theatric tone and attitude, and for the sake of creating a dramatic surprise utters and proposes absurdities which Blanche herself might have shrunk from. The effect, altogether, is as if the whole party, after having led a logical and respectable existence in a reasonable world, had suddenly grouped themselves before the footlights of some obscure, provincial stage, and begun to enact a piece of melodramatic claptrap. What could Mr. James have been thinking of?

The only suggestion we can make in answer to this question is, that he desired to avoid the true artistic conclusion demanded by his premises; and the reason of this desire was a reluctance to undertake the description of a passionate situation. It was a situation the right treatment of which would have raised Mr. James's reputation as a novelist to a place among the highest. Bernard Longueville was not the man tamely to submit to a gross insult levelled at the woman to whom he was betrothed, nor was Angela the woman either to be so insulted, or, in the very heat of the moment, composedly to execute a knowing little manoeuvre of insight, and, at the same time, to devise a far-fetched and improbable scheme of reconciliation. She would have set the wrong right, no doubt, as a heroine should; but it would have been by some grand dilation of the spirit, overawing and paralysing the baser soul. As for Bernard, unless we are greatly mistaken, he would have beckoned Gordon out of the room, and would then have promptly and relentlessly kicked him downstairs. Men who are in love and engaged to be married have a strong sense of possession, which will make a champion of the veriest craven, upon occasion given. The result of Mr. James's reticence—to call it by no severer name—is this: that he loses all belief in his own characters, and that they consequently lose their lifelikeness; that the remaining situations are tamely described through the medium of Angela's letters, and that the novel ends prematurely and stagnantly. Upon the whole, it strikes us that the author may have altered the design which he had sketched out for himself at the beginning of the story. Granting that Gordon might have married Blanche, there is no reason shown why the union should have turned out a more harmonious one than it was made superficially to appear. In the presentation of Gordon's character, furthermore, no indication is given of any element which would lead him deliberately to abandon his wife to a lover, in order to obtain grounds for a divorce from her. But no author of Mr. James's abilities has a right to violate the modesty of nature, merely to save himself the trouble of being arduously observant of it. At his worst, however, he provokes a great deal of reviewing.

## [*Washington Square:* A Rigidity of Purpose]

Anonymous*

Mr. James has been weighed in the most exact critical balances, and has had his every quality and defect accurately and unanimously counted to him. We do not open his new book to see whether it is good or bad, for long experience and nicety of perception have secured for Mr. James an immunity from failure which the possession of far higher gifts would not alone have insured him. It is not a discovery to habitual students of his work that his characters lack roundess, or that he is not a robust writer. Had he been destined ever to produce a novel after the established English pattern, we should doubtless have had such a work in *Washington Square.* Here Mr. James has made what is superficially a new departure. He has followed the track of custom so far as to select a situation solid and practical enough for the literary purposes of Mr. Trollope, characters which are in no way exceptional or problematic, and a *dénouement* so natural and so easily foreseen as to be almost a surprise in the case of a writer from whom

*Reprinted from *Lippincott's* 27 (February 1881):214–15. The first three sentences of the review have been omitted.

we have come to look for the bizarre and the unexpected. But except these few outward and visible signs there is nothing to distinguish *Washington Square* from its predecessors. It is not a whit more substantial or realistic, and it not less fine in touch. The chief result of this compromise with commonplace appears in a certain perfunctory air which the book wears. Even its epigrams suggest habit rather than spontaneity, and we feel as if the author had cramped his opportunity for being brilliant and *spirituel* when he planned a novelette containing only one character who is professedly clever. Even this personage, Dr. Sloper, suffers from isolation and lack of friction, and somehow fails to impress us as sufficiently luminous for a man who has absorbed the entire epigrammatic power of one of Mr. James's books. He is too consistently ironical. We should be sorry to think (though we believe certain wounded countrymen of the author regard Mr. James himself as an attestation of the fact) that the natural affections are killed by irony, as those of Dr. Sloper and his daughter appear to have been. There is a rigidity of purpose, in fact, about the whole book which strikes us as over-conscientious. The drama is absolutely confined to four personages, who uphold their respective and somewhat dreary roles with stoical firmness and resignation. No minor characters appear upon the scene to break the singleness of the effect, and the inference is irresistible that in 1840 (the time at which the story is laid) solitude reigned in Washington Square, and all its houses, save one, kept their shutters hermetically sealed.

# [*Washington Square:* A Most Refractory Provinciality]

Anonymous*

*Washington Square* . . . is one of Mr. Henry James's smoothly written, super-analytical, nothing-if-not-literary and upon the whole mildly pleasing novels. There has always been an air about Mr. James's writings which somehow gives the feeling that it is artificial, assumed for the occasion, and this assumption while evidently aiming at cosmopolitan breadth projects and accentuates a most refractory provinciality. His effort to appear to be writing down at his philistine countrymen and countrywomen from a vast aristocratic distance is so obvious, so strained and so incessant that it is beginning to take on the look of almost threadbare affectation. No genuinely intelligent and well-informed American believes for one moment that Mr. James has any special call to the chair of American Manners in the world's college, or that he has any particularly divine insight into the mysteries of Old World social refinements. Your well-bred American never insists upon his breeding, as Mr. James makes him do; and the chief trouble with Mr. James's style, as contradistinguished from his generally admirable

*Reprinted from the *Independent* 47 (30 May 1895):737.

diction, is an overwrought assumption (of breeding down from the original elect) which roots itself in European castles and palaces and mansions of the Vere de Veres. *Washington Square* is the work of a supremely clever literary artisan, self-conscious, artificial in every sense of the word and thoroughly un-American in all his sympathies and aspirations. As a fiction it is commonplace; as a verbal figment it is admirable.

## [*Washington Square:* A Turn-of-the-Century View]
Anonymous*

In 1880 came *Washington Square,* which must rank as one of the author's significant novels. One can think of no one else who could have written it, who could have used the spareness, the dullness of its material with such effect. Surely no heroine ever had less in her favour, than plain Catherine Sloper, yet we follow the conversion of her humble deference into a kind of heroic obstinacy with absorbed attention. "Her dignity was not aggressive; it never sat in state; but if you pushed far enough you could find it." The dignity disengaged itself at last, as a hard determination, from the pulp of her sad crushed sentimental spirit, and it is the slow creation of that hardness, not by the cruelty of fate, nor from her lover's falseness, but by the injustice of the father she had trusted and admired, which makes her story so engrossing. He had killed something in her life, and she turned its coffin into a kind of altar. Not consciously. It is the essence of her pathos that she seems never more than numbly conscious of what she feels. The whole story is a miracle in monotone; of the monotonous in life treated unmonotonously.

*Reprinted from the *Edinburgh Review* 197 (January 1903):59–85.

## [*The Portrait of a Lady:* A Masterly Painting of Moral and Intellectual Atmosphere]
John Ashcroft Noble*

The dominant qualities in the work of Mr. Henry James render that work intensely interesting to critical persons with a turn for analysis, but are, one would think, less calculated to attract the novel-reading crowd. He has a passion for perfection in the *technique* of craftsmanship, and a rather too unreserved disdain for what would be considered by the Philistine mind much more essential conditions of success in fiction. There is surely

*Reprinted from the *Academy* 20 (26 November, 1881):397–98.

something both illogical and perverse in the argument that, because many novels have become popular in spite, or even in virtue, of their bad qualities, all popular qualities must, therefore, be necessarily bad; and yet it is impossible to avoid the thought that much of Mr. James's work is the result of conscious or unconscious reasoning of this kind. He cultivates an artistic asceticism, or purism, or whatever it may be called, which, it must be admitted, is occasionally irritating even to those who are not worshippers of Dagon. It may not be well, for example, to subordinate all other interest to plot interest; but plot interest is not altogether contemptible. A novelist has to tell a story, though he has also to do other things which may be intrinsically better worth doing; and a story is not told when, as in *The Portrait of a Lady*, the last page of the third volume leaves all the threads of narrative hanging loose without even an attempt to unite them. Mr. James not only disappoints his readers, but does injustice to himself when he implicitly assumes that the interest aroused by the lady whose portrait he draws will be so lukewarm as to inspire no curiosity concerning the outcome of a great crisis in her history. Still, though in this and in one or two minor matters, Mr. James's stories are less imaginatively satisfying than they might be, the "peculiar difference" of his work is so valuable, so interesting, and at the same time so rare that one wants space for adequate celebration of it, and can spare none for complaint that some things are absent which we can get in plenty elsewhere. To note one achievement among many, I think that nothing in this book or in its predecessors is more remarkable than the masterly painting of moral and intellectual atmosphere— the realisable rendering not of character itself, but of those impalpable radiations of character from which we apprehend it long before we have *data* that enable us fully to comprehend it. As soon as we fairly see Mr. James's personages we have an impression, vague but sufficing, of their full possibilities, so that when we part from them we feel that they have not surprised or disappointed us, but have proved themselves consistent and homogeneous; and what makes this peculiar "effect" so valuable and interesting is that it is attained not by the hackneyed tricks and contrivances of ordinary fiction, but by the honest and direct workmanship which generally contents itself with a broad, fairly recognisable veracity devoid of anything like subtlety of portraiture. In *The Portrait of a Lady* the handling combines lightness and precision of touch in a way which is all but unique in contemporary English fiction, all the impressive effects of strong emphasis being achieved by that delicate accentuation which is as reposeful to the mental eye as the harmony of low-toned colours is to the physical. The most ambitiously conceived character in the book, Madame Merle, is perhaps the least successful; but the heroine is a very masterly portrait, and the account of her relations with Osmond before and after her marriage is full of psychological interest. Henrietta Stackpole, the female journalist, and her admirer, Mr. Bantling, are delineated with that high comedy humour which is becoming rarer every year; and the same fine quality, mingled with a strain of genuine and not too insistent pathos, appears in the delightful study of Ralph Touchett. We have not lately had so clever or so enjoyable a novel as *The Portrait of a Lady*.


# [*The Portrait of a Lady* as Pictorial Art]

Anonymous*

*The Portrait of a Lady,* by Henry James, Jun., fulfills all the technical conditions that are essential for the production of a perfect portrait in oil, save those that are mechanical or manual, and manifests clearly enough how successfully the pen may compete with the pencil in the sphere of pictorial art. Undoubtedly, in dealing with form and color, the pencil has the advantage of appealing directly to and delighting the eye, and the impressions it is thus able to make upon us are instantaneous and permanent; but it is subject to limitations which do not circumscribe the range or hamper the freedom of the pen. For however admirable a portrait in colors may be, it can present its subject in one only of his attitudes, it must drape him in an unvarying garb, it must environ him with accessories that become monotonous under their unchanging fixedness, and it can only reproduce the expression that he wore at a single moment of his life. In his contention with the limitations of his art, the painter, among other devices of technical detail that we need not specify, has been obliged to resort to the expedient of repeated sittings, so that his work shall not reflect a single fleeting or momentary play of expression, but shall combine those regnant and characteristic expressions which reflect the man when at his best, and which may be caught by studying him in different moods and fluctuations of feeling and temperament. An artist with the pen has no need to resort to this expedient, as Mr. James demonstrates in his continuous and sustained portraiture of the heroine of his long and fragmentary but profoundly interesting tale. Instead of her repeated sittings being condensed into one final touch, which necessarily sacrifices far more than it preserves, each contributes to the completeness of the picture without detracting from its unity. And the result is a vivid and life-like portrait of a woman at different stages of her life from girlhood to womanhood, as she is insensibly influenced by varying local, personal, and social environments, or by the teachings of sweet or bitter experience, but yet ever remaining intrinsically the same, and notwithstanding the shipwreck of some of her ideals, throughout preserving her cherished illusions and her distinctive and winsome individuality. Besides this elaborate portrait, several other subsidiary and contrasted portraits are introduced of men and women who came into the life of the heroine, and alternately checkered it with cloud and sunshine, which, like the

*Reprinted from *Harper's New Monthly Magazine* 64 (February 1882):474.

principal figure, are painted in rich but delicate colors, and are noteworthy for the clearness and definiteness of their outlines, and for their display of emphatic but not violent contrasts.

# [*The Portrait of a Lady:* James's Masterpiece]

Edgar Fawcett*

Into [*The Portrait of a Lady*], as it seems to us, Mr. James has poured his soul, and given the world something that it will not soon let die. . . . It is the longest thing that he has written, but it is also the most majestic and unassailable. Its heroine is a character whose misfortunes are the imperative catastrophes resultant from her own ideal strivings. Unlike Roderick Hudson, Isabel Archer does not recklessly sow the seed of her own future torments. She makes a pitiable error, but she makes it in all womanly faith and sincerity. She is a beautiful, talented, exceptionally lovable girl, and suddenly, at a period when she desires more than ever before to wrest a fecund and splendid victory from the usual aridity of life—to ennoble herself by subjugating herself—to live a power for good and to die somehow perpetuating such a power—at this very period, we say, she is lifted from the inertia of longing to the possibility of achievement. A fortune is left her, in a most unexpected manner; vistas of new purpose are opened to her; the prospect is dazzling at first; she hardly knows what she shall do with these charming, golden opportunities. She does what nearly every woman of her personal graces would do under the same conditions. Out of four suitors . . . she selects a man whom she marries, believing him a paragon of wisdom, virtue, taste, refinement, notability. He is poor, and it is a comfort for her to feel him so. For this reason he and she shall be yoked, all the more, in exercise of noble end. Her love, which is a reverence, becomes a horror of disappointed discovery. The whole novel is a sort of monumental comment upon the dread uncertainties of matrimony. Isabel's husband, whom she believed of a spirit equally lofty and amiable, turns out a frigid self-worshipper, a creature whose blood is ichor, whose creed is an adoration of *les usages*, whose honor is a brittle veneer of decorum, beneath which beats a heart as formally regular as the strokes of a well-regulated clock. He has married her with very much the same motive as that which might prompt him to buy a new bit of antique *bric-a-brac* at slight cost from a shrewd dealer. He is a virtuoso, a collector, a person who puts immense value upon all exterior things, and he considers life, happiness, matrimony, womanhood, principle, even divinity itself as an exceedingly exterior thing. Isabel's amazement, her grief, her dismay, her passionate mutiny, and her final bitter resignation, constitute the chief substance of

*Reprinted from "Henry James's Novels," *Princeton Review*, 14 (July 1884):82–85.

this remarkable book. But much more than this goes to make the book, as a thousand turrets, traceries, illuminations and sculptures go to make a great result in architecture. It is a book with a very solid earth beneath it and a very luminous . . . sky above it. It is rich in passages of quotable description, and no less rich in characters of piercing vividness. It contains more than one "portrait of a lady," as it contains more than one portrait of a man. Madame Merle, the perfectly equipped woman of the world, the charmer, the *intrigante*, the soft-voiced, soft-moving diplomatist, and yet (as we feel more than we are really told) the force for ill, the adulteress, and the arch-hypocrite—Madame Merle, we say, is incomparably depicted. Again, the dying Ralph Touchett, with his mixture of the cynic and the humanitarian, with his love for Isabel alike so exquisitely concealed and revealed, with his patience, his outbursts of regret, his poetry of feeling, his inalienable dignity and manhood, is an astonishingly striking conception. He exists, to our knowledge, nowhere else in any pages of fiction. He is the high-tide mark of what Mr. James can do with a human individuality, and he represents what Mr. James likes most to do with one. We all must recognize him if we have lived and thought. As the author first presents him to us, we involuntarily recall having seen someone who looked just like him. This may not be true, but the sensation of having met Ralph Touchett before is none the less insistent, and proves how marvellous is Mr. James's faculty for hitting off with a few airy or rough touches the physical "points" of his fellow-creatures. . . .

But, after all, tho he and Isabel are the two triumphs of the book, they are merely the crown of a perfect edifice; all the rest of the structure is of a correspondent excellence. The demure little Pansy, with her unswerving propriety, her devout, filial faith, her enormous sense of rule and law and obedience, is a picture of puritanic simplicity whose tints should last for other generations than ours. So, too, Lord Warburton, as regards crisp and potent yet harmonious and secure character-painting. He is the Liberal English peer to a fault,—with mind enough to understand that his position is absurd, yet with inherited pride enough to preserve an unblemished caste. Quotation, in *The Portrait of a Lady,* is a dangerous temptation. Every page offers abundant chance for it, filled as every page is with epigram, thought, knowledge of the world, glancing play of humor and sportive resilience of fancy.

# Henry James, Jr., and the Modern Novel                    J. H. Morse*

We reviewed lately in these columns the last of Henry James's novels, *The Portrait of a Lady,* and summed up briefly what seemed to us to be

*Reprinted from the *Critic* 2 (14 January 1882):1.

the leading characteristics of that tantalizing story. But we hardly like to leave the matter without some more general considerations regarding the author and his work. He is so much the creation of the modern or scientific methods—so representative of them in the world of romance—that he almost makes a school of novel-writing by himself. He is neither American nor French, much less English, in his treatment of life, but is realistic, almost materialistic, as opposed to spiritual and imaginative. Perhaps his natural antagonism is transcendentalism. The human character is to him mechanical. All its springs can be touched. If there is any power behind—any mighty force that moves even machinery, he fails to see it, or to believe in it. What lies on the surface he sees; what he can get by taking the machine to pieces, he gets at with remarkable precision. He certainly excels in portrait-painting, and his excellence grows. He improves in every fresh work. His dissection of moods, of motives, of sections of life is as minute and neat and complete as one could desire. His observation takes a wide range, and his eye is keen for shading in character. To find fault with his results one must get away from the fascination of immediate inspection. The artistic work is too exact and polished. There is no flaw in the workmanship. The neat, epigrammatic French academician could not make more compact dialogue, could not exclude from a sentence more rigorously all superfluous epithet. The most rigorous realist would fail to find any trace of sentimentality. His personages are all earth-born, and no high celestial essence ever bears the gross earthy particle to which it is attached beyond the reach of gravitation. Indeed, the spiritual becomes earthy, the ethereal materialized, the Newtonic theory of gravitation prevails and all comes down together. One is astonished to find how essentially matter-of-fact love and aspiration and all upward forces are. Sometimes one is more than astonished; he is chagrined and hurt. He feels cheated. But when he looks again at the analysis, he finds there is no cheat. It is all there in nature—the grossness, the heaviness, the earthy. If it is some ambitious, calculating love which the reader would chide, he has only to turn to his sister or his first-cousin, instead of the lovely girl he left in the last ball-room, to find the model which the artist has chosen, and he recognizes the main truth of the picture.

This is the trouble. The technique is perfect; but we quarrel with it. It satisfies the intellect and the observing faculties. It satisfies the man at the club-window; but it does not satisfy the heart. The heart idealizes; it puts in qualities and colors which re-create the picture; but when the artist looks about for the pigments, he fails to find them. It is the story over again of the unilluminated painter who puts into the landscape all there is to be seen, all that can be reduced to visibility and tangibility, and yet leaves out the peculiar effect of atmosphere and light—

> The light that never was on sea or land,
> The consecration and the poet's dream.

What is it that is left out? If we read any sketch by Hawthorne—"Old Ticonderoga," for instance—as against any chapter of James's, we are conscious at once of the value of imagination in novel-writing. It is easy to see that Mr. James lacks all this weird and beautiful faculty as it existed in Hawthorne—that is, he lacks the spiritual quality. He does not come within a hundred leagues of him; and yet the technique in Hawthorne is perfect; the description is exact, as far as it goes. There are plenty of details left out which Mr. James would put in; but there is one thing put in which Mr. James leaves out, and that one thing makes the whole beauty and charm of the picture. What is it? It is equally easy to see that our author has none of the pathos of Dickens. He cannot approach him, and he would not if he could. It is to him unreal. He cannot analyze and find it in nature. It belongs to the intangible, invisible; and Mr. James lives wholly in the world of scientific reality. Ralph Touchett has something as nearly akin to pathos as anything in James, but the writer is half ashamed of it. We can equally well assert that our novelist has none of the broad humor of Walter Scott—that intense human element which so rolls and rollicks in good nature. He has wit, but no strong, rich humor. He can be sarcastic to a degree, but never genial, like Thackeray. So that, with humor and pathos and spiritual imagination left out, we leave him not Thackeray, nor Dickens, nor Scott, nor Hawthorne; but he is still Henry James—acute, witty, incisive, flashing, entertaining, provoking, interesting, but not warming, or delighting, or elevating us a particle. We can read him by the hour and be fascinated, but not touched strongly. We quarrel eternally with his conclusions, but can seldom justify ourselves in words for the quarrel. We feel keenly and resent the loss of the element of warmth and color, of human sweetness and sympathy. Whenever he attempts to paint what is noble, he lessens the beauty of nobility; and whenever he touches upon high sentiment, high sentiment loses in some degree its disinterestedness. There is certainly in us all some general quality better than all our detail; and in the true artist we have a right to expect the power to discover and reproduce this quality. It is, after all, the power of breathing life into his mechanism. As the methods of scientific thinking do much to eliminate the spiritual action of the imagination, so the methods of scientific analysis of character have a tendency to eliminate the life-principle in all representation of human action.

# Henry James, Jr.                    William Dean Howells*

. . . The art of fiction, has, in fact, become a finer art in our day than it was with Dickens and Thackeray. We could not suffer the confidential

*Reprinted from the Century 25 (November 1882):28–29. This excerpt of Howells's essay (pp. 25–29) contains the ideas that sparked contemporary controversy.

attitude of the latter now, nor the mannerism of the former, any more than we could endure the prolixity of Richardson or the coarseness of Fielding. These great men are of the past—they and their methods and interests; even Trollope and Reade are not of the present. The new school derives from Hawthorne and George Eliot rather than any others; but it studies human nature much more in its wonted aspects, and finds its ethical and dramatic examples in the operation of lighter but not really less vital motives. The moving accident is certainly not its trade; and it prefers to avoid all manner of dire catastrophes. It is largely influenced by French fiction in form; but it is the realism of Daudet rather than the realism of Zola that prevails with it, and it has a soul of its own which is above the business of recording the rather brutish pursuit of a woman by a man, which seems to be the chief end of the French novelist. This school, which is so largely of the future as well as the present, finds its chief exemplar in Mr. James; it is he who is shaping and directing American fiction, at least. It is the ambition of the younger contributors to write like him; he has his following more distinctly recognizable than that of any other English-writing novelist. Whether he will so far control this following as to decide the nature of the novel with us remains to be seen. Will the reader be content to accept a novel which is an analytic study rather than a story, which is apt to leave him arbiter of the destiny of the author's creation? Will he find his account in the unflagging interest of their development? Mr. James's growing popularity seems to suggest that this may be the case; but the work of Mr. James's imitators will have much to do with the final result.

In the meantime it is not surprising that he has his imitators. Whatever exceptions we take to his methods or his results, we cannot deny him a very great literary genius. To me there is a perpetual delight in his way of saying things, and I cannot wonder that younger men try to catch the trick of it. The disappointing thing for them is that it is not a trick, but an inherent virtue. His style is, upon the whole, better than that of any other novelist I know; it is always easy, without being trivial, and it is often stately, without being stiff; it gives a charm to everything he writes; and he has written so much and in such various directions, that we should be judging him very incompletely if we considered him only as a novelist. His book of European sketches must rank him with the most enlightened and agreeable travelers; and it might be fitly supplemented from his uncollected papers with a volume of American sketches. In his essays on modern French writers he indicates his critical range and grasp; but he scarcely does more, as his criticisms in *The Atlantic* and *The Nation* and elsewhere could abundantly testify.

There are indeed those who insist that criticism is his true vocation, and are impatient of his devotion to fiction; but I suspect that these admirers are mistaken. A novelist he is not after the old fashion, or after any fashion but his own; yet since he has finally made his public in his own way of storytelling—or call it character-painting if you prefer—it must be conceded that he has chosen best for himself and his readers in choosing the form of fiction for what he has to say. It is, after all, what a writer has to say rather than what he has to tell that we care for nowadays. In one manner or other the stories were all told long ago; and now we want merely to know what the novelist thinks about persons and situations. Mr. James gratifies this philosophic desire. If he sometimes forbears to tell us what he thinks of the last state of his people, it is perhaps because that does not interest him, and a large-minded criticism might well insist that it was childish to demand that it must interest him.

I am not sure that my criticism is sufficiently large-minded for this. I own that I like a finished story; but then also I like those which Mr. James seems not to finish. This is probably the position of most of his readers, who cannot very logically account for either preference. We can only make sure that we have here an annalist or analyst, as we choose, who fascinates us from his first page to his last, whose narrative or whose comment may enter into any minuteness of detail without fatiguing us, and can only grieve us when it ceases.

# [The Storm over Howells's Praise of James]
George W. Curtis*

Mr. Howells must be disposed to swear that he will never do another good-natured thing. Some months ago he wrote a paper upon Mr. Henry James, Jun., giving in a most friendly and pleasant manner his estimate of that gentleman's talent and work, and naturally expressing some views upon fictitious writing in general, with casual comments upon some famous story-tellers. The paper was written in the most quiet tone, but it has raised an uproar. Indeed, nothing that Mr. Howells has ever written has caused such commotion. He has been accused of depreciating plots in stories because he has no invention, and of decrying great names that he may exalt little men. He is charged with uttering a counterfeit theory of novel-writing to enrich his own reputation and that of Mr. James. In fact, these two excellent and inoffensive writers are represented as a pair of accomplished literary "cracksmen" who are bent upon breaking into the inner treasury of Fame, and carrying off her choicest prizes for themselves. The virulence of the assault upon Mr. Howells for writing the paper, and upon Mr. James for being written about, recalls the feeling with which a couple of clever, well-dressed, and high-mannered boys are sometimes regarded by the crowd of Dr. Birch's young friends.

The turmoil touches the ludicrous point in an article in the London *Quarterly Review,* which actually describes Mr. Howells's paper as a crafty

*Reprinted from *Harper's Monthly* 66 (May 1883):791–93. A few passages that merely emphasize Curtis's points have been omitted.

puff of his friend James and himself. The *Quarterly* sneers at them as pretentious novelists advertising themselves energetically; and with a wholly unnecessary bitterness it girds at the "artificial mannerisms" and "tawdry smartness" of their tales, even stooping to speak of the "pretty portrait" published with Mr. Howells's paper, until the reader can not avoid the suspicion that some personal malevolence goads the writer to a tone as destitute of literary courtesy as it is of critical discrimination. It is surely a severe arraignment of the reading public of the two English-speaking countries to represent them as charmed with the works of a pair of feeble, dawdling, mutually admiring coxcombical pretenders.

The views which Mr. Howells holds of literary art, of fiction, and of novel-writers may be sound or unsound, according to the reader's own opinions of those subjects. But they are the honest opinions of a man who by charming the literary taste of his time has gained the public ear, and they are expressed with perfect courtesy and refinement. They are neither disproved nor disturbed by a sneer that he is envious of Thackeray, and that he is a whipster striking at Walter Scott. When Mr. Howells says that the stories were all told long ago, and that now we wish mainly to know what the novelist thinks about persons and situations, he means to say, as we understand him, that analytic fiction is more agreeable to the literary taste of the time than descriptive fiction. This does not seem to be very wide of the the truth. What is it but saying that the novel of adventure like Smollett's, and even the historical novel of Scott, are less to the public mind than the critical, observing, moralizing story of George Eliot and Thackeray? Mr. Howells says that we should not permit a writer nowadays to stop and preach as Thackeray does in his novels. But Thackeray good-humoredly chides himself for the practice, while, for our own part, we think it one of his delightful traits, and could no more spare the sermon than the text.

To represent Mr. Howells as decrying the great masters of his art is absurd. He is merely noting the changes of taste and the new stage of development, and he points out why, to an age which is introspective and analytical, a critical talent in fiction is not less attractive than a creative talent. The wrong done to Mr. Howells lies in regarding his paper upon Mr. James as a complete body of doctrine upon novel-writing, and the expression of his estimate of novel-writers. . . .

The *Quarterly Review* reproaches Mr. Howells and Mr. James that their stories are not American in the sense that Brockden Brown's and Cooper's and Hawthorne's are American, but that they introduce us to Europeanized Americans, which adds nothing to the knowledge of American character. Apparently the *Quarterly Review* thinks a novel to be American if it deals with the prairie and the Indian, the Puritan, and the city of Washington. Certainly such a novel may be American, as the stories of Cooper and Hawthorne attest, but not necessarily, as Campbell's "Gertrude of Wyoming" proves. It has escaped the *Quarterly*'s attention, perhaps, that nothing is more distinctively interesting in American life than the effect upon its development of European influence. Civilized America, as the *Quarterly* may remember, is in its origin, European. . . .

The pinchbeck imitations of foreign follies in this country, indeed, are as ludicrous as the sage assertion of Americans who admired the Second French Empire that things would never be in proper order here until a monarchy should be well established. But the Europeanized American, in whatever form he may be viewed, is as distinctive an American figure, and as legitimate a study for the satirist, the novelist, or the philosopher, as Billy Bowlegs, or Leather-stocking, or a party boss. Daisy Miller, on the other hand, although a mere sketch, a study, is quite as distinctively American as any heroine in Cooper's novels, while the women in Mr. Howells's stories, if not of the highest type of womanhood, are intrinsically Yankees.

Meanwhile that gentleman must be greatly amused by the commotion which his comments upon Mr. James and the literary taste of the age have produced. Neither of these gentlemen is likely to be diverted or perverted from his own course by loud denunciation of his canons of literary art or by caustic depreciation of his literary work. No men who write the English language to-day have a higher estimate of that art, or are more thoroughly and carefully trained in its exercise. In this they are like Hawthorne and Irving. But the abstract question of comparative genius is always a thankless one. . . .

## *The Bostonians*                                              Anonymous*

Mr. Henry James calls *The Bostonians* "a novel," and as we suppose that the characters are fictitious, and as the work is one in three volumes, perhaps he may be justified by convention in so terming it. But anything less like the ordinary novel than *The Bostonians* has not appeared in our day,—even from his own pen. *The Bostonians* is a wonderfully clever book, so clever in many parts even in execution, and so original in conception, that one can almost pardon the questionable tedium of a large portion of the second and third volumes, from which we get the impression that a comparatively slight study has been put under a microscope, and rendered in all the extended dimensions of an artificially magnified image. Only the opening and the close of the book are really effective, and they are almost as effective as it is possible for such a study as this in novel situations and novel characters to be. But between the opening and the close are long tracts of carefully studied delineation, in which the reader does not seem to get any further, but only to traverse again and again the same rudely

*Reprinted from the *Spectator* 59 (20 March 1886):388. The edition under review is the three-volume London edition published by Macmillan & Co. A long quotation describing Dr. Prance has been omitted.

pioneered and yet half desolate track,—a track of thought curiously blend-
ing half-matured ideas and aspirations with elaborated earnestness and refined passion, a track of enthusiasm going quite beyond the bounds of any
kind of wisdom, though quaintly mixed with elevated and even delicate
sensibilities. And all these elements are combined in Mr. Henry James's
picture with a very graphic delineation of spurts of Yankee shrewdness and
vulgar ostentation. *The Bostonians* consists chiefly of a truly wonderful
sketch of the depth of passion which has been embodied in the agitation of
woman's wrongs and woman's rights,—a depth of passion which it is hardly
possible for us in England to associate with anything short of religious fervour. Miss Olive Chancellor is the central figure of this agitation. She herself has nothing of the agitator in her, except so far as the real passion
which burns in her makes her willing to devote herself wholly to the right-
ing of those real or fancied wrongs. She herself is proud, shy, and refined,
profoundly sensible of the disgust which all the vulgarities of organised
movements and largely advertised philanthropies are calculated to excite in
such minds as hers, but none the less eaten up with the notion that if
women could but become what they ought to be in society and the State,
all the worse evils of our day would have disappeared at once. It is hardly
possible to speak with too much admiration of this powerful sketch of a refined, passionate, reserved woman, loathing the vulgar side of publicity,
and yet so eager for what she thinks the great reform of the age, that she
is launched into the vulgarities of the trading Yankee philanthropist against
her will, and in spite of the most lively sensation of horror and reluctance.
Her consuming desire for a friendship that should amount to a passion, her
steadfast and self-forgetting devotion when she finds such a friendship, her
deep and fierce jealousy when it is threatened by her friend's liability to a
stronger passion, and the tragic collapse both of the tie and of the great
mission on which the two friends had embarked, beneath the blighting influence of this stronger love, are painted with a force and originality such
as even Mr. Henry James has never before exhibited in an equal degree.
The contrast, too, between Olive Chancellor, one of those women who
"take life hard," and Verena Tarrant, one of those women who "take life
easy" and who yet reflect so meekly the stronger wills with which they
come into contact, that they are liable to present the false appearance of
sharing the deeper passions and embodying the fanatical enthusiams of
their friends, is very powerfully drawn. The reserved, reticent, enthusias-
tic, passionate girl, of perverse culture and misdirected zeal,—the true
Bostonian of illuminate earnestness and neological enthusiasm,—is contrasted on the one side with her own sister, a sister of the light-minded,
fashionable type, and on the other side with this charming, sparkling, eloquent, easy-going friend of hers, who has a sort of gift for attractive elocu-
tion and vivid fascination, and who, as the other hopes, will become the
medium for utilising and popularising all her own fervour and knowledge.
And again, there is a fourth feminine, or quasi-feminine, figure, intended

to furnish us with a contrast to both Olive Chancellor and Verena Tarrant,—the lady-doctor, Dr. Prance, whose matter-of-fact, dry intelligence is portrayed with all Mr. Henry James's humour and subtlety. All four are genuine Bostonians,—Olive Chancellor, a Bostonian of that most remarkable type in which the fiery Calvinism of old Massachusetts has undergone an intellectual transformation into one of the hybrid social enthusiasms of this half-baked century; Mrs. Luna, a fashionable, selfish Bostonian, who has a horror of these intellectual and moral knight-errantries; Verena Tarrant, a Bostonian formed to some extent by the atmosphere of public movements and progressist excitements, of whom the habit of the platform has taken a superficial hold, without in the least derogating from the softness of her womanly heart; and Dr. Prance, a Bostonian of the rigidly scientifically type, whose dry intelligence despises all the Quixotisms of the day, while her Yankee shrewdness warns her that it is hardly safe publicly to denounce them. Of these four figures, Olive Chancellor's is much the most original and powerful, but Doctor Prance is the most effective and finished. . . . And to this quadruple sketch of Boston womanhood there is added yet a fifth, in some respects the most pathetic of all,—that of the good, misty-minded, self-forgetful, worked-out old philanthropist, Miss Birdseye, who has believed in so many progressive movements that she has lost almost all hold on individual character, and goes about tendering her aid indiscriminately to almost every society which asks it in the name of what seem to be benevolent and progressive principles. Mr. Henry James has rarely presented us with anything more beautiful than the last scenes of this innocent old lady's life. His touch is usually more or less cynical; but while he makes some fun of Miss Birdseye when he first introduces her, the last scenes of her life are full of beauty and true pathos.

We could not give any adequate illustration of the cultivated fanatic and of her eloquent friend in any one extract, and must refer our readers to the book itself for the very powerful study of this pair of characters. But we must say that Mr. Henry James has fallen so deeply in love with his own study, that he is tempted to dwell on it and almost maunder over it, till it bores his readers; and it is not till we get to the second half of the third volume that the picture of the struggle between the fanatic friend and the imperious lover, for the heart of Verena Tarrant, rises to the highest point of interest and power. The close of the book is singularly effective, though, as usual, Mr. Henry James snuffs out the light of his story with a disagreeable sort of snap in his last sentence. He has apparently almost repented himself of having thrown so much true feeling into the death-scene of Miss Birdseye, and he makes up for it by breaking-off, with perhaps even more than his usual *brusquerie*, the love-story of Verena Tarrant. On the whole, though we can truly say that we have never read any work of Mr. Henry James which had in it so much that was new and original, we must also say that we have never read any tale of his that had in it so much of long winded reiteration and long drawn-out disquisition. Perhaps that, too, is in its way a reflection of the thin, long-drawn elaborateness of Bostonian modes of thought.

## [*The Bostonians:* A "Comprehensive Condemnation"]      Anonymous*

*The Bostonians* is ponderous. To the best of our recollection no work by Mr. James can compare with it in monotonous and oppressive solidity. The humorous portions themselves—and the patches of humor are numerous—have not an exhilarating effect; and the book can only be defined as dismal. Mr. James has chosen a disagreeable subject and developed it at inordinate length, with hardly an attempt to relieve the prevailing lowness of tone by contrasting episodes, and with less than his usual felicity in the description of character and the analysis of motives. The personages to whom he presents us are a group of female emancipators, inspirational speakers, magnetic healers, and miscellaneous lecture-room reformers, and there are flashes of excellent satire in the sketches of their talk and manners; but we have so much of their company and so little of anything else, we are asked to enter so often into their states of mind and to busy ourselves so much with their crudeness, vulgarity and weakness, that they become inexpressibly tiresome. Long before we are half through the book we feel as if we had been shut up for a whole evening with a party of very voluble progressive thinkers in a third-rate boarding-house. It was a great blunder quite to fill a novel with disagreeable persons and unpleasant incidents. There is nobody in *The Bostonians* with whom it is possible to feel a spark of sympathy, nobody from whose counterpart in real life we would not flee as from a stupendous bore.

From this comprehensive condemnation we certainly do not except the heroine. Verena Tarrant, who has been trained by an odious humbug, her father, to pose as a public rhapsodist, and yet possesses a fresh girlish charm, generosity and frankness, is an impossible supposition to begin with, and Mr. James does not make her plausible by his exceedingly minute statement of her feelings. Mr. Howells treated a similar idea in one of the very best of his novels, *An Undiscovered Country,* and he did it with far more skill and far more poetical feeling than Mr. James exhibits in this over-wrought but under-done study. We hardly know how Mr. James understands his heroine, but she appears to the outside world as a girl of a shallow nature and a weak will, who is always under somebody's control, whose perceptions are not acute, and whose ideals are neither high nor refined, yet who takes a desperate resolution in the last scene of which only

*Reprinted from the *New-York Daily Tribune,* 28 March 1886, 6. A few sentences at the end of the review have been omitted.

a strong character would have been capable. We are told that she was fascinating; but none of her actions are attractive, and her talk is the jargon of a public performer with a "gift." Her connection with Olive Challoner [sic], who believes in the girl's destiny as a prophetess of the great cause of woman's rights, lavishes upon her a passionate affection, and makes it her own mission to keep her from debasing and distracting associations, has in it the elements of a tragedy, which indeed is imperfectly outlined in the last chapter. Miss Challoner is by far the strongest personage in the story. But unfortunately Miss Challoner is also the most repulsive. Her grim fanaticism almost passes the bounds of sanity: the pathos of her struggle to keep Verena, and her cruel defeat, is spoiled by our constant consciousness that Miss Challoner was an appalling nuisance. All her traits, except her savage devotion to a mistaken idea, are unlovely. When she appears among the "Bostonians" the temptation to skip becomes almost irresistible.

If Mr. James had desired to discredit his own theory of the novel, to convince us that the construction of a story is worth while after all, and that the dissection of morbid consciences and the description of common and unpleasant persons and things are not the highest aims of art, he could have contrived no better argument than the publication of the "Bostonians." We have said enough to show that his principal characters are not worth much pains; the subordinate actors, including the hero, are of slight consequences and are slightly treated. As for the story, that does not move at all until about the four-hundredth page. Then Mr. James hurries things to an end, as he generally does when he is tired of his work. In this case, however, he winds up with a violent and sensational scene which has not been justified beforehand by anything in the course of events or in the development of the characters. . . .

## *The Princess Casamassima*                    Richard F. Littledale*

The criticism which best fits Mr. Henry James's new novel is . . .— the picture would have been better if the painter had taken less pains. He is a convert, and an ardent one, to the great French literary heresy, that it is of much more consequence how a thing is said than what it is that is said; and the result is that he produces works which are admirable examples of style, and are devoid of the faintest glimmer of interest. And in the present case, he has yielded to yet another of his besetting temptations—a fatal prolixity and minuteness of detail so that one cannot see the wood for the trees. The book is as long as two ordinary novels, and there is no apparent reason why it might not be continued to ten times its actual length. It is

*Reprinted from the *Academy* 30 (13 November 1886):323. The edition under review is the three-volume English edition.

rather a gallery of portraits than a story, and the portraits are very carefully individualised. But the very profusion of detail, the multiplicity of touches, like too much cross-hatching in an engraving, detracts from the vigor and definiteness of the original outline, and diminishes the reader's power of realisation. This is especially true of the heroine—one of Mr. James's international cosmopolitans; but very much the kind of personage who would be more at home under the treatment of an author whose canons of art are widely unlike those of Mr. James—Ouida herself. More successful, though scarcely generic enough for a type, is Millicent Henning, the London girl of the shopwoman and factory-hand class, who is very cleverly conceived, and not so painfully elaborated as the princess, because occupying a less important place. Lady Aurora Langrishe, the shy and nervous philanthropist, is also well sketched, and so is a shrewd-witted bed-ridden sister of one of the men actors. The hero, Hyacinth Robinson, a young fellow born in disastrous circumstances, and never fully escaping to a happier position, is over-elaborated almost as much as the heroine, and equally fails to arouse active interest. When Mr. James leaves narrative, politics, and dialogue, and sets himself to paint London street views, his touch is vivid and sympathetic; and one almost pardons him the tedious and arid stretches of mere verbiage, as one lights on these rare and welcome oases.

## [*The Princess Casamassima:* James as Mere Observer]

Anonymous*

Henry James's new book, *The Princess Casamassima*, contains six hundred closely-printed pages,—a statement which may seem all the more alarming when it is added that there is hardly any story. The pages are filled out with conversations and descriptions, so clever—so brilliant, indeed—that you are exasperated with yourself for taking only a languid interest in them. Perhaps this is because the characters are so realistically unreal. Mr. James concerns himself only with the actual world of today: he carefully eschews the ideal characters, the romantic incidents, which the finer art of the modern novelist has taught him to abandon. He banishes from his stage Harlequin and Columbine, Prince Charming and the Fairy Godmother; he lays his scene in modern London, attends carefully to all the accessories, and sustains the local color with admirable art. Yet the illusion is incomplete. Hyacinth Robinson, Paul Muniment, Lady Aurora, the Princess herself,—all these characters who talk so much and do so little and are so cleverly manipulated,—strike you not as real men and women, but as ingenious manikins who excite curiosity by the closeness with which they simulate life. You are never really deceived by them, but you feel as

*Reprinted from *Lippincott's* 39 (March 1887):359.

if at any moment you might be deceived. When their creator lays bare their inner selves and explains the motives of their actions, he does not appear in the light of a social philosopher probing the secret springs of human action, but rather of an inventor explaining the mechanism by which his puppets are made to play their appointed parts. The book makes one sigh for the methods of those great masters whom Mr. Howells has told us are of the past,—for the confidential attitude of Thackeray or the mannerism of Dickens. Here is a novel which glances at some of the most important and far-reaching problems of the present, whose chief characters are conspirators plotting against the existing social order and discussing the wrongs of the oppressed,—material enough, one would think, for stirring incident, and ample opportunity for pointing a moral, expressing a conviction, or delivering a warning. Yet the author's attitude is that of a mere observer: he preserves throughout the calm, superior air of one who has outgrown emotion and enthusiasm; he looks upon his fellow-beings only as available literary material. What does he believe? Does he hate? Does he love? If you prick him does he bleed? These questions cannot be answered from his work.

## [*The Princess Casamassima:* A Great Novel]

Anonymous*

We find *no* fault with Mr. Henry James's *Princess Casamassima:* it is a great novel; it is his greatest, and it is incomparably the greatest novel of the year in our language. . . . From first to last we find no weakness in the book; the drama works simply and naturally; the causes and effects are logically related; the theme is made literature without ceasing to be life. There is an easy breadth of view and a generous scope which recall the best Russian work; and there is a sympathy for the suffering and aspiration in the book which should be apparent even to the critical groundlings, though Mr. James forbears as ever, to pat his people on the back, to weep upon their necks, or to caress them with endearing and compassionate epithets and pet names. A mighty good figure, which we had almost failed to speak of, is the great handsome shop-girl Millicent Henning, in whose vulgar good sense and vulgar good heart the troubled soul of Hyacinth Robinson finds what little repose it knows.

Mr. James's knowledge of London is one of the things that strike the reader most vividly, but the management of his knowledge is vastly more important. If any one would see plainly the difference between the novel-

*Reprinted from *Harper's* 74 (April 1887):829. A review of the narrative and description of the characters has been omitted.

ist's work and the partisan's work, let him compare *The Princess Casamas-sima* and Mr. W. H. Mallock's last tract, which he calls *The Old Order Changes.*

## [*The Tragic Muse:* Or
## *The Idiot Asylum?*]

George Saintsbury*

We have sufficient respect for Mr. Henry James to review him frankly—the greatest compliment that can be paid to a novelist. And, therefore, we shall say at once that, to our thinking, *The Idiot Asylum* would have been a better title for his new book than *The Tragic Muse.* Such a company of, by their own showing, imbeciles in word and deed has rarely been got together by a writer of great talent. We remember long ago an innocent critic-without-knowing-it who, casting in despair a book aside, exclaimed: "I can't make out why anybody does anything!" A similar lamb of the flock might with justice make a similar remark on *The Tragic Muse.* There are about two people in it—Peter Sherringham, the diplomatist, and his sister, Julia Dallow, a wealthy widow—who, though the former is besot-ted with a mindless actress, and the latter with a backboneless coxcomb, are alive, and human, it being indeed extremely human and alive to be so besotted. But the actress and the coxcomb and his mother, the correct Lady Agnes, and his sisters (one pretty and *sympathique,* the other plain and dense), and his friend Mr. Gabriel Nash, who is a kind of caricature of a long series of other caricatures, and the rest of them, are such things as nightmares are made of. They come, like the language that they talk, of constant imitation and re-imitation, not of real life or of anything like real life, but of thrice and thirty times redistilled literary decoctions of life. As for the language just mentioned, Mr. James, who was always clever at a wonderful kind of American *marivaudage,* has this time "seen himself" at his very best hitherto, and gone we hardly know how much better. Some-body "smiles like a man whose urbanity is a solvent." Somebody else had "a nose which achieved a high free curve." A third "acquitted herself in a manner which offered no element of interest:" but a fourth "remained con-scious that something surmounted and survived her failure—something that would perhaps be *worth taking hold of.*" Fancy "taking hold" of "something" which "surmounts and survives" a "failure" which is also an "acquittal without an element of interest!" It is all very well for smart un-dergraduates and governesses, who have read Mr. Meredith without the ghost of an understanding, and Mr. Stevenson with a keen relish for exactly the things which are not good in him, to attempt distinction by this sort of thing. But Mr. Henry James really might give us something a little more

*Reprinted from the *Academy* 38 (23 August 1890):148.

like English sense and a good deal less like French-American rigmarole. We cannot honestly say that there is much in the story or the characters of *The Tragic Muse* to redeem this fatal fault; but even if there were, it would probably still be fatal. . . .

# [*The Tragic Muse* and the New Novel]                    William Dean Howells*

The fatuity of the story as a story is something that must early impress the story-teller who does not live in the stone age of fiction and criticism. To spin a yarn for the yarn's sake, that is an ideal worthy of a nineteenth-century Englishman, doting in forgetfulness of the English masters and grovelling in ignorance of the Continental masters; but wholly impossible to an American of Mr. Henry James's modernity. To him it must seem like the lies swapped between men after the ladies have left the table and they are sinking deeper and deeper into their cups and growing dimmer and dimmer behind their cigars. To such a mind as his the story could never have value except as a means; it could not exist for him as an end: it could be used only illustratively; it could be the frame, not possibly the picture. But in the meantime the kind of thing he wished to do, and began to do, and has always done, amidst a stupid clamor, which still lasts, that it was not a story (of *course*, it was not a story!), had to be called a novel; and the wretched victim of the novel-habit (only a little less intellectually degraded than the still more miserable slave of the theatre-habit), who wished neither to perceive nor to reflect, but only to be acted upon by plot and incident, was lost in an endless trouble about it. Here was a thing called a novel, written with extraordinary charm; interesting by the vigor and vivacity with which phases and situations and persons were handled in it; inviting him to the intimacy of characters divined with creative insight; making him witness of motives and emotions and experiences of the finest import; and then suddenly requiring him to be man enough to cope with the question itself; not solving it for him by a marriage or a murder, and not spoon-victualling him with a moral minced small and then thinned with milk and water, and familiarly flavored with sentimentality or religiosity. We can imagine the sort of shame with which such a writer, so original and so clear-sighted, may sometimes have been tempted by the outcry of the nurslings of fable, to give them of the diet on which they had been pampered to imbecility; or to call together his characters for a sort of round-up in the last chapter.

*Reprinted from *Harper's Monthly* 81 (November 1890):639–41. A few introductory lines of the section dealing with James have been left out.

The round-up was once the necessary close of every novel, as it is of every season on a Western cattle ranch; and each personage was summoned to be distinctly branded with his appropriate destiny, so that the reader need be in no doubt about him evermore. The formality received its most typical observance in *The Vicar of Wakefield*, perhaps, where the modern lover of that loveliest prospect of eighteenth-century life is amused by the conscientiousness with which fate is distributed, and vice punished and virtue rewarded. It is most distinctly honored in the breach in that charming prospect of nineteenth-century life, *The Tragic Muse*, a novel which marks the farthest departure from the old ideal of the novel. No one is obviously led to the altar; no one is relaxed to the secular arm and burnt at the stake. Vice is disposed of with a gay shrug; virtue is rewarded by innuendo. All this leaves us pleasantly thinking of all that has happened before, and asking, Was Gabriel Nash vice? Was Mrs. Dallow virtue? Or was neither either? In the nineteenth century, especially now toward the close of it, one is never quite sure about vice and virtue; they fade wonderfully into and out of each other; they mix, and seem to stay mixed at least around the edges.

Mr. James owns that he is himself puzzled by the extreme actuality of his facts; fate is still in solution, destiny is not precipitated; the people are still going uncertainly on as we find people going on in the world about us all the time. But that does not prevent our being satisfied with the study of each as we find it in the atelier of a master. Why in the world should it? What can it possibly matter that Nick Dormer and Mrs. Dormer are not certainly married, or that Biddy Dormer and Sherringham certainly are? The marriage or the non-marriage cannot throw any new light on their characters; and the question never was what they were going to do, but what they were. This is the question that is most sufficiently if not distinctly answered. They never wholly emerge from the background which is a condition of their form and color; and it is childish, it is Central African, to demand that they shall do so. It is still more Central African to demand such a thing in the case of such a wonderful creature as Gabriel Nash, whose very essence is elusiveness; the lightest, slightest, airiest film of personality whose insubstantiality was ever caught by art; and yet so strictly of his time, his country, his kind. He is one sort of modern Englishman; you are as sure of that as you are of the histrionic type, the histrionic character, realized in the magnificent full-length of Miriam Rooth. *There* is mastery for you! There is the woman of the theatre, destined to the stage from her cradle, touched by family, by society, by love, by friendship, but never swayed for a moment from her destiny, such as it is, the tinsel glory of triumphing for a hundred nights in the same part. An honest creature, most thoroughly honest in heart and act, and most herself when her whole nature is straining toward the realization of some one else; vulgar, sublime; ready to make any sacrifice for her art, to "toil terribly," to suffer everything for it, but perfectly aware of its limitations at its best while she provisionally contents herself with its second-best, she is by all odds so much more perfectly presented in *The Tragic Muse* than any other like woman in fiction, that she seems the only woman of the kind ever presented in fiction.

As we think back over our year's pleasure in the story (for we will own we read it serially as it was first printed), we have rather a dismaying sense of its manifold excellence; dismaying, that is, for a reviewer still haunted by the ghost of the duty of cataloguing a book's merits. While this ghost walks the Study, we call to mind that admirable old French actress of whom Miriam gets her first lessons; we call to mind Mrs. Rooth, with her tawdry scruples; Lady Dormer, with her honest English selfishness; Mrs. Dallow, with her awful good sense and narrow high life and relentless will; Nick's lovely sister Biddy and unlovely sister Grace; Nick himself, with his self-devotion to his indefinite future; Sherringham, so good and brave and sensible and martyred; Dashwood, the born man of the theatre, as Miriam is the born woman; and we find nothing caricatured or overcharged, nothing feebly touched or falsely stated. As for the literature, what grace, what strength! The style is a sweetness on the tongue, a music in the ear. The whole picture of life is a vision of London aspects such as no Englishman has yet been able to give: so fine, so broad, so absolute, so freed from all necessities of reserve or falsity.

## [*The Tragic Muse:* The Infinite Variety of Mind]

Anonymous*

If Mr. James were, like his only English rival in the art of fiction, Mr. Stevenson, naturally impelled to write chiefly stories of adventure, he would get more applause than he does for his beautiful manner and exquisite style. Many instinctive censors of literature believe that Stevenson's stories are all action, therefore great; that James's stories are all rest, therefore fine-spun inanity. This sort of comment leads one to suppose that people who are not continually rolling down stairs must not consider the charge of torpidity an aspersion, and that nothing ever is accomplished in life by less violent methods. Most of the people in *The Tragic Muse* are exceedingly careful of their steps, and yet they achieve a good deal. Nicholas Dormer gives up fine political prospects and a great marriage for the sake of a beggarly art; Peter Sherringham, after much vacillation, is ready to fling over diplomacy and the star of an ambassador for love of the Tragic Muse; the Tragic Muse herself, Miriam Rooth, never dreams of giving up anything, but holds fast to her one idea, much to her worldly advantage. It is true that the two men and most of the subordinate characters are less

*Reprinted from the *Nation* 51 (25 Decmber 1890):505–56.

interesting for what they do than for what they think, for mental activity preliminary and subsequent to physical. Mr. James is, in fact, guilty of selecting complex creatures—creatures who are centuries away from savage simplicity—and of devoting his greatest energy to the exhibition of the storehouse of their complexities, the mind. He finds an infinite variety of mind, and its tricks are vastly more surprising and entertaining than a conjurer's tricks, which we see but do not in the least understand. There is the dull, ponderous, prejudiced mind of Lady Agnes; the naive mind of her daughter Biddy, its ingenuousness crossed by inherited worldliness; the worldly mind of Mrs. Dallow, with innumerable shades, refinements, and even contradictions of worldliness; the mind of Peter Sherringham, her brother, very like hers, but the contradictions heightened by greater possibility of passion; the mind of Nicholas Dormer, slow like his mother's but much less under control, capable of no end of fantastic flights; last, the mind of Gabriel Nash, serenely philosophical, but nebulous, unreliable, elusive.

Nash is nothing but a mind, a sort of incarnation of wisdom gathered through observation, the sharpness and justice of which have never been impaired by feeling. The other minds are only parts of substantial beings for the most important parts, most subtle and intricate, altogether most worthy of one whose avowed profession is the complete representation of men and woman. But Mr. James realizes that approximately primitive people, people who do more and better than they think, are still to be found in the world, often making great bustle and exciting wild curiosity. The Tragic Muse is one of these. Of mixed race, with a not distant Jewish strain, vagabond from her birth, beautiful, polyglot and poor, she turns instinctively to the stage, where her natural advantages can be most brilliantly utilized and the disadvantages of circumstance most speedily conquered. Enormously vain, with imperturbable self-assurance, showy, hard, not ungenerous, capable of assuming every emotion and incapable of feeling any not connected with public applause and the receipts of the box-office—such is the Tragic Muse, by far the most brilliant and faithful representation of the successful modern actress that has ever been achieved in English fiction.

# Twentieth Century Essays

## Roderick Hudson

Richard Poirier*

Comedy in *Roderick Hudson*, which James considered his first novel, is the result, almost invariably, of the dramatic confrontation of two opposing kinds of sensibility. The first of these, most clearly seen in the character of Roderick, is egotistical and self-interested, and it expresses itself by an extravagant disregard for the feelings and the needs of other people. The excessive and theatrical way in which characters with this kind of sensibility usually speak is an indication that their view of things is limited, that it is uncomplicated and unmodified by any consciousness that there are, possibly, other views. Their sensibilities allow them to express only those attitudes in which they have a vested interest, so that the style in which they speak shows little evidence of an unencumbered intelligence. Their talk, as a result, tends to caricature them, to turn them into Types. Roderick talks like the Young Temperamental Artist; Mrs. Light, like the Long Suffering Mother; Mr. Leavenworth, like the American Millionaire Abroad. Melodramatic is the term which can properly define this sensibility, and when the term is used in discussing this novel it is meant to refer to any stock expression of stylized intensity. The expression of intense feeling becomes stylized in *Roderick Hudson* because of the exclusion from it of language which would militate against the insistence of the person speaking that what he is saying is of supreme importance, even as we see, to the contrary, that it is narrow-minded and self-absorbed.

All of the characters in the novel express themselves melodramatically except Cecilia, Mary Garland, Christina Light, and Rowland Mallet. The last of these, and the most important by virtue of his being the observer of all the action in the novel, represents the kind of sensibility which is opposed to melodrama and its moral equivalents: fixity and confinement of awareness, and the self-regarding consistency of expression which never takes other possible ways of feeling into account. Rowland is pre-eminently

*Reprinted from *The Comic Sense of Henry James: A Study of the Early Novels*, by Richard Poirier, © Richard Poirier, (New York: Oxford University Press, 1967), 11–43. Reprinted by permission of the author.

sane and reasonable, and he is above all selfless. His selflessness is apparent in his desire to help others, and he is clearly self-sacrificing in his attempts to preserve the engagement between Roderick and Mary, even though he is himself in love with her. Like all the admirable people in James, he is interested more in the quality of what he does than in its practical results. This, in James's view of conduct, is the ideally reasonable attitude towards experience. Those of his characters who have it are distinguished from those who do not by their indifference to the often painful consequences of an obedience to personal ideals. In this respect, Christina Light, a character of most perplexing deviousness, is yet one of the commendable figures in the novel. She tries to give up the social triumph of marriage to a Neapolitan Prince in order to satisfy herself that she is capable of doing something less palpably successful but more personally satisfying. In doing this she is motivated by the desire to emulate the integrity and fine intelligence which at their first meeting she recognizes in Mary Garland. Such characters as Christina and Rowland do not express themselves melodramatically. Indeed, they are given instead to irony and sarcasm in the attempt to expose the limited ambitions of those around them and the absurd intensity of their action and speech in pursuit of these ambitions. Because Rowland is the ever-present witness of all the action, the virtues which attend his sensibility are always conspicuous in the novel, and serve as a standard by which the expressions of the opposing and melodramatic sensibilities are rendered comic. This is true even when Rowland, who is not a remarkably witty man, makes no direct comment on what is happening. Because of him, the novel is a comic melodrama, the melodrama being inherent in most of the characters and much of the action, the comedy being a matter of our acceptance, through Rowland, of standards by which melodrama is judged as a vulgar expression of insufficient sensibility.

The plot of *Roderick Hudson* shows us the defeat, in terms of practical satisfaction, of Rowland and Christina by the forces of selfishness and irrationality with which they try to contend. This can be expressed in another way, which accurately enough describes the dramatic movement of the novel, by saying that comedy, which dominates the opening, is defeated by melodrama, which it tries to exorcise but which dominates the conclusion. The novel opens in Northampton, Massachusetts, where Rowland is visiting his cousin Cecilia before leaving for Europe. She introduces him to Roderick Hudson, a highly temperamental youth whose work as a sculptor shows such promise of genius that Rowland offers almost immediately to take him to Rome for study. In this he is at first opposed by Mrs. Hudson, Mr. Striker, the boy's employer, and Mary Garland, the girl who loves him. Rowland within a few days falls in love with Mary, but he tells no one, and when he learns on the voyage to Europe that Roderick successfully proposed to her just before sailing, he is put in a most uncomfortable position. He can make no avowal whatever of his own feeling, and he must,

out of love for Mary, feel even more responsible for the emotional as well
as the artistic security of Roderick. So far as Roderick's art is concerned,
Rowland has little, at first to worry about, and he has the pleasure of being
the patron of the most promising young artist in Rome. He is less successful in keeping Roderick free of the damaging experiences of romantic and
alcoholic escapades, however, and when Roderick meets Christina Light,
presumably the most beautiful woman in Europe, he is the victim of an
unmanageable infatuation which threatens to ruin his life, his art, and,
though he never thinks of this, the happiness of his betrothed. Christina
resembles Roderick in that a brilliant future is also being planned for her,
not so much by herself as by someone else, her mother. Her position is
somewhat different from Roderick's, however, in that her mother is not a
selfless patron, as Rowland is, and she does not want the kind of career to
which her mother is committing her. Regardless of Christina's wishes, Mrs.
Light is determined to marry her to Prince Casamassima, but she succeeds
in forcing Christina into the marriage only by revealing to her, with the
threat of public exposure, that she is illegitimate. Her father is the Cavaliere who, for years, along with Mrs. Light and Christina's dog, has seemed
merely a part, and an easily patronized one, of Christina's colourful entou-
rage. In his extreme disappointment at the loss of Christina, Roderick suffers a moral and psychological breakdown, confirming the earlier prediction
of the cynical artist Gloriani. He has to be taken to Florence for recupera-
tion, where he is joined by his fiancée and his mother. Mrs. Hudson holds
Rowland responsible for Roderick's difficulty. Dissatisfied with Florence,
the party moves north to Switzerland where, by accident, Roderick meets
Christina and her new husband. When he tells Rowland that he plans to
follow Christina, there ensues a violent argument in which Rowland confesses his love for Mary and tells Roderick, finally, that he is an insufferable
egotist. Roderick wanders off, and in the middle of a tempestuous Alpine
storm falls or jumps to his death from a cliff. The novel ends with a brief
account of Rowland's ennui after Roderick's death, as revealed by his spo-
radic trips to Northampton, where he sees Cecilia and, now and again,
Mary Garland. He is, so he tells us at the very end, not restless but merely
patient.

   If the plot of the novel shows us the defeat, in terms of their practical
utility, of those ideals of conduct and feeling which Rowland represents, it
does so in no abstract, sentimental, or allegorical way. These ideals—
selflessness, reasonableness, and a recognition that one's best aspirations
might actually be served by practical failure—exist as part of our experience of the novel by being inseparable from our responses to the emotional
complexity of the characters. In fact, they are often shown to be the result
of a character's psychological incapacity. Christina's ideals, to cite an example, evolve not from any intellectual recognition or intuitive moral awareness on her part, but from deeper personal needs which tend to create that
awareness. She decides to give up the Prince because she feels that this is

the sort of superior action that Mary Garland, under similar circumstances, might perform. Such an act is typical of Christina's propensity, in her search for some ideal of noble self-realization, to assume different moral and dramatic postures in the way an actress might assume a given role. "I think she's an actress," remarks Madame Grandoni, "but she believes in her part while she is playing it."[1] It is, therefore, ironic that her most serious attempt to dramatize her idealism should be thwarted by the standard excuse of the theatrical villain: the excuse of the irregularity of birth. She is the victim of what Madame Grandoni calls, in the final revision of the novel, an obloquy which "is now mere stage convention and melodrama."[2] Her theatrical inclinations, which express a touching desire to put herself in a position, even if it is a fictitious one, which she can admire more than the merely socially exalted position her mother wants for her, are precisely what make her an easy victim of a threat of disgrace couched in such a conventionally theatrical way. In the characterization of Christina at this early point in his career, James shows the logic behind one of the most disturbing features of his work: the reason why an Isabel Archer or a Hyacinth Robinson will *act* in a way that seems destructive of the very ideals for which he has eloquently declared himself. The apparent contradiction is, we shall see, of crucial importance to a critical judgment of James's art. As in the case of Christina, the given act has its source in the same psychological anguish that creates the belief in the ideal. In the novels before *The Bostonians*, however, such a method of investing characters with ideals and of making them the very standard-bearers of the author calls only for our recognition or commendation and for little more. The early novels do not reward excursions into Gestalt psychology.

None the less, it is not possible to show the nature of James's achievement in this first novel or to demonstrate the way in which comedy contributes to that achievement without seeing how the standards which Rowland represents, the same standards by which comic judgment is passed on most of the action, have their source in his personal psychology and in some of its misfortunes. The sort of calm reasonableness and good sense which his continuous presence brings into every scene provides, to repeat, a comic contrast to the pervasive melodramatic action. But his rationality and tolerance are in part suggestive of those "powerless-feeling young men,"[3] in Mr. Dupee's phrase, who preoccupy James in some of the stories written before *Roderick Hudson:* John Ford of *The Story of a Year* (1865), who relinquishes claim to his fiancée because he might be killed in the war, the wealthy young artist of *A Landscape Painter* (1866), whose wife understandably tells him at the end of the story "I am a woman, sir! Come *you* be a man!"[4] and, most notably, Roger Lawrence of *Watch and Ward* (1871) who, like Rowland, is introduced at the very beginning with the information that one romantic disappointment has made him take a vow of celibacy, and who exhibits throughout the story an integrity which is obscurely associated with a fear of sexual and romantic involvement. It is not at all certain in these earlier efforts that James is aware of the psychological peculiarities of his heroes, and, whether he is or not, it is obvious that he can do no more than present them. They are peripherally stimulating without being substantially involved in the main meanings. Rowland's peculiarities are treated in a different way. They are so presented as to give those standards which he represents the concreteness of a specific emotional necessity. This may explain the careful and extended treatment, in the opening chapter, of Rowland's background and personality. Some explanation is apparently needed since, in what is the best early critical study of James, Joseph Warren Beach complains that the author takes nearly a dozen pages "to tell us all he knows of Rowland Mallet and his antecedents—all he knows, and much more than we care to know at the time or shall ever have need for knowing."[5]

The combination in Rowland of the dispassionate man, as in his toleration of Roderick, with the man of great unexpressed feelings, as in the reticence of his love for Mary Garland, the cast of mind which reveals itself in his insistence to Roderick on the connection between virtuous conduct and artistic success, and the temperament which submits itself to the life of reason as the way to the sources, if only by subsidizing artists, of creative beauty—these elements in James's characterization are made a part of Rowland's particular family inheritance. And that inheritance is, in turn, described as a part of what James knew to be a not uncommon American and European heritage. To that extent, Rowland's character is inescapable, his particular values being an expression of sentiments which are associated with the mellowest evidences of American Puritanism. James observes that he had originally sprung "from rigid Puritan stock" (R. H., p. 9). In the passage which follows this remark, the language ironically shows the modification, in the lives of Rowland's forebears, of what is generally meant by the word "rigid." The irony reveals what James, after Hawthorne, but with more urbane humour, could recognize as the complications behind Puritanical rigidity. Rowland considered his mother a saint, for example, not primarily because for years she stoically endured an unhappy marriage, but because at her death, though only then, she revealed that during her silence she had actually cultivated a "private plot of sentiment" (R. H., p. 13). Her example may help to explain Rowland's inability to express his romantic attachments to Cecilia and to Mary as something more distinctly rooted in his personality than an abstract, and therefore dramatically unvigorous, sense of honour. In the career of his maternal grandfather, however, there is even more persuasive evidence of the close connection between Roland's standards of conduct and the inherited and largely unconscious elements in his motivation:

> He had sprung from rigid Puritan stock, and had been brought up
> to think much more intently of the duties of this life than of its privileges
> and pleasures. His progenitors had submitted in the matter of dogmatic
> theology to the relaxing influences of earlier years; but if Rowland's

youthful consciousness was not chilled by the menace of long punishment for brief transgression he had at least been made to feel that there ran through all things a strain of right and of wrong, as different, after all, in their complexions, as the texture, to the spiritual sense, of Sundays and weekdays. His father was a chip of the primal Puritan block, a man with an icy smile and a stony frown. He had always bestowed on his son, on principle, more frowns than smiles, and if the lad had not been turned to stone himself, it was because nature had blessed him, inwardly, with a well of vivifying waters. Mrs. Mallet had been a Miss Rowland, the daughter of a retired sea-captain, once famous on the ships that sailed from Salem and Newburyport. He had brought to port many a cargo which crowned the edifice of fortunes already almost colossal, but he had also done a little sagacious trading on his own account, and he was able to retire, prematurely for so sea-worthy a maritime organism, upon a pension of his own providing. He was to be seen for a year on the Salem wharves, smoking the best tobacco and eying the seaward horizon with an inveteracy which superficial minds interpreted as a sign of repentance. At last, one evening, he disappeared beneath it, as he had often done before; this time, however, not as a commissioned navigator, but simply as an amateur of an observing turn likely to prove oppressive to the offi-cer in command of the vessel. Five months later his place at home knew him again, and made the acquaintance also of a handsome, blonde young woman, of redundant contours, speaking a foreign tongue. The foreign tongue proved, after much conflicting research, to be the idiom of Am-sterdam, and the young woman, which was stranger still, to be Captain Rowland's wife. Why he had gone forth so suddenly across the seas to marry her, what had happened between them before, and whether—though it was of questionable propriety for a good citizen to espouse a young person of mysterious origin, who did her hair in fantastically elabo-rate plaits, and in whose appearance "figure" enjoyed such striking pre-dominance—he would not have had a heavy weight on his conscience if he had remained an irresponsible bachelor; these questions and many others, bearing with various degrees of immediacy on the subject, were much propounded but scantily answered, and this history need not be charged with resolving them.

(R. H., pp. 9–10)

The ironic comedy in this passage depends upon the implied contrast between the connotations, with all they allow us to anticipate about the subsequent statements, of the terms "rigid Puritan" and "primal Puritan block," and the account of actual conduct, not only of the Captain but of the somewhat pruriently curious community of Salem. As I have suggested, this is essentially the method of comedy in the novel as a whole, though the terms of the contrast are different and, usually, sharper and more broadly comic in their application than they are here. This kind of comedy is, in a superficial way, reminiscent of Jane Austen. Her habit is often to introduce us to a character or a situation with an epithet or a sententious maxim, and then to qualify it ironically by subsequent dramatic action. The most ready example, the opening sentence of *Pride and Prejudice*, is no more ironically modified by what follows it than is the assertion here about "rigid Puritan stock." The passage in James involves a comic interplay between implication and the initial assertion. The purpose of this technique is to show the connection between seemingly disparate things: between the rigidity mentioned at the beginning as a factor in Rowland's background, and the very unrigid luxuriousness of the figure who is described at the end as one of his direct ancestors. The humour derived from making this connection comes close to turning his grandmother's *enbonpoint* into a comic metaphor.

To see a similarity here to the manner of Jane Austen is to recognize that, by and large, it is a similarity only in technique, in verbal play, and in ironic modulation of tone. More interesting and more important is the fact that despite an affinity between them in the use of certain resources of language and grammar, Jane Austen and Henry James are quite dissimilar in the points of view from which they see the comedy in any particular act. In Jane Austen, the ironic variety of possible interpretations is made possible by her adherence to a stable set of social conventions. If we are to appreciate her comedy, we must accept the structure of her society. This means not that we have to read a book on Regency England, but that we have to be convinced of the effectiveness, in the drama of the novel, of the words by which Jane Austen represents that society and its values. In doing this, she always addresses us from inside the social conventions she presents. Her narrative voice, usually witty, sometimes crisply derisive, and always authoritative, reveals her confidence that social processes will ultimately confirm and even enforce the good sense of her judgments. Even when she uses a spokesman for her values who suffers from a certain amount of social alienation, like Fanny Price in *Mansfield Park*, Jane Austen's humour is never the result of social attitudes impinging from outside the world she creates. This is not true of Henry James. There will be occasion later in this chapter to show that this difference explains, in part, how those standards are created by which James can render comic judgments, and serious judgments which are not comic, upon the experience of his characters. For the moment it is enough to remark, on the basis of this passage, that James addresses us from outside any part of the society with which he is dealing. Neither Rowland's grandfather and his wife nor the town are spared by the ironies which are directed down on them from a point of detached social and intellectual cosmopolitanism. James explicitly disavows, for example, the kind of questions "the neighbours" asked about the grandfather's conduct: "this history need not be charged with resolving them." By contrast with James's attitude, the town is amusingly provincial—"the foreign tongue proved, after much conflicting research, to be the idiom of Amsterdam," and the propriety of its speculations is highly dubious. The sytle, rather than any assertion, establishes James's superiority to all the values expressed either by the town or by the objects of their scrutiny and judgment, Mr. and Mrs. Rowland. This is achieved partly by an exaggerated pomposity of language by which James makes fun simultaneously of the parochial suspiciousness of the town and of the provoking foreignness of Mrs. Rowland.

The peculiarity in Rowland's background is the more comic in that it is productive of pleasures not in what we might assume to be its opposition to Puritanical rigidity but actually through and by means of it. There is in Rowland's inheritance the custom, not unnoticed as a feature of Puritanism, of making moral and financial responsibility the agent of quietly nurtured and very private self-indulgence of feeling: "He was seen for years on the Salem wharves, smoking the best tobacco, and eying the seaward horizon with an inveteracy which superficial minds interpreted as a sign of repentance." By following the straight and narrow, the "rigid," he comes into possession of "redundant contours," "fantastically elaborate plaits." It is exactly such a sequence—even the terminology is suggestive of sculpture—which Rowland recommends to Roderick for the production of art. The compassionately observed difference between Rowland and his grandfather is that the latter was able to act out for himself the seemingly contradictory impulses of his nature, while Rowland, we are told, is an "awkward mixture of strong moral impulse and restless aesthetic curiosity" (R. H., p. 15), the observer who, like Ralph Touchett, must subsidize the kind of life he cannot lead. James's characterization of Rowland gives a psychological reality and a human solidity to standards of reason, intelligence, and selflessness. More than anyone else in the novel, Rowland has the indispensable virtue required of all of James's heroes: a capacity for caring more about the quality of an experience than about its practical rewards.

It is now possible to show the techniques by which the qualities represented by Rowland are expressed through the comedy. A most useful instance of this occurs at the beginning of the novel during a conversation about Rome between Rowland and Cecilia. Here we see Rowland's own standards turned against him by his satirically minded cousin. During this conversation, Rowland does not live up to those elements in his character which make him useful to James as an observer of the action. The comedy is a means of correcting him, as it were. It is as if James were saying to us what the discussion of Rowland's characterization has already suggested: that as his observer Rowland stands for certain values of perception and spiritual generosity, but that he represents these not because James imposes them on him from the outside, so to speak, but because his very individual emotional complications find expression only in his adherence to these values. He discovers them as a result of his own psychological limitations. These limitations prevent him from being passionate either in conduct or in speech, and they keep him from being a very artistically creative person. When he fails to comprehend his own nature and pretends to be these things, he is himself rendered momentarily absurd by the same standards which make Mrs. Light continually absurd. The comedy directed against Rowland in this instance is a muted example of how in the rest of the novel comedy is used through him to evaluate conduct. Relevant to this is a significant addition to the conversation in the revised edition. To the second sentence of the quotation given below James adds to Rowland's remarks the line "you must have noticed the almost priggish ecstacy with which those who have enjoyed it talk about it" (R. H. rev., p. 6). "Priggish ecstacy" is an embarrassingly apt description, as James in adding it might have meant to suggest, of Rowland's own tone as he nears the end of his little speech:

> "I did a good many things when I was in Europe before, but I did not spend a winter in Rome. Every one assures me that this is a particular refinement of bliss; most people talk about Rome in the same way. It is evidently only a sort of idealized form of loafing: a passive life in Rome, thanks to the number and the quality of one's impressions, takes on a very reasonable likeness to activity. It is still lotus-eating, only you sit down at table, and the lotuses are served up on rococo china.
>
> "It's all very well, but I have a distinct prevision of this—that if Roman life doesn't do something substantial to make you happier, it increases tenfold your liability to moral misery. It seems to me a rash thing for a sensitive soul deliberately to cultivate its sensibilities by rambling too often among the ruins of the Palatine, or riding too often in the shadow of the acqueducts. In such recreations the chords of feeling grow tense, and afterlife, to spare your intellectual nerves, must play upon them with a touch as dainty as the tread of Mignon when she danced her egg-dance."
>
> (R. H., pp. 6–7)

A combination of somewhat effeminate sententiousness and preciosity characterizes this speech. Rowland is, in the modern phrase, trying too hard, and Cecilia immediately catches the disconcerting pretentiousness of his tone:

> "I should have said, my dear Rowland," said Cecilia, with a laugh, "that your nerves were tough, that your eggs were hard!"
>
> (R. H., p. 7)

The significance of Rowland's remarks about Rome as a prevision of what happens there to Roderick is obvious enough, but I am primarily concerned with indicating how Cecilia's irony and laughter effectively prevent Rowland from laying claim to the intensities of feeling which his speech evokes. The feelings are, as his reference to Mignon unintentionally betrays, operatically theatrical. And theatricality suits Rowland's character, as Cecilia and as we know it, very clumsily.

The representative significance of this exchange between Rowland and his cousin is confirmed by another revision in the dialogue. James lets Cecilia clarify the point of her sarcasm by having her add that she takes exception to Rowland's talk about Rome "with all recognition of your eloquence" (R. H., rev., p. 6). Like many of James's revisions, this is by way of an interpretive comment which clarifies what is already dramatically suggested. Eloquence of speech, which James explicitly remarks upon in Roderick and Mrs. Light, is a stylistic symptom in *Roderick Hudson* of personal irresponsibility, of showing, through addiction to language too florid for ordinary sensible discourse, that a character has a deficient sense of his obligations to other and to the complexities of a given situation. The characters in this novel who speak most naturally and with little verbal flourish all have a feeling of attachment to things less obsessively selfish than say, Mrs. Light's ambition for Christina.

In using style to dramatize varieties of egotism and selfishness, James has in mind something like a secular version of Mr. T. S. Eliot's idea in *After Strange Gods* that uncurbed self-expression can be an evidence of heretical sensibility, of "powerful personality uncurbed by any institutional attachment, or submission to any objective beliefs."[6] The relevance of Eliot's remark to *Roderick Hudson* is that he makes the point, for which he may be indebted to Matthew Arnold,[7] that stylistic disorders are an indication of moral and psychological ones. Yet it is even more interesting that Eliot's references to "institutional attachment" and "objective belief" are totally unsatisfactory as descriptions of the standards by which we judge so-called "heretical" sensibility in James. Eliot is talking not about James but about Hardy, and while the relevance of such terms to Hardy is also, to my mind, very much in question, the irrelevance of them to James is not. For a standard such as "institutional attachment," James would substitute "sensitivity," "intelligence," and some word which would describe an attachment, largely, to an ideal of personal sacrifice; for "objective beliefs" he would offer us the practice of art, very directly in this novel and in the stories of the nineties; and for the exposure of "heretics" against these, he would give us the judgments of comedy.

In so far as they have any life in the novels, James's "institutions" and "beliefs" do not depend, in Eliot's sense, upon systems of value outside the work. They are, as in the case of Rowland, bound within dramatized human limitations and deficiencies. Thus Rowland's exchange with Cecilia, this early in the novel, is admirably contrived to accomplish two things at once: to reveal in Rowland the tendency towards self-indulgent theatricality, which his presence in the novel renders comical in others, and to purge him of it by way of showing him, and us, through a gentle irony, that such self-expression is neither natural for him nor to be expected of him. In this way Rowland becomes James's agent for bringing comedy to bear on any tendency towards egotistical feeling or its literary expression in melodramatic verbiage. Rowland, as I have already suggested, does not comment satirically or ironically on all the action that is to be so rendered. Very often he is personally responsible for comic observations and judgments, but more often he is used in the way Joyce in *Dubliners* will sometimes use his sensitive observers: he is present and we are aware, even when he stands apart from the action, of the way in which everything that is said might be measured, though Rowland might not be able to do the measuring, against the kind of sensibility we know him to have. In this way, James's subject in *Roderick Hudson* is like the subject of a painting consisting always, as he remarks in the Preface, in "the related state, to each other, of certain figures and things."[8]

Possibly because *Roderick Hudson* has not been thought one of James's more demanding efforts, criticism has been curiously consistent in failing to see the character of Rowland as James asks us to see it or to agree to the importance of his function in the novel. There is a general tendency to refer to his "solemnity," as if it were an allegorical vice and not part of a complex character, and no one has seen that his "solemnity," for which I would substitute the word "rationality," is the means of creating not a solemn but a comic judgment on the action. Joseph Warren Beach, as a natural result of his objection to the amount of attention given to Rowland, expresses a resentment at "being cheated of the experience of Roderick by having it shown us through the judicial optics of Rowland."[9] Mr. T. S. Eliot, whose criticisms of the novel are accepted some thirty-three years later by Mr. F. W. Dupee,[10] complains without any regard to James's irony and critical discrimination in his characterization of Rowland, that James fails to "see through the solemnity he has created in that character [and] commits the cardinal sin of failing to 'detect' " him.[11] That the acceptance of such inadequate views of Rowland has damaging consequences for an understanding of what is accomplished in the novel as a whole, and specifically by the uses of comedy, is apparent in a recent study by Mr. Leo B. Levy. Mr. Levy's book on James, called *Versions of Melodrama*, has many good observations on the melodramatic element in the novels and plays, but he fails to see, and so does Mr. Jacques Barzun in his article, "Henry James, Melodramatist,"[12] that James uses melodrama more often than not with a comic intention. This is especially true in *Roderick Hudson*, largely because of the way in which James makes use of Rowland. If it were not for Rowland, the novel actually would be what Mr. Levy says it is, a work of "simple, dramatic display" in which "Roderick's attitudinizing produces the form of dramatic significance without the substance."[13] He feels, as does Pelham Edgar,[14] that the wild irregularity of Roderick's genius is dramatized for its pictorial possibilities, and that the picture is not substantially conditioned by Rowland. Only Miss Cornelia Kelley[15] and Mr. F. R. Leavis[16] adequately consider the novel in the light of James's own assertion in the Preface that "the centre of interest throughout *Roderick* is in Rowland Mallet's consciousness, and the drama is the very drama of that consciousness."[17]

The explanation for so much critical misapprehension on this point, with the attendant assertions that Roderick is more dramatically compelling than Rowland or that Rowland is a fairly uninteresting, even priggish, man, is not to be found in the novel. Roderick's conduct, colourful and pathetic as it is, is also made repetitious and tedious, and he is so self-indulgently and theoretically will-less ("Do I succeed—do I fail? It doesn't depend on me") (R. H., p. 208) that he could not, like Milly Theale, struggling with her fate by "contesting every inch of the road," provide the "soul of drama." That "soul," James remarks in the Preface to Wings of the Dove, is the portrayal, as we know, of a catastrophe determined in spite of opposi- tions."[18] The "oppositions" in Roderick Hudson are all of Rowland's mak- ing, and it may be that the novel would be more considerable if Roderick were intelligently enough engaged by his own problems not to be satisfied with excusing them by the remark that he is "incomplete" (R. H., p. 234). Rowland tells us little more about Roderick's trouble, except that his in- completeness is a matter of his having no heart, and Roderick remains a mystery to himself and to us even at the end. He does not, therefore re- main insignificant, but his significance is a result of his stimulating the drama of Rowland's consciousness. That consciousness is itself incomplete, in the ways already indicated, in that it depends upon Rowland's accepting the fact that certain kinds of experience and the expression of certain depths of feeling are denied him. This restriction actually enhances his use- fulness as the observer of the action. He becomes the dramatic center of the novel by virtue of his feelings of incompleteness, and his attempt some- how to make up for his inadequacies is evidence of his capacity to contend with fate. His fate, like that of most Jamesian heroes, is his character. In his conception of Rowland, James seems to feel much the way Santayana[19] did when, in opposition to Bergson, he stated his preference for the life of reason despite its incompleteness:

> a certain sort of life is shut out by reason, the sort that reason calls
> dreaming or madness; but he [Bergson] forgets that reason is a kind of
> life, and that of all the kinds—mystical, passionate, practical, aesthetic,
> intellectual—with the various degrees of light and heat, the life of reason
> is that which some people may prefer. I confess I am one of these.[20]

The denial to Rowland Mallet of a "certain sort of life," and his natural congeniality, given his background and temperament, with the life of rea- son is the burden of the ironies and the sympathetic discriminations which go into his characterization from the beginning of the novel. He is denied, quite expressly in the conversation with Cecilia, both eloquence and melo- dramatic self-expression, and it is this which gives him his place, among the characters in the novel as a morally responsible individual.

This moral responsibility expresses itself comically through stringently literary means: by comic insinuations about what can be called the prose style of the people with whom Rowland is in contact. Rowland, with a cer- tain literalness of mind, is not always intentionally funny about such mat- ters, but by making use of this tendency towards literalness James very of-

ten contrives a double joke: at the expense of the person talking to Rowland
and at the expense of the undeviatingly calm rationality of Rowland's view
of things. An obvious example of this occurs when the Cavaliere visits him
with the news that Chistina has refused to marry the Prince:

> "Miss Light has committed a great crime; she has plunged a dagger
> into the heart of her mother."
> "A dagger!" cried Rowland.
> The Cavaliere patted the air an instant with his fingertips. "I speak
> figuratively. She has broken off her marriage."
>
> (R. H., p. 353)

Quite often, however, Rowland himself should be given the credit for
the ironic wit with which exaggerated expression is treated in the novel.
This is especially true in his dealings with Roderick. When Roderick first
appears, for example, he makes the sort of utterance which soon becomes
characteristic of him: "I can't be slow if I try," he tells Cecilia, who has
merely remarked that he walks too fast, "There's something inside me that
drives me. A restless fiend" (R. H., p. 19). The ironic comedy to which this
remark is submitted is fairly broad, but this is not uncharacteristic of the
comedy throughout the novel. Nor is it uncharacteristic that the counter-
point should be in this case between verbal exaggeration and a contrasting
unintimidated calmness. The contrast is given particular emphasis by the
fact that while Roderick is speaking Rowland is reclining in a hammock,
pretending to allow Cecilia's child, Bessie, to rock him to sleep. When he
hears Roderick's evocation of the fiend, he attempts to get up—"I want to
see the gentleman with the fiend inside of him," he tells Bessie—only to
be told by the child that "It's only Mr. Hudson" (R. H., p. 19).

The scene on the porch in Northampton is the first of many similar
instances in which James elicits an amused scepticism towards Roderick's
attitudinizing. We are encouraged to take a comic, though tolerant view of
him by the very fact that Rowland continues to do so even after he begins
to express great admiration for his talent. His admiration, like Cecilia's does
not prevent his responding, with his own version of Cecilia's "long, light,
familiar laugh," to any "peculiarly striking piece of youthful grandiloquence" (R. H., p. 23). Part of the justification for Rowland's inability to
take Roderick's grandiloquence seriously—to take it, that is, as an indication of dangerous egocentrism—is to be found not only in his natural tolerance of Roderick's youthfulness but also in the fact that Roderick himself
seems to see the comedy inherent in his own extravagance of feeling and
in the hyperbole of his expression. This is clearly the case when he tells
Rowland about the interview with his mother in which he informed her of
his plans to go to Rome:

> "She had the advantage of me, because she formerly knew a portrait-
> painter at Richmond, who did her miniature in black lace mittens (you
> may see it on the parlor table), who used to drink raw brandy and beat

his wife. I promised her that, whatever I might do to my wife, I would never beat my mother, and that as for brandy, raw or diluted, I detested it. She sat crying for an hour, during which I expended treasures of eloquence."

(R. H., pp. 39–40)

Throughout the early part of the novel and until the beginnings of Roderick's dissipation in Rome, such utterances as these are comic partly because we do not believe that they actually express anything substantial about Roderick. They reveal an excess of youthful spirit and his tendency to tell, in the manner of a boy, tall stories about himself. When he describes his parting with Mr. Striker—"I bid good-by here, with rapture, to these four detested walls—to this living tomb"—Rowland is described as "correcting a primary inclination to smile" (R. H., pp. 41–42). Rowland later comes to recognize that Roderick's verbal exaggeration is not a joke, a bit of gulling, but evidence instead of a deeply troubled personality and an "extraordinary insensibility to the injurious effects of his eloquence" (R. H., p. 391). It does not follow as a consequence of this insight that Roderick's melodramatic speech ceases to be comically rendered, or that Rowland withholds his irony when he is confronted with it. The comedy remains essentially the same, but, as the novel continues, its significance is modified by developing dramatic circumstances. From being largely a commemoration of Roderick's "eloquence," as an evidence of his youthful protest about the cramping circumstances of Northampton, the comedy becomes satirically derisive of it, as an evidence of his submission to the equally cramping circumstances of his own temperament:

"Pity me, sir; pity me!" he presently cried "Look at this lovely world, and think what it must be to be dead in it!"
"Dead?" said Rowland.
"Dead, dead; dead and buried! Buried in an open grave, where you lie staring up at the sailing clouds, smelling the waving flowers, and hearing all nature live and grow above you! That's the way I feel!"
"I am very glad to hear it," said Rowland. "Death of that sort is very near to resurrection."

(R. H., pp. 424–25)

In this exchange Rowland is the man of literal imagination by an act of choice: his first response—"Dead?"—has the ring of his reply to the Cavaliere's statement about Christina's plunging a dagger into her mother's heart, but here he is, as it were, exploiting his native tendency towards literalness in the interests of a sarcastic judgment upon Roderick's feeling. His final response becomes witty because he pretends to "believe" what Roderick tells him, calmly insisting, however, on a different and equally absurd interpretation of it.

Rowland's comedy, a matter of putting his rationality at the service of dramatic irony, is similarly used to expose the theatrical verbalizations of

Mrs. Light. She asks his help in forcing Christina to accept the Prince, and while doing so she describes Christina's characteristic way of handling her fiancé:

> "Christina has treated him as you wouldn't treat a dog. He has been insulted, outraged, persecuted! He has been driven hither and thither till he didn't know *where* he was. He has stood there where you stand—there, with his name and his millions and his devotion—as white as your handkerchief, with hot tears in his eyes, and me ready to go down on my knees to him and say, 'My own sweet prince, I could kiss the ground you tread on, but it ain't *decent* that I should allow you to enter my house and expose yourself to these horrors again.'"
>
> R. H., p. 364

With the same tone of satiric and urbane rationality used in his replies to Roderick, the tone of a sophisticated man making very wide and innocent eyes, Rowland can only respond to Mrs. Light with the observation that "It would seem, then, that in the interest of Prince Casamassima himself I ought to refuse to interfere" (R. H., p. 365).

Generally, however, it is Christina whose irony serves, in a more direct fashion than Rowland's, to expose the pretentiousness of her mother's speech and the fraudulence of the sentiments behind it. She has, in James's description, a "languid, imperturbable indifference (R. H., p. 137), which presents itself to us as a cynical and seductive version of Rowland's intelligent imperturbability. When she is sitting for Roderick, to give an instance, he remarks that Rowland had shown his disapproval of an earlier work by looking as if he were wearing a pair of tight boots. Mrs. Light immediately takes the opportunity to remark to Christina:

> "Ah, my child, you'll not understand that. You never yet had a pair that were small enough."
>
> "It's a pity, Mr. Hudson," said Christina gravely, "that you could not have introduced my feet into the bust. But we can hang a pair of slippers round the neck!"
>
> (R. H., pp. 165–66)

The explicit expression by Rowland, and to a lesser extent by Christina, of wit and irony as a response to melodramatic speech so habituates us to the process that James can depend upon our finding comedy in exaggerated uses of language even when no one directly points it out to us. This is usually the case when a character is acting so much in defiance of reasonable and natural manners that he becomes a grotesque. In the characterization of Mrs. Light, James shows her development towards comic grotesqueness as she becomes more and more imbued with the absolute primacy, to the exclusion of all moderation, of her ambitions for Christina. When Christina opposes her she complains to Rowland:

> "If ever a woman was desperate, frantic, heartbroken, I am that woman. I can't begin to tell you. To have nourished a serpent, sir, all

these years! To have lavished one's self upon a viper that turns and stings her own poor mother! To have toiled and prayed, to have pushed and struggled, to have eaten the bread of bitterness, and all the rest of it, sir—and at the end of all things to find myself at this pass. It can't be, it's too cruel, such things don't happen, the Lord don't allow it. I'm a religious woman, sir, and the Lord knows all about me. With his own hand he had given me his reward! I would have lain down in the dust and let her walk over me; I would have given her the eyes out of my head, if she had taken a fancy to them. No, she's a cruel, wicked, heartless, unnatural girl."

(R. H., p. 362)

This speech needs no ironic observation from Rowland or Christina to have its comic absurdity made obvious to us. It is a burlesque of the feelings it expresses, a fact noticeable in the sudden failure of verbal inspiration ("and all the rest of it, sir"), and in the obvious parodies of Biblical language. Her evocations of martyrdom and heavenly reward do more than satirize the hysteria and pretensions of a woman corrupted by her ambitions. They reveal something like Eliot's description of the "heretical sensibility" as one which is not bound in its exorbitant self-expression to any "institutional attachment." But we have seen that such phrases do not have much to do with James, and no one would consider the comedy in Mrs. Light's religiosity significant merely because it is blasphemous. We are back to the question of what does give the comedy its significance.

If Mrs. Light is a grotesque figure, then by what standards? To say that she is grotesque by the standards of what we know about life is not a literary judgment. The "life" exists only in the novel, if it is to be a part of that organized experience by which the author makes anything resembling the complex distinctions about conduct of which comedy is capable. This, essentially, would be James's view of the matter, and it would explain why Mrs. Light is not, by his definition, a grotesque figure in the Dickensian sense. Writing about *Our Mutual Friend* in 1865, he observes that Dickens does not, as does James himself, reveal the grotesqueness of a character by contrasting it *within* the world of the novel with representations of "sound humanity." The implication is that if we are to respond to the eccentrics in Dickens's novel, we ourselves must do the job of relating them to a reality which we experience not in the novel itself but in the world outside it:

> What a world were this world if the world of *Our Mutual Friend* were an honest reflection of it! But a community of eccentrics is impossible. Rules alone are consistent with each other; exceptions are inconsistent. Society is maintained by natural sense and natural feeling. We cannot conceive a society in which these principles are not in some manner represented. Where in these pages are the depositaries of that intelligence without which the movement of life would cease? Who represents nature? Accepting half of Mr. Dickens's persons as intentionally grotesque, where are those exemplars of sound humanity who should afford us the proper measure of their companions' variation?[21]

"A community of eccentrics is impossible"—such a proposition is the essential *raison d'être* of *Roderick Hudson*. It explains why Rowland's consciousness is the centre of the drama; why, as it is remarked at the beginning, the comedy in the novel is given its significance by the measuring of one kind of sensibility by another, and why, finally, within each kind of sensibility James is careful to discriminate, again by the use of comedy, the kinds and degrees of "sound humanity."

## II

Any larger observations about the significance of comedy in *Roderick Hudson* involve an account of James's relationship to an important problem in American and English fiction. This problem involves the creation in a given novel of a society which will adequately bear a resemblance to life as we know it, and which will, at the same time, be capable of involving itself in actions which give us the dramatic experience of certain values or ideas. It is possible, in terms of this problem, to make a general distinction between American and English fiction. To begin with, it is worth remarking on the uniqueness of George Eliot's announcement in 1871 that the subject of *Middlemarch* had to do with a "certain spiritual grandeur illmatched with the meanness of opportunity."[22] Before George Eliot the English novel with the exception of Charlotte Brontë,[23] did not question the belief that aspiration could be satisfied within a society that in its fictional existence was an image of society as it actually did exist, with its traditions, manners, and suppositions about the virtues of one kind of conduct as against another. The situation in the major American novelists of the nineteenth century can be stated quite differently: individual aspiration requires for its expression a society which is only tangentially connected with the kind of society within which English novelists could dramatize the personal destinies of their heroes and heroines. As a result, the most significant body of American fiction, as it was produced by Hawthorne, Melville, and Twain, has been romantic in the sense adduced by Hawthorne in his Preface to the *Blithedale Romance* in 1852. He remarks that his

> present concern with the socialist community is merely to establish a theatre, a little removed from the highway of ordinary travel, where creatures of his brain may play their phantasmagorical antics without exposing them to too close a comparison with the actual events of real lives.[24]

Hawthorne's "theatre, a little removed" is observable even in some of his works which are involved directly with social and historical propositions as in the best of his short stories, "My Kinsman, Major Molineux," where the young boy becomes aware of his American identity through a series of dream-like experiences and by witnessing a real but seemingly phantasmagorical pageant. Hawthorne's "theatre" is not unlike James's "balloon of experience" which, in his definition of "romance" in the Preface to *The American*, he pictures as "tied to the earth" by a "rope of remarkable length."[25] Such a conception of the romantic removal of experience to a position where it will not be exposed to "too close a comparison with the actual events of real lives" explains in large part the "raft" of *Huckleberry Finn*, the Pequod of *Moby Dick*, the screened "office" within an office of Melville's *Bartleby*, and later, the "woods" in *The Bear* and the "bull-ring" in Hemingway. Each of these places of removal sets the stage for a reordering of the social hierarchies which exist outside it. The reordering is accomplished in terms of aspirations and achievements which cannot express themselves in a society based upon practical utility and traditional manners. In every case, however, the "removed stage" of action, the "balloon" is in fact, tied to earth, to a society in the novel which is a reproduction of the kind of society in which the characters would ordinarily live. Huck's raft is not, for example, cut off from civilization. He carries inside him the vocabulary and the values of that civilization, and the dramatic excitement of the novel is partly a linguistic one. There is a question of Huck's being so caught up in other people's words that he will forfeit that freedom of feeling which his idyllic existence with Jim has given him. The novel is, in that sense, about Huck's enslavement to the kind of world to which his "balloon," his raft, is tied in the hard knots of words and phrases, and their attendant values, which bewilder him whenever he tries to unravel his impulses.

Ideally, Hawthorne's description of the method of *The Blithedale Romance* did not mean that the experience in a work of fiction so removed itself from comparison with "real lives" that the result was allegorical, with the characters disengaged from the kinds of responsibility which would ordinarily attach to their actions. It was a fear of this, however, which explains why in his study of Hawthorne, published in 1879, the year of his first extensive revision of *Roderick Hudson*, James expresses certain objections, which Miss Cornelia Kelley very adequately describes,[26] about the tendency in Hawthorne towards romantic allegory. He complains, for example, that the characters in *The House of the Seven Gables* are "figures rather than characters" and that they are "all types, to the author's mind, of something general."[27] James's reservations about allegory and about the grotesques in Dickens are of a piece: "Who represents nature?"[28] This takes us to James's own literary practice. In a novel like *Roderick Hudson* he attempts to deal with the kind of experience which American fiction customarily dramatizes by removing the theatre of action from the "highways of ordinary travel" and, at the same time, to give a strongly realistic image of society as it is normally conceived and experienced. It is my contention that in the attempt to put these two kinds of society in conjunction—the romantically removed and the realistically presented—James naturally found himself involved in the writing of comedy.

The equivalent in James of "the threatre a little removed" is the society of what we can call the elect, of those people of high intelligence and selflessness of whom Rowland is an example. He stands for certain qualities, it has been shown, not in any sense allegorically but as they exist in and because of distinctly realistic human frailties. His idealistic faith in the "essential salubrity of genius" (R. H., p. 47) is shown to be not an absolute standard, unfortunately impossible of achievement, but a delusion bred of his need to believe it. This does not make his ideal less commendable, but only the less romantic, the less "removed" from that "natural feeling and natural sense" which James commends in the comment on Dickens. For this reason it does not seem true in this novel, or in the world of James as a whole, that he is, in Joseph Warren Beach's phrase, like "some visionary Platonist [content] to refer each item of conduct to an absolute standard of the good and the beautiful."[29] The thing that makes James's work slightly different from most of those in the idealistic and romantic tradition of Emerson, Hawthorne, and Melville, and relates him, though eccentrically, to Jane Austen and George Eliot, is that his "absolute standards" can only be called "visionary" in a very indirect way.

James is most intellectually congenial not with the aspiring visionaries, like Roderick or Isabel, but with those people who, made wise rather than cynical by experience and by their own limitations, are optimistically dedicated to helping them out. Rowland, Valentin in *The American*, and Ralph in *The Portrait*, all occupy a middle ground between the detached visionaries, the people who are, so to speak, actually up in James's "balloon," and the systematized society down on the ground. Through them we see the latent ironies of the one and the comic stupidities of the other, and are witness to the tragedy which attends the necessary failure of the visionaries in their attempt to give something more than merely imagined existence to their ideals. In the consciousness of a man like Rowland—the man of many travels, the man who makes his own society, the cosmopolitan—we are shown the struggle between those who excite his imagination, as they excite James's, by seeming for some brief while really to achieve an individual fulfilment of their ideals, and those who represent conventionality and who measure individual fulfilment by the standards of social and economic practicality. The struggle is such that the excesses on either side can become comic, as in the case of Roderick, with his contempt for the suggestion that he is responsible to anything *except* his ideal. The visionaries can become as comically limited in their view of experience as those whom we might call the utilitarians. As Roderick observes of himself in the revised edition, "I'm an ass unless I'm an angel" (R. H. rev., p. 204).

James's comedy in *Roderick Hudson* results, in large part, from his attempt to keep the "balloon of experience" tied to the earth, to keep what he considered the necessary conjunction of the "free" world and the "fixed" world. The terms "free" and "fixed" are James's own. They occur in a passage from the Preface to *The Spoils of Poynton*, in which there is a clear indication of the connection in James's mind between comedy and the social structures which he creates in his novels:

> Thus we get perhaps a vivid enough little example, in the concrete, of the general truth, for the spectator of life, that the fixed constituents of any reproducible action are the fools who minister, at the particular crisis, to the intensity of the free spirit engaged with them. The fools are interesting by contrast, by the salience they acquire, and by a hundred other of their advantages; and the free spirit, always tormented, and by no means triumphant, is heroic, ironic, pathetic, or whatever, and, as exemplified in the record of Fleda Vetch, for instance, "successful," only through having remained free.[30]

The terms in this passage are helpful only if we keep in mind that they should not be used for statically schematic descriptions of the way James places his characters in relation to one another. They help us to describe what is going on at "the *particular* crisis," and to be aware of the polarities between which, in the dramatic movement of the novel, his characters may move. The one dependably placed character is the moderate man in the middle, though we have seen in the case of Rowland that even he can be made to look foolish when he talks unlike himself. In *Roderick Hudson*, then, the term "fixed" can apply at the beginning to Mr. Striker and to Mrs. Hudson, in the sense that they represent conventional repressions upon Roderick's freedom of movement and do so by expressing themselves in a "fixed" and, therefore, comic way: Mr. Striker is clearly a kind of humour, the New England man of practical good sense, and Mrs. Hudson exploits all the conventions of the deserted mother. By introducing these two people with somewhat disrespectful comic phraseology, James quite literally "fixes" them in certain peculiarities to which they, and James, are to remain confined. We take too much pleasure in Mr. Striker's oddity ever to want him to express anything but that oddity. He is described as having "interminable legs" with which he every so often kicks the air, at the same time that he comments on the proposed advantage of Roderick's using Italian models with the observation that "I suppose they're no better made than a good tough Yankee," (R. H., p. 55), and, a bit later, on Rowland's generous offer of help to Roderick, with the remark that "I'm a self-made man, every inch of me!" (R. H., p. 58). Similarly, Mrs. Hudson is introduced as "empty-handed save for the pocket-handkerchief in her lap, which was held with an air of familiarity with its sadder uses" (R. H., p. 47). These pictorially comic introductions occur in the scene in Northampton in which the very subject of Roderick's freedom—his trip to Rome—is being discussed. The use of Mr. Striker and Mrs. Hudson as "fixed constituents" who "minister to the free spirit engaged with them" is a matter not only of their moral stand on Roderick's departure, but of their actual literary existence, the comic "fixity" which James imposes upon them. Because they are as they are, Roderick, in this particular scene, is a "free spirit," and it is in seeing him in the context of the particular "fools" of Northampton that Rowland can justifiably overlook his friend's excessive expressions of freedom from conventional social behaviour.

*Roderick Hudson* is by way of a comment on both American and English fiction with respect to their various ways of dramatizing the relationships between aspiring characters and the conventions of the society in which they live or from which they try to escape. Does a novelist, under these circumstances, merely adopt the values of the romantic rebel? And, if he does that, will he not forfeit the necessary presence in the novel of sound and realistic intelligence by which the actions of such characters can be seen with compassion but also with discrimination? Or is he to accept the conventions of a society, reproduced in the particular novel from actual life, and from that point of view regard the actions of his romantic heroes? Were he to do that, then his imagination would not even be engaged by the aspirations of such characters, by their desire to escape what George Eliot calls the "meanness of opportunity" which traditionally constituted society has to offer. In *Roderick Hudson,* James sets the pattern for his later works by using a character like Rowland—a Mr. Allworthy who is not a country squire but a world wanderer who makes his own society wherever he happens to visit. James puts him very much in the middle, using his intelligence and his freedom from all commitments, except those of reason and selfless benevolence, as the standards by which he can direct irony in both directions, either at fixed society on the one hand or aspiring romantics on the other.

Society, as an organized pattern of conventions and of assumptions about what is worth striving for, is reduced in this novel to comic fixity—in Mr. Striker, Mrs. Hudson, Mr. Leavenworth, who is described with a comic picturesqueness not unlike that used on the latter two, and in Mrs. Light. Mrs. Light is as much a grotesque as Mr. Striker because she is equally undeviating, though more impassioned, in her belief in the value of those practical rewards which are an expression of traditional social hierarchies. On the other hand, the aspiration of a character like Roderick exerts a great appeal on James and on his elected observer, particularly when it exercises itself within the confinements by which the socially "fixed constituents" threaten, often with good intention, to stifle it. But such aspiration is in itself the subject of comedy: of gentle and admiring irony at the innocent optimism with which it can at first express itself and of more satiric irony when it becomes egotistical self-assertion. When this happens, aspiration becomes grotesque because it violates those standards of "natural sense and natural feeling" which James considers necessary, in his remarks on Dickens, to "the maintenance of society."[31] "Society" on those terms is a very uncomplicated thing. Henry Fielding often talks about "natural feeling," but he also talks about affection and amiability within the limits of social status and conventions, and he does so in a way which we never find in James, unless, as in *The American*, he is being satiric. "Natural sense and natural feeling" exist in James not in society, as it is thought of usually in the English novel, but rather in those select individuals who gather together in wholly extemporised and usually expatriate groups to form a "society." This "society" exists to serve, if only by subsidy or by good talk, the cause of freedom in its disengagement from fixity, of romance in its attempt to impose itself upon realism. And it exists, too, to consider patiently why at the end of each novel the cause of freedom has somehow failed.

The two characters, Rowland and Christina, whom I have previously shown to be responsible for most of the direct verbal sarcasm and irony in the novel, are also the two who represent, in humanly fallible form, the absolute standards of full consciousness and of willingness to be selfless in the interest of an ideal. Their presence as well as their own verbal expression sets the standard by which comedy can exist in this novel. In summation of this there is a passage in the Preface to *The Princess Casamassima* which gives a clue to James's own awareness that his comedy might operate in the way I have described. James's method, to recapitulate briefly, is to have all the characters measured by their relationship to an ideal of awareness and selflessness. While showing that even in the best of them there are deficiencies in these virtues, he gives to those who come closest to the ideal in any given novel the function of providing a rationale, a pattern of feeling and intelligence, which is like that supplied in Jane Austen by coherent social values. By their distance from the "society" of these highly endowed individuals, the other characters are rendered relatively more or less comic and, at the extreme distance, grotesque. In his Preface, James is commenting on the value of having his characters in a state of "bewilderment," of not having them even at their best "too *interpretative* of the muddle of fate, or in other words too divinely, too priggishly clever."[32] None of the characters can be ideally conscious of what is going on around him and remain humanly and dramatically useful. But there are degrees of "bewilderment," and there is a kind of stupidity which means that a character may not be bewildered at all, the stupidity which keeps him from being conscious of more significance than he can handle. Mr. Striker is thereby less "bewildered" by Roderick than Rowland is, and he is perfectly right in his predictions that Roderick will succeed no better in Rome, finally, than he did in Northampton. Mr. Striker is right, but he is also, by James's standards, "stupid." James relates all this very specifically to comedy, and gives us what, so far as I know, is his most explicit account of the way in which comedy reflects the seriousness of his intentions:

> The whole thing comes to depend thus on the *quality* of bewilderment characteristic of one's creature, the quality involved in the given case or supplied by one's data. There are doubtless many such qualities, ranging from vague and crepuscular to sharpest and most critical; and we have but to imagine one of these latter to see how easily—from the moment it gets its head at all—it may insist on playing a part. There we

have then at once a case of feeling, of ever so many possible feelings, stretched across the scene like an attached thread on which the pearls of interest are strung. There are threads shorter and less tense, and I am far from implying that the minor, the coarser and less fruitful forms and degrees of moral reaction, as we may conveniently call it, may not yield lively results. They have their subordinate, comparative, illustrative human value—that appeal of the witless which is often so penetrating. Verily even, I think, no "story" is possible without its fools—as most of the fine painters of life, Shakespeare, Cervantes and Balzac, Fielding, Scott, Thackeray, Dickens, George Meredith, George Eliot, Jane Austen, have abundantly felt. At the same time I confess I never see the *leading* interest of any human hazard but in a consciousness (on the part of the moved and moving creature) subject to fine intensification and wide enlargement. It is as mirrored in that consciousness that the gross fools, the headlong fools, the fatal fools play their parts for us—they have much less to show us in themselves. The troubled life mostly at the center of our subject—whatever our subject, for the artistic hour, happens to be—embraces them and deals with them for its amusement and its anguish: they are apt largely indeed, on a near view, to be all the cause of its trouble. This means exactly, that the person capable of feeling in the given case more than another of what is to be felt for it, and so serving in the highest degree to *record* it dramatically and objectively, is the only sort of person on whom we can count not to betray, to cheapen or, as we say, give away, the value and the beauty of the thing. By so much as the affair matters *for* some such individual, by so much do we get the best there is of it, and by so much as it falls within the scope of a denser and duller, a more vulgar and more shallow capacity, do we get a picture dim and meagre.[33]

To be "capable of feeling in the given case more than another of what is to be felt for it" is to be "free" in the best sense, "free" from the different forms of self-absorption which are to be found in all the characters in this novel except Rowland, Christina, and Mary. They are the only ones capable of that "enlargement" of consciousness which permits them to see that their own conduct and other people's involves complex responsibilities to an ideal of selflessness which, by the standards of most other characters in the novel, is impractical. The deeply felt expression of this ideal neutralizes what might otherwise be considered melodramatic absurdity. As a result, Rowland, without engaging our comic sense, can risk his neck climbing a rock to pick a flower for Mary when such an act, attempted earlier by Roderick for Christina, appeared madly theatrical and self-dramatizing. And so, too, we are given nothing to laugh at in the extremely melodramatic circumstances of Roderick's death—in dark and storm on the Swiss Alps while his distraught and hysterical mother swoons at his absence. Even at the moment when he has at last come to see the injuriousness of his egotism, he becomes the victim of tempestuous forces which seem, as they destroy him, also to dignify, in some ultimate way, his destructive submission to the forces of irrational feeling inside him. In mourning for him, Rowland "the most rational of men was for an hour the most passionate" (R. H., p. 480). The conclusion of the novel shows us how, in their imagination of what Roderick *might* be, James no less than Rowland reveals a "consciousness subject to fine intensifications and wide enlargement."

The ideals which are the positive standards behind the comedy are also those which allow us to be finely aware of the pathos of Roderick's death, to get the most out of it. To do that we must see beyond the excitement of the death itself to something more important: the effect upon the consciousness of Rowland Mallet. It pays to express the matter brutally— that what happens to Rowland in life is more important than Roderick's death—because James is a novelist of extraordinary toughness in giving the lie to the notion that we are obliged to "feel" for things because they demand it of us in a loud and conventional voice. The lamentations of Mrs. Hudson at the disappearance of her son are, for example, rendered in a way that makes her coarseness of mind and emptiness of head more rather than less offensive. "We care," James writes in the Prefaces, "our curiosity and our sympathy care, comparatively little for what happens to the stupid, the coarse and the blind."[34] We pity Roderick at the end of the novel because, though he is at times all these things, he yet leaves recorded on the consciousness of Rowland Mallet some of his fineness and his promise. But the ending of the novel is such that we finally "care, our curiosity and our sympathy care," for what happens to Rowland. The last sentence of the novel adequately explains what happens to him; "I assure you," he tells Cecilia, "I am the most patient" (R. H., p. 482). It is not clear whether he is patient in the expectations, which clearly will not be realized, of Mary Garland's love, or whether he is "patient" because he expects nothing. As we shall see, this is the final plight of the characters who matter most in each of the novels through *The Portrait of a Lady*. It is a patience akin to death, in which fineness of impulse loses confidence in its social efficacy. This, parenthetically, explains why so many of James's good people are unmarried and remain so. That is the destiny of the hero of James's next novel, *The American*, and it is significant that there, as in *Roderick Hudson*, much of the comedy comes from the fact that at the centre of the action is a man who has such confidence in the effectiveness of his good intentions that it can be said of him, as of Rowland, that he is betrayed by his sense of humour, his willingness to suffer "fools" because he cannot imagine that they might contaminate the value and the beauty of things in which he trusts and believes.

## Notes

1. *Roderick Hudson* (Boston, 1876), p. 176. Hereafter the novel will be designated *R. H.* and page references to it will be included in the text.

2. *Roderick Hudson* (London, 1921), p. 369. Subsequent references to this edition will to *R. H.* rev., and pagination will be indicated in the text.

3. F. W. Dupee (New York, 1951), p. 61.

4. *A Landscape Painter* (New York, 1919), p. 67.

5. Joseph Warren Beach, *The Method of Henry James* (New Haven, 1918), p. 191.

6. T. S. Eliot, *After Strange Gods* (New York, 1934), p. 59.

7. Arnold's "theory of style . . . was actually a theory of morality," according to Lionel Trilling, *Matthew Arnold* (New York, 1939), p. 159. See also pp. 30–31.

8. *The Art of the Novel*, ed. R. P. Blackmur (London, 1950), p. 5.

9. Beach, p. 197.

10. See Dupee, *Henry James*, pp. 88–89.

11. T. S. Eliot, "The Hawthorne Aspect," in *The Question of Henry James*, ed. F. W. Dupee (London, 1947), p. 132.

12. See Dupee, *The Question of Henry James*, pp. 261–73.

13. Leo B. Levy, *Versions of Melodrama: A Study of the Fiction and Drama of Henry James, 1865–1897* (Berkeley, 1957), pp. 18–19.

14. See Pelham Edgar, *Henry James: Man and Author* (Boston, 1927), pp. 232–7.

15. See Cornelia Kelley, *The Early Development of Henry James* (Urbana, 1930), pp. 182–94.

16. See F. R. Leavis, "Henry James's First Novel," *Scrutiny*, XIV (September, 1947), 295–301.

17. *The Art of the Novel*, p. 16.

18. *The Art of the Novel*, p. 290.

19. James, when asked if he would come to luncheon to meet Santayana, is reported by Logan Pearsall Smith to have replied: "Come! I would walk across London with bare feet on the snow to meet George Santayana." This report appears in *The Legend of the Master*, compiled by Simon Nowell-Smith (New York, 1948), p. 83.

20. George Santayana, *Winds of Doctrine* (New York, 1913), p. 29.

21. Unsigned review of Dickens's *Our Mutual Friend*, *The Nation*, I (December 21, 1865), 787. The review is reprinted in a very useful collection of James's essays and reviews, *The Future of the Novel*, ed. Leon Edel (New York, 1956), pp. 75–80.

22. George Eliot, *Middlemarch*, (Everyman, ed) I, xv.

23. See the excellent discussion of Charlotte Brontë in an article by George Armour Craig, "The Unpoetic Compromise," *English Institute Essays*, 1955, ed. Mark Schorer (New York, 1956), pp. 31–41.

24. Nathaniel Hawthorne, *The Blithedale Romance*, in *Hawthorne's Works* (Boston, 1883), V, 321.

25. *The Art of the Novel*, p. 13.

26. See Cornelia Kelley, pp. 250–6.

27. *Hawthorne* (New York, 1879), p. 121.

28. See footnote 21.

29. Beach, p. 149.

30. *The Art of the Novel*, pp. 129–30.

31. See footnote 21.

32. *The Art of the Novel*, p. 64.

33. *The Art of the Novel*, pp. 66–7.

34. *The Art of the Novel*, p. 62.

# Rereading *The American:*
# A Century Since
James W. Tuttleton*

Very late in life, in 1913, Henry James gave Stark Young two lists of his "advanced" novels; they constituted the "beef and potatoes" of his art, while the tales were the delectable "little tarts." At the head of the more advanced second list was *The American,* followed by *The Tragic Muse, The Wings of the Dove, The Ambassadors,* and *The Golden Bowl.* James of course intended Young to read *The American* in the much-revised New York Edition; otherwise, he remarked, Young would forfeit "half," or much more than half, my confidence." Clearly James thought highly of his novel of the American in Paris. Yet Robert Herrick, the novelist who visited James in 1907, while the New York Edition was in preparation, remonstrated with the Master about his "re-touching" of *The American.* His ground for the protest was "the respect one owed to one's past, living, or buried, and the impossibility of this sort of resurrection by breathing the breath of one's present life into what for good or ill had been done and finished under another inspiration, as a different if inferior person."[1]

James, however, was absolutely adamant about the importance of his revisions. He told Herrick: "I shouldn't have planned the edition at all unless I had felt close revision—wherever seeming called for—to be an indispensable part of it. I do every justice to your contention, but don't think me reckless or purblind if I say that I hold myself really right and you really wrong." His "duty to his older creations," according to Herrick, called for "nothing less than a complete 're-writing' of these earlier and primitively simple efforts in the later manner—the manner of the amanuensis and the 'overtreatment!' "[2]

The point of this contention between the two novelists has the highest significance for literary criticism. Which is the preferable form of the novel, *The American* as James wrote it in 1875–76, or as he revised it in 1907? (There has been little discussion, in a century of criticism, over whether it is necessary to choose between them.) Unquestionably some of James's critics have preferred the later version of the book, or at least deferred to James's rigorous insistence. Royal A. Gettmann has argued that "it is wrong . . . to assume that James the Reviser mercilessly manhandled the works of James the First."[3] Commending the revisions as "a moral act of the highest kind," Isadore Traschen has praised the extent to which the retouching "enlarged on character and theme through the use of recurrent images; images in the original were transformed into emphatic symbols." And he has praised the extent to which the revisions introduced into the novel the "poetic mode" of the major phase.[4]

*Reprinted from the *Henry James Review* 1 (Winter 1980):139–53, with the permission of the *Henry James Review* and the author.

Such defenses of the Master's revisions have not always been widely accepted. In my judgment, the *doubtful* retouchings constitute a distinctive irritant to readers who are familiar with both texts. While James, as he put it in the Preface to *Roderick Hudson,* "nowhere scrupled to re-write a sentence or a passage on judging it susceptible of a better turn," a number of the "better turns" in *The American* seem worthy of calling into question. The alteration of Newman's "clean shaved" cheek to "he spoke, as to cheek and chin, of the matutinal steel" is, in my view, a dubious felicity. The bluntly effective "You killed your husband" strikes one as much overdrawn in the revision "You cruelly killed your helpless husband." And the transposition of "he was too short, as he said, to afford a belly" into "he was too short a story, as he said, to afford an important digression" strikes this reader, at least, as a literary affectation. Perhaps a more balanced assessment is that offered by Louis Auchincloss, who has observed that "in the nondialogue, or descriptive passages the revisions are largely improvements, and that in the dialogue passages they are not." Beyond this, he finds "no essential difference in any of the characters or in any incident of the plot. It is the same story with essentially the same interpretations and the same emphases."[5]

Without doubt, some of James's revisions are improvements. And for those who wish to make direct comparisons, the recently published Scolar Press facsimile of the holograph revisions is available.[6] But since the revisions are so extensive, no mere emendation of the original, incorporating the changes, is possible; and James's critics, as well as his editors, must therefore make a determination as to the appropriate text to offer for criticism. I frankly go on record as preferring the early version of the novel, the book as young James essentially wrote it in Paris in the mid-1870s. In this regard, I concur with Leon Edel, who has observed that the New York Edition of *The American* "is almost another book" which "lacks the pristine qualities, the visual sharpness, and the intensity with which Henry, feeling himself as good as the Europeans, wrote this tale in a Paris that kept him at arm's length."[7] Consequently, in the remarks that follow, I shall refer only to the early version of the novel as prepared for the Norton Critical Edition series.[8]

From a review of all the known contemporary magazine reviews and subsequent essays in criticism of the novel, one perceives that a number of pertinent issues have surfaced or resurfaced during the century or so of the novel's existence. In this centennial essay I propose to look at merely *some* of these issues, to indicate representative viewpoints, and to formulate some notions of my own that will, I trust, throw additional light on James's intentions and execution.

First, *The American,* as I have argued elsewhere, is a novel of manners juxtaposing for analysis the mores of an aristocratic French society with the comparative mannerlessness of the American traveler in Paris, specifically a Western businessman who has amassed a sudden fortune and has come abroad to cultivate aesthetic interests and, it turns out, to find a wife.[9] A great deal has been written about this "international theme"—by Edel, Cargill, Vanderbilt, and others—so that it is perhaps not necessary here to belabor these oft-discussed matters. The interested reader will find a directive to opinions on these and other issues in the notes.[10]

But there are one or two matters relevant to the international theme and to the way it is *constructed* that, it strikes me on further reflection, have not been sufficiently elucidated in the criticism. One has to do with the frequency and extent of James's technique of doubling, or parallelism. The number of paired contrasts in the book is striking: natural vs. titled nobility; democracy vs. royalism; renunciations of revenge in business and in love; American vs. French conceptions of "honor" (with the further contrast of the meaning of "honor" to the aristocrat Valentin and to the *petit bourgeois* M. Nioche); the parallelism of contrastive marriages; the walls of the *hôtel* vs. the convent walls, etc.

It is clear, for example, that the central "marriage theme" is developed simultaneously on two fronts: both Christopher Newman and Noémie Nioche are in search of a spouse. What is striking about this parallel is that significantly different intentions animate these two characters. In the case of Noémie, James deploys the familiar theme of marriage as an avenue to greater wealth and upward social mobility. In novels where love is obstructed by class barriers, money is of course crucial, and James gives it its due in the dilemma faced by father and daughter over her dowry. M. Nioche puts the matter succinctly: " 'Ah, monsieur, one doesn't get a husband for nothing. Her husband must take her as she is; I can't give her a sou. But the young men don't see with that eye.' " Newman may advance an American viewpoint in suggesting that " 'your young men are very shabby. . . . They ought to pay for your daughter, and not ask money themselves' " (53–54), but the custom of the country, in France, is the necessary *dot*. But in reply to Newman's generous offer of money to provide the dowry, in exchange for a half dozen execrable copies, Noémie remarks: " 'What sort of husband can you get for twelve thousand francs? . . . Grocers and butchers and little *maîtres de cafés!* I will not marry at all if I can't marry well' " (64).

Newman's counsel (" 'I would advise you not to be too fastidious' " [64]) doubles back upon him with irony when we come to consider the height of his own marital ambitions. But the trajectory of the plot with Noémie Nioche is established in this exchange, and her subsequent conduct, however vulgar and immoral, is directed to the end of escaping the poverty of the *petite bourgeoisie*—if not as an affluent wife, then at least as an aristocrat's mistress. In the end, she comes closer to her goal than Newman to his, she having successively brought in tow both a French count and an English lord.

The plot line associated with Newman, however, does not deal with the usual theme of upward social mobility, greater wealth, or improved social status. For one thing, Newman is immensely rich—much richer than the Bellegardes. Second, he has no interest in the social status of the aristocratic family with which he becomes involved. His aim is not to enter the sacred circle of the Faubourg St. Germain but rather to possess Claire, to draw her out of its narrow confines, and to offer her, in recompense, the whole wide world. This is indicated in his telling the young marquise that he really does not want to come into the family by way of marriage: " 'I only want to take Madame de Cintré out of it' " (144). In this respect, the book differs from those novels of manners in which the energies of the *nouveau riche* are directed toward gaining an entry into society. Newman has no interest in the Bellegardes' social status because he has no interest in "society," and, as an American democrat, he thinks that he is as good as anybody, is in fact "nature's nobleman."[11] Instead of the usual motive, then, James defines Newman's intention in terms of acquisition.

As a businessman, Newman has risen to the top of the financial world through making and selling wash-tubs and leather, through stock deals and like transactions, some apparently rather cut-throat. He has made a pile high enough to enable him to renounce the blood-thirstiness of Gilded Age business practices and to "assimilate" Europe. Practically speaking, he believes that "Europe was made for him, and not he for Europe. . . . The world, to his sense, was a great bazaar, where one might stroll about and purchase handsome things; but he was no more conscious, individually, of social pressure than he admitted the existence of such a thing as an obligatory purchase" (66).

The principal purchase in question is of course a wife. And there is no mistaking the acquisitiveness evident in Newman's whole courtship of Claire de Cintré. He advises Mrs. Tristram, for example, that " 'To make it perfect, as I see it, there must be a beautiful woman perched on the pile, like a statue on a monument. She must be as good as she is beautiful, and as clever as she is good. . . . I want to possess, in a word, the best article in the market' " (44). This degree of fastidiousness, in view of the commercial advice he gives to Noémie Nioche, is bound to reverberate with irony. For while he believes that any desire can be realized—with enough determination, energy, and cash—he obviously does not know the height of exclusiveness of which the Bellegardes are capable. I suggest that it is this detached commercial acquisitiveness that renders Newman ineffective as the dynamic, successful lover his American reviewers wanted him to be. His failure to sweep Claire off her feet, whatever the piddling impediments of French snobbishness, has always seemed a problematic aspect of his characterization.[12] His desire for a wife is in fact willed, for he is not a sufficiently passionate man. He is not a Don Juan. And in this respect Urbain may be right in calling Newman's persistence in trying to retrieve Claire a mere "audacious pertinacity."

## II

In the service of this plot—doubled as it is through the parallelism of Newman's and Noémie's marital ambitions—James strikes off a glittering array of suggestive symbolism derived from the visual arts, literature, music, and mythology. These have been the subject of some critical notice, although a full-scale treatment of James's allusive technique yet remains to be done.[13] On one level, of course, the world of art—the great masters, the magnificent museums—is sketched in by James in order to underline the bewilderment of a businessman who has just discovered "a very rich and beautiful world," one that "had not all been made by sharp railroad men and stock-brokers" (75). What should be made of this dazzling discovery is enough to give our hero an "aesthetic headache" (17). But for the reader it is a pleasure to observe the uses to which specific paintings are put by the author, whose lead characters are intent on matrimony.

The motif of marriage is continually reinforced, for example, by a network of allusions to paintings by Titian, Raphael, Murillo, Veronese, and others. Murillo's beautiful moon-borne Madonna is the first painting to come under Newman's scrutiny in the Louvre, although, "baffled on the aesthetic question" (19), he admires Noémie's copy as much as the original. That James should have set up, at the outset of the novel, a symbol resonant with the notion of divine motherhood, innocence, and purity suggests two things: both Newman's aspiration to a certain kind of wife, and a contrast (yet to become apparent) with Noémie, who passes in the course of the action from the condition of a coquette to that of a contemptible prostitute. James's symbolic intent is suggested with a brilliant economy of means in a sentence near the end of Chapter 1: "Mademoiselle Noémie had collected her accessories, and she gave the precious Madonna in charge to her father, who retreated backwards out of sight, holding it at arm's-length and reiterating his obeisances" (25). This comment crystallizes in a single sentence the notion of chaste virtue, the father's responsibility for preserving it, his inability to do so, and his fawning obsequiousness. Later, when she destroys one of her copies by painting two crimson daubs on it, so as to create "the rough indication of a cross," we have been alerted to James's motif of appearance and reality: she is a poor imitation of the Madonna. Her remark about the cross (" 'It is the sign of truth' " [133]) is spoken without any deep understanding of the truth of virtue and self-sacrifice implicit in the Christian faith.

Another work of art—Paul Veronese's portrait of the marriage feast at Cana—is put to a like use in the opening of Chapter II. In this scene, Newman sits before the depiction of Christ's first miracle and finds that the painting "satisfied his conception, which was ambitious, of what a splendid banquet should be" (26). James observes what it is that attracts Newman: "In the left-hand corner of the picture is a young woman with yellow tresses confined in a golden head-dress; she is bending forward and listening, with the smile of a charming woman at a dinner-party, to her neigh-bour. Newman detected her in the crowd, admired her, and perceived that she too had her votive copyist—a young man with his hair standing on end. Suddenly he became conscious of the germ of the 'collector' " (26). This scene too adumbrates, in a symbolic way, several matters to follow. The recognition of a beautiful woman, the votive attention, the marriage, the splendid banquet, wifely charm at a dinner party, the wife as an object of the collector's mania—all of these take on full form as the plot unfolds, but are here simply noted with a symbolic compression that suggests how rap-idly James's art had matured since *Roderick Hudson.*

Both of these art works depict the Holy Family or the subject of mar-riage in the context of the Gospels and radiate, therefore, sacred associa-tions. What are we to make of them? I do not believe that James was a religious symbolist along the lines suggested by Quentin Anderson's *The American Henry James.* But the multiplication of other art works sacred to the Christian faith does beguile the critic's curiosity. The allusion to Noé-mie's study of the "Madonnas and St. Johns" (60), in the context of New-man's question about her being a coquette, reminds us that if the Madonna is an image of virgin purity and Noémie will come to a bad end, St. John lost his head through the betrayal and sexual treachery of Salome, even as Valentin loses his life in part as a consequence of Noémie's machinations.

In the context of this conversation about her imputed immorality, Noémie proposes, as a commission, a picture of the Marriage of St. Cather-ine. That Newman's marriage of Claire will be sanctified by her saintliness seems to be authenticated as we get to know Claire. Indeed, as Newman later says, " 'She is my dream realised' " (106). But more than a little irony inheres in James's choice of Saint Catherine's marriage when, after the Bel-legardes have broken faith, Urbain remarks, " 'I think my mother will tell you that she would rather her daughter should become Soeur Catherine than Mrs. Newman' " (250). Catherine of Siena (1347–80) is well known in the hagiographies for her mysticism and asceticism. Claire's renunciation of the world, not to speak of her renunciation of marriage to Newman and of the motherhood of his children, is therefore interestingly implied by the reference. From Saint to Sister is, indeed, Claire's direction in the novel.

Yet, as it turns out, Catherine is not the name elected by this beautiful woman who takes the veil. In the last chapter of the novel, we and New-man discover, from Mrs. Tristram, that, on her twenty-seventh birthday, Claire " 'took the name of her patroness, St. Veronica. Sister Veronica has a lifetime before her!' " (304). Veronica, we are reminded, was the holy woman of Jerusalem who gave to Christ, on his way to Calvary, a handker-chief. Ever afterward, it is said, the handkerchief bore his image. (Indeed, any cloth so bearing an image of Christ is called a veronica.) While her fi-ancé's name is Christopher—or Christ-bearer—no elaborate one-for-one parallels should be sought in these religious allusions. It is enough to say that they are consciously dropped in passing for associative value and that they suggest the notions of purity, virtue, and asceticism associated with Claire (the antithetical associations being pertinent to Noémie) and the notions of betrayal and emotional agony associated with Newman.

The alteration of the religious name from Catherine to Veronica may associate the anguish of Newman with the passion of Christ, but these matters cannot be carried too far. Otherwise, we would have to do something improbable with Newman's use of the language of Pontius Pilate, when, in speaking to Valentin of M. Nioche, he says, " 'if the old man turns out to be a humbug, you may do what you please (with Noémie). I wash my hands of the matter' " (136). James, as an inheritor of some of Hawthorne's moral interests, knew enough to avoid his predecessor's overdevelopment of such images. An excess of the fanciful element was not consistent with James's sense of realism in fiction, and in the biography *Hawthorne*, soon to be published, James criticized Hawthorne on this very point. In *The American*, as elsewhere, James merely indulges the liberty of a free irony in playing with the latencies of suggested meaning.

That Newman is not meant to be a serious analogue to Christ is suggested by the symbolism of two other *objets d'art* alluded to in the novel. The first is a fan which is nervously opened by old Madame de Bellegarde in the scene where Newman threatens to stage an engagement party at his hotel, featuring the singer Madame Frezzolini and "all the first people from the Théâtre Française" (170). As she pales before this prospect, the old Marquise opens an antique fan on which is painted "a fête champêtre—a lady with a guitar, singing, and a group of dancers round a garlanded Hermes" (171). The old lady's horror at an uncivil public revel—to which will be invited the likes of Miss Kitty Upjohn, Miss Dora Finch, General Packard, and C. P. Hatch—with Newman, The King of Leather and Wash-Tubs, as an American avatar of the garlanded Hermes, Greek God of Commerce—is wittily suggested by the latent implications of this old fan.

The second symbolic art work is the gift Newman purchases for the Reverend Mr. Babcock, a New England minister who has come to France on funds supplied by his congregation for moral and cultural self-development but who finds Europe to be "impure" and Newman to be wanting in a sufficient "moral reaction" to their experiences. In response to Babcock's long letter charging him with hedonism, Newman purchases for him "a grotesque little statuette in ivory, of the sixteenth century, which he sent off to Babcock without a commentary. It represented a gaunt, ascetic-looking monk, in a tattered gown and cowl, kneeling with clasped hands and pulling a portentously long face. It was a wonderfully delicate piece of carving, and in a moment, through one of the rents of his gown, you espied a fat capon hung round the monk's waist." That James intends us to see a latent meaning in this gift (as well as in the other *objets d'art*) is suggested by the curious questions posed by the author: "In Newman's intention what did the figure symbolise? Did it mean that he was going to try to be as 'high-toned' as the monk looked at first, but that he feared he should succeed no better than the friar, on a closer inspection, proved to have done? It is not supposable that he intended a satire upon Babcock's own asceticism, for this would have been a truly cynical stroke. He made his late companion, at any rate, a very valuable little present" (73). These alternative possibilities reflect Hawthorne's familiar trick of the multiple interpretation of symbolic objects and actions but do not, I submit, carry Hawthorne's characteristic heavy freight of allegorical meaning.[14]

## III

A number of literary allusions, fairy tales, folk legends, and myths complement the symbolic artworks so as to suggest, without developing, other layers of meaning. One of the most textually significant is the allusion to *Faublas,* a book which Newman reads to avert insomnia at the Croix Helvétique, where Valentin lies dying. This recondite title alludes in shortened form to *Les Amours du Chevalier Faublas,* published by Jean Baptiste Louvet de Couvray in Paris in 1821. The full title is a more suggestive gloss associating the loves of Valentin and Newman. But by 1907, when the New York Edition was prepared, James had concluded that the abbreviated allusion was too obscure and that the full title was too cumbersome and explicit, with the effect that he altered the name of the book, in revision, to *Les Liaisons Dangereuses,* a work by Choderlos de Laclos published in 1782, the title of which provided a more evident, expressive ironic association.

Not so textually significant, but an allusion nevertheless suggestive of the improbable romanticism of Newman's courtship, is the Duchess's remark that Newman's " 'real triumph . . . is pleasing the countess; she is as difficult as a princess in a fairy tale' " (190). At the engagement party, as Urbain introduces Newman to his peers, James remarks that "If the marquis was going about as a bear-leader, if the fiction of Beauty and the Beast was supposed to have found its companion-piece, the general impression appeared to be that the bear was a very fair imitation of humanity." Despite the civilities of the aristocracy, Newman is obliged to ask himself, " 'Am I behaving like a d——d fool?' " (191). Much of the time, unfortunately, in that salon and on that occasion, he is.

That Newman will not prove to be the prince who can carry off the princess is suggested by another fairy-tale allusion. At one of the dinner parties, Newman arrives at the *hôtel* de Bellegarde just in time to hear Claire de Cintré finish reading a story to her young niece: " 'But in the end the young prince married the beautiful Florabella . . . and carried her off to live with him in the Land of the Pink Sky. There she was so happy that she forgot all her troubles, and went out to drive every day of her life in an ivory coach drawn by five hundred white mice. Poor Florabella,' she explained to Newman, 'had suffered terribly' " (137–38). F. V. Bernard has astutely argued, on the basis of other evidence, that the Land of the Pink

Sky is America.[15] But Newman is not to be the princely deliverer who will transport Claire from suffering in Paris to the joys of San Francisco. And the denouement of the plot is appropriately adumbrated in Claire's remark, a few minutes later: "I have very little courage; I am not a heroine. . . . I could never have gone through the sufferings of the beautiful Florabella. . . . not even for her prospective rewards" (138). In this admission Newman's fate is sealed.

Valentin's allusion to King Cophetua and the beggar-maid puts additional emphasis on the impossible fairy-tale courtship of Newman. In discussing the exalted character of the family, which descends from the ninth century, Valentin remarks that the young women had, with only a few exceptions, always married into old families. Best of the exceptions was the ancestor in the middle ages who had " 'married a beggar-maid, like King Cophetua. That was really better,' " Valentin remarks: " 'it was like marrying a bird or a monkey; one didn't have to think about her family at all. Our women have always done well; they have never even gone into the *petite noblesse*. There is, I believe, not a case on record of a misalliance among the women' " (103). This remark, like Claire's observation that she is no heroine, aptly adumbrates the dissapointment of the hero at the end. The allusion, however, is charged with an ironic paradox. For it is Newman who has the kingly wealth, of course, while the Bellegardes are financially "forlorn"; but it is the Bellegardes whose aristocratic status will effectively deprive Newman, nature's nobleman, of an opportunity for kingly "condescension."

The American hovers on the borderline between high comedy and tragedy, while ultimately descending into a doubtful melodrama. But that James, early in the book, wanted to invest the forthcoming denouement with tragic overtones is suggested in Mrs. Tristram's comparing Claire to Desdemona in *Othello*.[16] Just after Newman has met Claire for the first time, and she has not absolutely foreclosed further meetings, Mrs. Tristram congratulates Newman and remarks of Claire: " 'No woman was ever so good as that woman seems. . . . Remember what Shakespeare calls Desdemona: "a supersubtle Venetian." Madame de Cintré is a supersubtle Parisian. She is a charming woman, and she has five hundred merits; but you had better keep that in mind' " (117). One is struck with that verb in the first sentence: *seems*. It alerts the sensitive reader to a possible discrepancy between the appearance and the reality of Claire's goodness. And Mrs. Tristram's suggestion that Newman keep in mind Claire's supersubtlety has the effect of forewarning us that Madame de Cintré may be entirely capable of commanding the resolution of the eventual conflict. But aside from that, implicit in the Desdemona allusion is the notion of the betrayal of a lover. Desdemona is entirely innocent of treachery to Othello, of course, but Madame de Cintré's decision to enter a convent, however victimized she is by her family, represents a failure of courage which effectively betrays and repudiates Newman's love for her.

The destructiveness of women who victimize men and prevent the fulfillment of love is suggested in Mrs. Tristram's allusion to Keats's "La Belle Dame sans Merci," on the occasion when she tells Valentin that he reminds her of the "knight-at-arms, / Alone and palely loitering." Valentin replies with elaborate facetious courtesy but suggests that " 'it is good manners for no man except Newman to look happy' " (192). This connection of Newman and Valentin with the beautiful ladies without mercy not only forecasts how both will suffer in love but constitutes a part of the subtext of feelings and associations negative to marriage.

The setting for Valentin's confession to Newman that he has come within an inch of " 'taking that girl [Noémie] *au sérieux*' " (198) is a performance of Mozart's *Don Giovanni*. Both are putative Don Juans. The conversation among the principals about the opera sets up a series of parallels among the characters of the opera and of the novel, in which, above all, Newman is the Don Juan whose pursuit of Claire as Donna Elvira will be obstructed by Urbain as the man of stone, with the ironic reversal that Newman will be the one forsaken, not Donna Elvira. James is not content to let the reader draw the parallels in this scene but points them himself. In this, I believe, there is a failure of the young writer's trust in his readers. But the operatic analogues are in any event unmistakable and constitute another adumbration of the end of the novel.

William Dean Howells complained to James that in his previous stories the promised marriages had had a way of evaporating. Indeed, they did, for marriage in *The American*, as in previous works, seems hardly a consummation devoutly to be wished. A brief look at the several marriages in the novel is enough to trouble the reader at the negativism with which James presented the estate of wedlock. Most criticism, however, has tended to center only on Newman's loss of Claire.

First, with respect to the Tristrams, it takes very little reading between the lines to discover how incompatible is this couple. Mrs. Tristram virtually detests her boorish husband, hankers after Newman, and, as the novel develops, suffers a good deal of jealousy over Claire's managing to take him away from her. James writes that "it was only a tenderly perverse theory of his hostess of the Avenue d'Iéna [Mrs. Tristram] that he was faithless to his early friendships. She needed the theory to explain a certain moral irritation by which she was often visited; though, if this explanation was unsound, a deeper analyst than I must give the right one. Having launched our hero upon the current which was bearing him so rapidly along, she appeared but half-pleased at its swiftness" (116–17). The "moral irritation" is plainly jealousy arising out of discontent at her marriage to a boor and out of a sense of loss represented by Newman's abandoning the confidences of her parlor *tête-à-têtes* for Claire's drawingroom.

That wives detest their husbands, that marriage partners may be cold, faithless, and unsympathetic, seems to be the latent subtext of this novel. Certainly the young marquise has little use for Urbain, although she is powerless before his familial authority. Still, she, like Mrs. Tristram, sees Newman as a likely romantic diversion. She asks him, " 'What do you think of my husband?' " confessing, " 'It's a strange question, isn't it? But I shall ask you some stranger ones yet' " (144). She urges him to form " 'an alliance, offensive or defensive,' " with her (145) and repeatedly tries to induce him to take her to the Bal Bullier, the "ball in the Latin Quarter, where the students dance with their mistresses" (202). Newman eventually comes to pity her, "especially since she was a silly, thirstily-smiling little brunette, with a suggestion of an unregulated heart. The small marquise sometimes looked at him with an intensity too marked not to be innocent, for coquetry is more finely shaded. She apparently wanted to ask him something or tell him something; he wondered what it was. But he was shy of giving her an opportunity, because, if her communication bore upon the aridity of her matrimonial lot, he was at a loss to see how he could help her. He had a fancy, however, of her coming up to him some day and saying (after looking round behind her) with a little passionate hiss: 'I know you detest my husband; let me have the pleasure of assuring you for once you are right. Pity a poor woman who is married to a clock-image in *papier-mâché!*' " (183). In this passage James may be drawing upon the French reputation, among Victorian Anglo-Americans, for what Matthew Arnold called French "lubricity." In any event, the scene marks one more marital failure in the book.

Madame de Bellegarde, the younger, is merely an aristocratic version, however, of Madame Nioche, Noémie's mother. If Noémie is a *"franche coquette,"* according to her father, " 'she comes honestly by it. Her mother was one before her!' " Madame Nioche is described as having deceived her husband under his very nose, " 'year after year. I was too stupid, and the temptation was too great. But I found her out at last. I have only been once in my life a man to be afraid of; I know it very well: it was in that hour! Nevertheless I don't like to think of it. I loved her—I can't tell you how much. She was a bad woman.' " And in alluding ominously to his " 'dark days, and my explosion with Madame Nioche,' " the old man remarks, " 'She was my purgatory, monsieur!' " (57).

While we may wish to consider the dubious source of these confidences about marriage, that the institution may be purgatorial for either or both parties is implied for very nearly every couple. Certainly it is for Claire as the wife of M. de Cintré. Married off at eighteen to an odious but wealthy man of sixty, whose money she renounced during a lawsuit brought by his family in which scandalous evidence tended to incriminate him in a fraud, Claire washed her hands of the money—and of marriage—"forever." Such is the disagreeableness of matrimony, in this novel, that it is hard to disagree with Valentin, who says of Claire that he does not see " 'why a widow should ever marry again. She has gained the benefits of matrimony—freedom and consideration—and she has got rid of the drawbacks. Why should she put her head into the noose again? Her usual mo-

tive is ambition; if a man can offer her a great position, or make her a princess or an ambassadress, she may think the compensation sufficient' " (108).

The ultimate horror of the married life is of course implied in the relationship of Claire's parents, the old marquis and marquise. That the wife
should have murdered her husband, in order to prevent his barring Claire's
marriage to the odious thief Cintré, translates mere marital discord, which,
as we have seen, is horrific enough, into heinous criminality. Babcock's
classmate who had studied architecture in Paris and who had "had a love
affair with a young woman who did not expect him to marry her" (69) begins to sound less scandalous than the marriages which are sketched in by
James.

It may be tempting to ascribe these marital disasters to the European
custom of the *mariage de convenance* in which the girl is "sold" for the
dowry, or in which her title, if she is noble, is traded for wealth. That much
is suggested by Mrs. Tristram, who remarks of Claire: " 'She has been sold
once; she naturally objects to being sold again' " (79). Newman cannot believe that " 'helpless [French] women are bullied into marrying men they
hate.' " But Tristram reminds Newman, to no avail, that " 'A great deal of
that kind goes on in New York. . . . Girls are bullied or coaxed or bribed,
or all three together, into marrying nasty fellows. There is no end of that
always going on in the Fifth Avenue, and other bad things besides. The
Mysteries of the Fifth Avenue! Someone ought to show them up' " (80).

All of these disastrous marriages may of course be seen as James's attempt to create the context that will prepare us for the ending (and, sec-
ondarily, to express his sympathy for the marriageable girl). But Leon Edel
has speculated suggestively on possible other reasons that led James to
break off Newman's marriage. Edel remarks that "having ruled out marriage for himself," James "found it genuinely difficult to offer it to those of
his heroes with whom he was in some way identified. The marriage tie, to
Henry's vision, was a tie which enslaved: and women represented a threat
to man's sovereignty. . . . To accept them as mates was to court . . . disaster."[17] But the election of the life of celibacy in the service of the imagination, James's choice of the so-called "high priesthood of art," seems less
likely a way of putting it than a downright aversion to an institution so implicitly full of duplicity, infidelity, and heartache—both for the women and
for the men.

## V

One of the issues of major significance evolving from James's conception of the character of Christopher Newman is indicated in the title—*The
American.* It is the issue of our "national character." James's English reviewers appear to have had no doubt that Newman, in the words of *The
Athenaeum* reviewer, was "a clever presentment of a characteristic type of
his countrymen, in search of adventures in the paradise to which good

Americans go." "The portrait of his countryman must of course be taken as accurate," *The Academy* reviewer remarked, "and is evidently sympathetic." Most English reviewers had little sympathy for Newman, but it is not clear whether the reason lay in Newman's vulgar Americanism or in James's general method of characterization, about which I shall say more later on.[18]

American reviewers objected to several aspects of Newman as "the" American. Before the serialization was even concluded, *The Nation* reviewer confessed to "a feeling of irritation at being called upon to take an interest in a specimen of a type which, as a type, is, to say the least, not aesthetically attractive."

The *Galaxy* reviewer continued the attack: "Mr. Christopher Newman is certainly a fair representative of a certain sort, and a very respectable sort, of American; but he is not such a man that Mr. James, himself an American living in Europe, is warranted in setting him up before the world as 'The American.'" And the reviewer for *The Catholic World* asked whether it was "commendable in American authors not merely to lampoon the national foibles which ought to be lampooned, but to paint an illiterate and audacious gawk in a pretendedly fine frame and label him a representative American?"[19]

With the passage of time, American readers have become less self-concious and less embarrassed about travellers abroad who are, as James put it elsewhere, "ill-made, ill-mannered, ill-dressed" and "by no means flattering to the national vanity." More recently the issue has resurfaced in Irving Howe's argument that the "notion that there is a 'national character' is impossible to defend as an abstract proposition." This is so, he argues, because the term is "relevant only to a country with a homogeneous culture," whereas America is "a country fractured into sharply varying regions."[20] Howe's point is well taken, but no one knew this better than James himself, who avoids the accusation by giving us a varied gallery of American types in this novel. The foils Tom Tristram and the Reverend Mr. Babcock, both Americans, suggest other "national types" in whom James took considerable interest. Much of James's success in portraying this reverse Christopher Columbus, discovering Europe, this "new man" created by the American continent, consists as much in Newman's individualized traits as in his being an assemblage of stereotypically "American" elements.

While the title of the novel invites us to consider Newman as a national representative, I believe that uneasy Americans are taken in if they reduce the significance of the title to that possibility. I should therefore like to offer a complementary interpretation of the title. Whatever its other implications, the name of the book expresses a distinctive attitude toward the hero: that of the Bellegardes and their aristocratic friends. For them, Newman is *the* American, the only American. There is no other in their circle. Few of them have ever met an American, although one remembers once having seen the great Dr. Franklin.[21] "The American" aptly describes how Newman is thought of by these Legitimists and Ultramontanes, who detest republicans, perpetuate the wig, carry on the "profuse white neck cloth of the fashion of 1820"(143), and believe in "the divine right of Henry of Bourbon, Fifth of his name, to the throne of France" (153). The term "the American" has the effect of expressing their sense of Newman's difference from them, of denying him an individual identity or name, of effectively placing him in the inferior status signified by his being common, foreign, and commercial. The title thus asks us—as James's witty phrasing so often asks us—to see Newman as he is seen by the aristocracy he is involved with. And the effect of this technique is to distance us from Newman, with whom in any event we cannot fully sympathize, since much of the time he is, as he suspects, " 'stepping about like a terrier on his hind legs' " (191). Viewed in this way, the title reflects that estrangement James himself felt from the society of the Faubourg St. Germain. He never did have a proper entrée into that society during this year in Paris, and he felt his foreignness even at the more sociable evenings with Mme. Viardot and Mme. de Blocqueville, who, with one or two others, constituted, he confessed as late as April 1876, the "very slender thread of my few personal relations."[22]

James's sense of isolation, of his being a spectator rather than an involved participant in the Parisian social scene, accounts in part for the tone he takes with his characters. Newman is masterfully, if ironically, individualized, and the portraits of Valentin, Mlle. and M. Nioche, Babcock, the old marquise and the Tristrams are masterful delineations of minor characters. But none of these characters, despite the mastery of James's technique, was particularly liked by his contemporaries. How could one "like" such disagreeable personae of the kind whom one would not wish to risk meeting in polite society? In essence, much of the criticism of the disagreeableness of the characters was a reflection of reviewers' hostility to the new mode, in realism, of psychological dissection. Characters subjected to the kind of emotional dissection provided by James, interfused as it was with sarscasm or irony, could not be "identified with," therefore could not be fully "sympathized with." "The story in itself is too slight to interest," observed *The Literary World,* "the *denouement* being evident at the outset; half the characters are utterly detestable, and the other half without attraction. No gentle reader will shed a tear or heave a sigh over the most tragic of its pages." The critic for the *North American Review* remarked its excessive intellectuality. While conceding that James was not one of those writers "who make the reader feel as though he were attending merely on a series of experiments,—a kind of psychological clinic," the critic felt that James's "delicate and subtle analysis" had the effect of attaching "almost altogether to the process, very little to its suggestions or results, and least of all to the characters that may have been its subjects."[23]

Claire de Cintré seemed an especially problematic character. *The Nation* reviewer observed that "the best thing of all, in our opinion, is the delicacy with which Madame de Cintré is drawn, with her shyness and gracious delicacy." But it was generally felt that she was a shadowy, lifeless character whose reason for accepting Newman was never quite shown. As *The Galaxy* put it, "Our only wonder is how a woman like Mme. de Cintré can be brought to look upon him with eyes of personal favor. We are speaking of a woman such as the figure of Mme. de Cintré stands for. For as to the heroine herself, her personality is of the vaguest. She leaves no impression of individuality upon us; we are told certain things about her, indeed, but she is almost a lay figure."[24]

James had a serious technical problem with Claire. He could not, as he was later to observe, resolve the plot problem by having her reject Newman. She had to be, as he put it, "an equal victim just as Romeo was not less the sport of fate for not having been interestedly sacrificed by Juliet." But Claire is no helpless and innocent Juliet. In fact, her decisions control the denouement and render even her powerful family helpless. But how could James have her take the decisive step of rejecting Newman in favor of the convent without her losing the reader's sympathy. "Since Madame de Cintré was after all to 'back out,' " James wrote, "every touch in the picture of her apparent loyalty would add to her eventual shame. She had acted in clear good faith, but how could I give the *detail* of an attitude, on her part, of which the foundation was yet so weak?" James confessed to having evaded the problem: "I preferred, as the minor evil, to shirk the attempt—at the cost evidently of a signal loss of 'charm'; and with this lady, altogether, I recognise, a light plank, too light a plank, is laid for the reader over a dark 'psychological' abyss. The delicate clue to her conduct is never definitely placed in his hand." Concluding the Preface, James threw up his hands at the problem of Claire, leaving "the record to stand or fall by [Newman's] more or less convincing image."[25]

If James's portrait of Newman as a national type provoked American readers to some indignation, his treatment of the French character has raised comparable objections. Neither the Bellegardes, at the apex of society, nor the Nioches, at the bottom, are attractively presented. And French critics, like other Europeans, have objected to James's establishing the innocence, moral superiority, and natural nobility of the "American" at the expense of the antithetical European.[26] James even added fuel to this fire with his later remarks on the moral character of the French aristocracy. In the Preface, James remarked in 1907 that the "way things happen is frankly not the way in which they are represented as having happened, in Paris, to my hero. . . . The great house of Bellegarde, in a word, would, I now feel, given the circumstances, given the *whole* of the ground, have comported itself in a manner as different as possible from the manner to which my narrative commits it. . . . They would positively have jumped then, the Bellegardes, at my rich and easy American, and not have 'minded' in the least any drawback." To the aristocrats' original crimes of mendacity and murder, that is to say, James added that of greed and, by way of explanation, remarked that "[s]uch accommodation of the theory of a noble indifference to the practice of a deep avidity is the real note of policy in forlorn aristocracies—and I meant of course that the Bellegardes should be virtually forlorn."[27] In other words, he had not really known the French aristocracy in the 1870's; if he had, he would have had the Bellegardes accept Newman and milk him for every sou they could get.

## VI

James's feeling that he had misunderstood the deep avidity of the French nobility led him to discourse at some length, in the Preface, between the "kinds," or modes, of realism and romance. I refer the reader to his extended discussion of the two, which has its own interest independent of this novel. But here I should like to argue a proposition that I have not seen sufficiently advanced in the criticism of the book: namely, that if there is in James's words an "affront to verisimilitude" in the novel, it is not the Bellegardes' eventually rejecting Newman; it is in their initially consenting to entertain his courtship for Claire at all. Commoners have in real life of course married into the French aristocracy; that is not the point. It is fictional consistency in characterization that is my point. Throughout the book as he wrote it, James was at great pains to characterize Urbain and the old Marquise as exceptionally proud, haughty, arrogant, mechanically polite, but intensely snobbish aristocrats. The family descend from the ninth century; they perpetuate the royalist tradition; there has never, as Valentin remarks, been a misalliance among the women. The conduct of Urbain and his mother is entirely consistent with their aristocratic caste, their familial pride, and their passion of blood—except in one respect: they weaken momentarily and countenance Newman's courtship of Claire. In my view, this lapse, the lapse from the putative hauteur of the family, is the point that fails of realism. How such a family, as James conceived them, could have permitted themselves even for a moment to suffer the lounging, slangy, socially illiterate American manufacturer of wash-tubs and leather goods is a nice question—one that James does not really wish us to ask. In fact, all of his prefatory remarks have the effect of leading us away from this central problem in the consistency of his characterization. I for one do not, therefore, find the Bellegardes' rejection of Newman a lapse into romance at all. Rather, the rejection redeems the novel from the fairy-tale conclusion toward which Newman's engagement was heading. The young James was closer to the truth than the elder when he told William Dean Howells in 1877 that the demands of realism required a breaking off of the match: "*Voyons:* it would have been impossible: they would have been an impossible couple. . . . We are each the product of circumstances and there are tall stone walls which fatally divide us. I have written my story from Newman's side of the wall, and I understand so well how Mme. de Cintré couldn't really scramble over from *her* side! If I had represented her as doing so I should have made a prettier ending, certainly; but I should have felt as if I were throwing a rather vulgar sop to readers who don't really know the world and who don't measure the merit of a novel by its correspondence to the same."[28]

James's 1907 Preface nails the unmitigated "romance" of the book to the Bellegardes' rejection of Newman. In my view, this is one of the Master's diversions; it obscures what are the more obivious affronts to realism. I refer to the elaborate trappings of the gothic mode implied by the concealed murder, the deathbed accusation, the incriminating note surfacing after many years, the duel of "honor," and the incarcerated heroine, whose imprisonment behind the walls of the Carmelite nunnery (together with the vow of silence!) strikes the American Protestant imagination as the ultimate horror. Here is romance aplenty. Walpole, Radcliffe and Monk Lewis could not have done better. I point to this whole assemblage of materials as really another signal instance of James's attempt to transform the sow's ear of sentimental romanticism into the silk purse of the "new realism." But the effort is not wholly successful, and James was surely right in remarking that the book has a hole in it almost large enough to sink it.

## VII

One other aspect of the novel's truth to life seems worthy of remark. I refer to James's late discovery that, at the time of composition, he had been "plotting arch-romance *without knowing it*" (my italics).[29] Whatever distinctions James intended in distinguishing between "realism" and "romance," my interest here is in what appears to be James's recovered affection for the romantic mode. In rereading the book at the time of revision, and in discovering the novel's "emblazoned flag of romance," he found that the novel yielded him "no interest and no reward" comparable to the recognition of how "romantic" he had been. By 1907, of course, the "war over realism," fought by Howells and James, Twain and DeForest, Howe, Eggleston, and many others, had been won. And, as the handbooks say, the realism of the 1870s had been "succeeded" by the starker naturalism of Norris, Crane, and others. There is therefore something poignant in the mature James's losing himself "at this late hour, I am bound to add, in a certain sad envy of the free play of so much unchallenged instinct" as he found in the youthful *The American*. James disclosed more than a little regret at the extent to which, throughout his career, the demands of "verisimilitude" had contained, if not restrained, his imagination: "One would like to woo back such hours of fine precipitation. They represent to the critical sense . . . the happiest season of surrender to the invoked muse and the projected fable."[30]

But the elderly James could no longer "invent" with the free, instinctive, "thoughtless" indifference to critical questions that had characterized his youth. Nor did he really wish to. His "whole faculty" had waked up, and he could no longer write so spontaneously. Why then, we may ask, did James not rewrite *The American* totally? Why did he not go beyond the level of the sentence, the phrase, the word—so as to eliminate the romantic elements of the book? Why did he not get rid of the gothic banalities? In my judgment the task was simply too formidable and would have involved not just revision but a complete rewriting, perhaps in the vein of *The Ambassadors*, perhaps under the constraints of verisimilitude that characterize the story of Lambert Strether.

The best that James could do was therefore to mount, in the Preface, a defense of the novel as one of the "mixed genre" varieties and to celebrate the kind of imagination capacious enough to interfuse both modes, realism and romance. He wrote in 1907 that he doubted "if any novelist . . . ever proposed to commit himself to one kind or the other with as little mitigation as we are sometimes able to find for him." He remarked that the interest of a great writer's genius is the greatest "when he commit himself in both directions; not quite at the same time or to the same effect, of course, but by some need of performing his whole possible revolution, by the law of some rich passion in him for extremes." And in contemplating those writers of genius who had worked both the realistic and romantic veins, "the men of largest responding imagination before the human scene," he singled out Scott, Balzac, and "the coarse, comprehensive, prodigious Zola" as writers for whom "the deflexion toward either quarter has never taken place," with the effect that the writer of genius in mixed modes "remains therefore extraordinarily rich" and washes us "successively with the warm wave of the near and familiar and the tonic shock, as may be, of the far and strange."[31]

The warm wave of the near and familiar unquestionably came through *The American* as originally written. Its source was that "high probity of observation" that made James a superb portraitist of realistic social types. But, clearly, James was enchanted by the discovery of the latent romanticism of his vision, and he wished to preserve it intact—not to rewrite it out of the novel—and so to represent himself (along with Scott, Balzac, and Zola) as committed in both directions simultaneously, by "the law of some rich passion in him for extremes."

Yet James did try to salvage the novel by making claims for Newman, in the Preface, that neither the early nor the much-revised late form of the novel can support. These claims tend in the direction of making Newman out to be one of the supersubtle fry of an "intenser consciousness." James insisted in the Preface that the interest of everything is all in *Newman's* "vision, *his* conception, *his* interpretation: at the window of his wide, quite sufficiently wide, consciousness we are seated, from that admirable position we 'assist.' He therefore supremely matters; all the rest matters only as he feels it, treats it, meets it."[32] It goes without saying that Newman is the focus of the book and that we are sympathetic to his plight. But this astonishing remark attempts to transform Newman and his drama into something like that of Strether in *The Ambassadors*, of whom the remark could be said to be literally true. Yet a protagonist of Strether's civility and sensitivity could never have come from Civil War battlefields, Western campfires, and the manufactory of wash-tubs. And certainly we *cannot* narrow our experience of the novel to *Newman's* "vision, *his* conception, *his* interpretation." If we do so we forfeit the wit and social comedy that are directed at him—not only by the other characters but *by James himself.* For Newman is above all else an incarnation of what James, in his essay "Americans Abroad" (1878), called that "profound, imperturbable unsuspectingness on the part of many Americans of the impression they produce in foreign lands." And much of the comedy of the novel occurs because "the impression produced is a good deal at variance with European circumstances."[33] But the elderly James, in the process of sounding and "dragging" the depths of his own creative past in order to reconstruct his intentions, in using "the long pole of memory" to "fish up such fragments and relics of the submerged life and the extinct consciousness" as could be pieced together, forgot how comic he had originally conceived Newman to be.[34] In reading the early version of the novel, that comedy clearly shines forth to us.

## Notes

1. *Selected Letters of Henry James,* ed. Leon Edel (London: Rupert Hart-Davis, 1956), p. 137; Robert Herrick, "A Visit to Henry James," *The Yale Review,* 12 (1923), 734.

2. *Selected Letters of Henry James,* p. 190; Herrick, p. 732.

3. Royal A. Gettmann, "Henry James's Revision of *The American*," *American Literature,* 16 (1945), 279–95. This essay, as well as several other essays to be mentioned, is reprinted in Henry James's *The American,* ed. James W. Tuttleton (New York: W. W. Norton, 1978). Cf. p. 476. Hereafter, citations from such reprinted essays will be indicated by the abbreviation *HJTA*.

4. Isadore Traschen, "Henry James and the Art of Revision," *Philological Quarterly,* 35 (1956), 46–47.

5. Henry James, Preface to *Roderick Hudson,* in *The Art of the Novel,* ed. R. P. Blackmur (New York: Scribner, 1934), p. 12; Louis Auchincloss, "The Late Jamesing of Early James," *Life, Law and Letters: Essays and Sketches* (Boston: Houghton Mifflin, 1979), pp. 94–95.

6. *The American.* Manuscript Revision, 1908. Facsimile. London: The Scolar Press and Oxford Univ. Press, 1975.

7. Leon Edel, "The American," *Henry James: The Conquest of London, 1870–1881* (Philadelphia: J. B. Lippincott, 1962), reprinted in *HJTA*, p. 424.

8. *HJTA*; cf. note 3. As indicated in my textual commentary to this edition, the manuscript of *The American* is no longer extant. The first form of the novel is therefore the serialized version published in the *Atlantic Monthly* between June 1876 and May 1877. The first American book edition was published on 30 April 1877 in Boston by James R. Osgood and Company. James revised the novel lightly for the first English book edition, published by Macmillan in 1879. Macmillan later brought out a collected edition of the novels in 1883, based on its 1879 text, which was not revised in its substantives. These, aside from the much-

revised New York Edition of 1907, constitute the significant forms of the text, which have been collated in preparing the Norton Critical Edition, for which the copy-text was the London 1879 edition. Properly edited and emended, as I have sought to do, this text has a greater directness and immediacy. The details of composition and the publication history of the novel may be found in the textual apparatus of that edition. Appended to the text are relevant items of correspondence, notebook extracts, all known British and American magazine reviews, a bibliography of secondary criticism, and a selection of twentieth-century criticism.

9. *The Novel of Manners in America* (Chapel Hill: Univ. of North Carolina Press, 1972), pp. 48–85.

10. Cf. Edel, *HJTA*, pp. 415–26; Oscar Cargill, "The American," *HJTA*, pp. 426–41; Kermit Vanderbilt, "James, Fitzgerald, and the American Self-Image," *Massachusetts Review*, 6 (1965), 289–304; Christof Wegelin, *The Image of Europe in Henry James* (Dallas: Southern Methodist Univ. Press, 1958); Frederick J. Hoffman, "Freedom and Conscious Form: Henry James and the American Self," *Virginia Quarterly Review*, 37 (1961), 269–85.

11. On Newman's "nobility," see H. R. Hays, "The Limitations of Christopher Newman," in *Henry James: The American*, ed. Gerald Willen (New York: T. Y. Crowell 1972), pp. 402–13; Constance Rourke, *American Humor: A Study of the National Character* (New York: Harcourt, Brace, 1931), p. 200; and Charles Sanford, *The Quest for Paradise: Europe and the American Moral Imagination* (Urbana: Univ. of Illinois Press, 1961).

12. *The Nation* reviewer observed that if Newman had really wanted Claire "all the mothers and brothers in Christendom would have no more guard for Madame de Cintré than half a dozen cobwebs"; and the *Scribner's* reviewer remarked that "it was an imperative condition that he should have *tried* to marry the woman he loved, and if he must fail, that his failure should be in no wise weak and spiritless." Cf. *HJTA*, pp. 392, 399.

13. The best work in this aspect of James criticism has been done by Edwin T. Bowden in *The Themes of Henry James: A System of Observation Through the Visual Arts* (New Haven: Yale Univ. Press, 1956) and by Viola H. Winner in *Henry James and the Visual Arts* (Charlottesville: Univ. of Virginia Press, 1970).

14. James's critique is summed up in his remark that "the faults" of *The Scarlet Letter* "are, to my sense, a want of reality and an abuse of the fanciful element—of a certain superficial symbolism." *Hawthorne* (New York: Collier, 1966), p. 101.

15. "James's Florabella and the 'Land of the Pink Sky,' " *Notes and Queries*, 13 (1966), 70. Bernard's otherwise astute identification is marred, however, I believe, by his attempt to adduce this allusion as evidence in support of John A. Claire's doubtful claim that Claire is the daughter of Mrs. Bread. Cf. Claire's "*The American:* A Reinterpretation," *PMLA*, 74 (1959), 613–18; reprinted in *Studies in The American*, compiled by William T. Stafford (Columbus: Charles E. Merrill, 1971), pp. 80–91.

16. Whether James is a comic, a tragic, or a melodramatic novelist, or some combination of all three, continues to vex his critics. Richard Poirier in *The Comic Sense of Henry James* and Ronald Wallace in *Henry James and the Comic Form*, among others, argue the first; Frederick Crews in *The Tragedy of Manners* poses the second; and Leo B. Levy in *Versions of Melodrama*, Jacques Barzun in "James the Melodramatist" (*Kenyon Review*, 5 [1943], 508–21), and Peter Brooks in *The Melodramatic Imagination* see James as essentially melodramatic. On the tragic implications of *Othello*, see Agostino Lombardo's "Henry James, *The American* e il mito di Otello," in *Friendship's Garland: Essays Presented to Mario Praz . . .* , 2 vols. (Roma: Edizioni di Storia e Letteratura, 1966).

17. Leon Edel, *HJTA*, p. 422.

18. *HJTA*, pp. 409, 410.

19. *HJTA*, pp. 389, 395, 409.

20. Henry James, "Americans Abroad," *HJTA*, p. 361; Irving Howe, "Henry James and the Millionaire," *HJTA*, pp. 442–43. Useful treatments of the topic are also to be found in

John Kinnaird's "The Paradox of an American 'Identity,' " *Partisan Review*, 25 (1958), 381, and in Frederick J. Hoffman's "Freedom and Conscious Form: Henry James and the American Self," *Virginia Quarterly Review*, 37 (1961), 269–85.

21. It may be argued that Mrs. Tristram is known to Claire de Cintré, thanks to the accident of their convent schooling together. But Mrs. Tristram is not a part of Claire's society: the friends of Urbain de Bellegarde do not know Mrs. Tristram or any other American. The friendship between the two women is merely the device by which James secures for Newman an introduction to Claire and a confidante to listen to his troubles. On Mrs. Tristram's function, see D. W. Jefferson's *Henry James and the Modern Reader* (New York: St. Martin's Press, 1964), pp. 89–90.

22. *Henry James: Letters,* ed. Leon Edel (Cambridge: Harvard Univ. Press, 1975), 11, 37.

23. Cf. *HJTA*, pp. 397, 404.

24. *HJTA*, pp. 392, 395.

25. *The Art of the Novel*, pp. 24, 38–39.

26. On reactions to James's view of the French, see Wegelin's *The Image of Europe in Henry James*, Jeanne Delbaere-Garant's *Henry James: The Vision of France* (Paris: Société d'Editions, 1970), and Alberta Fabris's *Henry James e la Francia* (Roma: Edizioni di Storia e Letteratura, 1969).

27. *The Art of the Novel*, pp. 34–36.

28. *Henry James: Letters*, 11, 104–5.

29. *The Art of the Novel*, p. 25. See also George Knox's "Romance and Fable in James's *The American*," *Anglia*, 83 (1965), 308–23.

30. *The Art of the Novel*, p. 25.

31. *The Art of the Novel*, p. 31.

32. *The Art of the Novel*, p. 37.

33. Cf. *HJTA*, p. 360.

34. *The Art of the Novel*, p. 26.


# James's *The Europeans* and the Structure of Comedy                    J. A. Ward*

*The Europeans* has received careful and intelligent attention from a number of critics. It is not the purpose of this essay to differ with other studies of the novel, most of which are indicated in the footnotes, but to examine the structure of the work, which has not been previously considered.

Any analysis of the structure of *The Europeans* should begin with the observation that it is essentially a comic novel. For one thing, it owes much to the well-made dramatic comedies of such nineteenth-century playwrights as Dumas *fils*, Augier, and Sardou, and also to the narrative romances of Feuillet and Cherbuliez.[1] Not only do the wit, the grace, and the situation of *The Europeans* suggest such works, but also the rigid con-

*From *Nineteenth Century Fiction* 19, no. 1 (June 1964):1–16. © 1964 by The Regents of the University of California. Reprinted by permission of the Regents.

struction, the careful balancing and juxtaposition of character types, and the rigorously logical progression of events (rendered scenically) to an inevitable conclusion. Also James draws freely upon much older comic patterns, such as the conversion of a traditional society by a group of young intruders to a fresher view of life and the triumph of the young lovers over the objections of their obtuse and narrow-minded elders.[2] In addition, *The Europeans* uses such venerable devices as the comic intrigue and the complicated and neat rounding-off. The atmosphere is pastoral, and the spirit is predominantly gay.

The clash of opposing social groups provides the central comic situation, and since the clash is for the most part resolved harmoniously, the prevailing view of life in the novel is comic, that is, faults exist to be laughed at, and errors exist to be corrected. In *The Europeans*, James gets closer to a purely comic vision of the international conflict than in any other novel, but it is a mistake to force the work into an exclusively comic pattern. Finally the novel is *sui generis* in its design. It has a conventional comic foundation, but the total effect is something different. James's conception of structure in this novel is organic, so that while he uses many of the usual motifs and compositional devices of comedy, he rejects those demands of a mechanical form that either misrepresent or have no bearing on the idea he wishes to develop.

The New England setting is of first importance in the comic mood of *The Europeans*. Though James frequently uses Europe for comic and satiric purposes—as when he exposes the provincialism of Henrietta Stackpole against the background of St. Peter's Cathedral—he never makes it the setting of a predominantly comic story. Even in the stories in which James invests Europe with the picturesque coloration of travel literature, he is unwillng to isolate the beauty of the past from the evil he usually associates with the past. But America in *The Europeans* is mainly a pastoral scene— a Forest of Arden or "green world"[3] suggesting the Golden Age not only to Felix Young, but also to the reader. Here is a world in which evil can exist only as something temporarily disagreeable. If the pastoral scene makes the gloom of the Americans additionally quaint and groundless (they are seen as Calvinists in Eden), it also provides an atmosphere in which young lovers can achieve bliss and in which innocence can never be sullied. The setting also colors our estimation of the Europeans; it prevents us from associating them with any Old World corruption. The casual, semi-rural Arcadia that James wishes us to accept as a Boston suburb of the 1840's[4] is in every way congenial to a humorous treatment of the international theme.

The comedy of *The Europeans* blends gentle, urbane satire of the Puritan temperament with a modulated evocation of the charms of innocence. The relaxed, mildly ironic tone lends an easy grace to the novel. The tone itself is a perfect vehicle—perhaps the principal reason for the excellence of the book. It is detached, yet genial, sympathetic yet neither serious nor sentimental, and it falls well short of either frivolity or cyncism. The narrative approach is old-fashioned, recalling Thackeray and Trollope rather than forecasting the later James. Throughout we hear the voice of the author gracefully and even ceremoniously telling his story and commenting on his characters. This voice is exceedingly tolerant, and yet it is witty at the expense of the characters; it gives a steady and barely perceptible control over our own judgement of the action, counseling us to refrain from both harsh judgements and suspicions that the story is merely trivial.

The experience which James renders in *The Europeans* is rather graver and less purely amusing than we commonly expect in comedy, and yet not grave enough to be something else—such as tragedy, melodrama, or even romance. James deliberately mutes the moral issues that he lingers over in other novels. If the tone is slightly unsteady, the reason is James's reluctance to falsify certain deeper realities that the situation seems to bring forth. For example, Gertrude Wentworth occasionally overreaches the simple role that James assigns her; she is hard-hearted and callous of others' feelings. This is a quality James often reveals in the American heroine,[5] but it is out of place in the translucent scheme of *The Europeans*. The novel softens and almost conceals the suggestions of unresolvable difficulties, but it does not omit them. The rigid structure and essential artificiality of classical comedy, the leisurely flow of the prose, and the unhurried lives of the characters make *The Europeans* a nearly perfect comic performance, but the novel remains something both more and less than comic. Even the neat resolution of the plots in the final half-dozen pages—in which four marriages are recorded, with Shakespearean finality and ceremony—does not disguise the special quality of the experience of the novel.

As in most comedy, James's principal technique is to represent his characters as undeviating simplifications. *The Europeans* is thus roughly an allegory, with each of the major characters representing a large aspect of the culture which has produced him. Yet a sense of complexity is achieved through James's characteristic technique of implying contrasts among characters and events. With the possible exception of Robert Acton, no single character is very complicated, but we can understand their significances only by perceiving how James has dramatically related each to each. For instance, Felix Young is an extremely simplified creation—in the mold of the gay young man of the well-made play—but to estimate his character we must consider his relation to the characters who frame him, not merely to his obvious foils, Mr. Brand and Mr. Wentworth, but also to Gertrude and to Eugenia. The structure follows from a revelation of complex inter-relationships among simple chracters, all latent within the obvious and basic contrast between Europe and America.

Superficially it would seem that the Europeans—Felix and Eugenia—are to be admired, and the Americans—the Wentworths, the Actons, and Mr. Brand—are to be pitied. Freedom is preferable to oppression, a positive view to a negative one, culture to barbarism, intelligence to irrationality, happiness to gloom, and art to a distrust of art. Read solely in such terms, the novel shows the gradual conversion of Gertrude and the final resistance of Robert Acton to the European temperament, and as a flat background to this central action the utter rigidity of all the other Americans. The mechanics of character selection and the logical movement of the plot are obvious.

Yet it is a distortion of the experience of the book to suggest where our sympathies should lie or to demonstrate which way of life "wins." The Europeans have a larger role than to expose the limitations of the Americans. Critics do not widely disagree in their assessments of the New Englanders, but there are extreme differences of opinion as to how Felix and his sister are to be regarded. Felix is usually accepted as a thoroughly congenial embodiment of European *joie de vivre,* but Eugenia has been judged both a selfish schemer for wealth and position[6] and a charming, graceful woman whose faults are essentially minor.[7]

Certainly the title characters are the major figures in the novel. Everything that happens is an effect of their plotting; the Americans merely react to them. As the causes of the action, they create the structure of the novel. In the opening chapters their mere presence provides a means of contrasting two cultures, but afterwards everything develops from their various intrigues and sub-intrigues. We witness not merely a static contrasting of opposing national views, but the direct and conscious influence of the Europeans upon the Americans.

James's characterization of the two Europeans largely accounts for the structure as well as the tone of the novel. Eugenia and Felix are essentially different from most of the other Europeans in James's fiction. Their distinctiveness consists in the apparent lightness with which they are handled; they seem—at least to the tastes of critics who share some of the Wentworths' bias—to get off too lightly. Detached as they are from the vaguely malignant European scene, Felix and Eugenia are remote from the evil atmosphere that shrouds such European characters as the Bellegardes and Richard de Mauves. It is not just that the genial tone and the pastoral vision of things prohibit any strong suggestion of the sinister and the portentous. The European background of Felix and Eugenia is only faintly and indirectly conveyed, and then it is suggestive of either Graustarkian fable and comic opera (how else is the reader to regard Eugenia's situation as morganatic wife of Prince Adolf of Silberstadt-Schreckenstein?) or of fancifully picturesque travel posters and provincial misconceptions of the bohemian life (Felix, we are told, has strolled through Europe with a band of carefree musicians). When Gertrude first sees Felix, she glances upward from a volume of *The Arabian Nights,* and the vision she beholds is as miraculous as the story she has been reading. Gertrude is naive, but the Europeans consistently behave in a manner in keeping with her fantasies. Also the Europeans are purged of ancestral evil. The connivances of Eugenia's remote brother-in-law are clearly not to be lingered upon; this is but a quaintness as extravagant and as charming as the childlike view of the Old World that fascinates Gertrude.

In one respect it is characteristic of James to represent Europe through such a pair as the good-natured Felix and the worldly Eugenia. In *The American,* for example, Valentin de Bellegarde has the same zest for life as Felix Young, while his brother and mother, like Eugenia, are much devoted to traditional manners. In *The American,* of course, the burden of manners is considerably heavier than in *The Europeans,* eventually oppressing even the frolicsome Valentin. Still the schematic arrangement of European characters in *The American* has much the same effect as in *The Europeans.*

Since Felix and Eugenia are removed from the hereditary guilt and rigid social apparatus that weigh upon the Bellegardes, they appear not only unusually free (more like Americans than Europeans) but also unusually simplified. Felix is the least credible character in the novel. He is childishly good-natured, single-mindedly bent on happiness, and thoroughly engaging and charming—a man with neither temper nor guile, seemingly incapable of thinking any but the most flattering of thoughts about anyone. Not only is he unrestricted by the demands of class that finally inhibit Valentin de Bellegarde, but he is free from the demands of any class or society, and yet at the same time highly civilized. He stands virtually alone in James as a man who has all of the benefits of worldliness but none of the faults.

With the Baroness, who likewise stands for a part of the generic European character, James has a more difficult artistic problem. For his intention seems to be to draw a thoroughly attractive kind of Madame Merle, and by extension to represent artfulness as an unequivocal good. But it is part of James's technique in sketching the Baroness to make her slightly ridiculous: she is so absurdly out of place in the world of the Wentworths that some of the amusement is at her expense—as in mock-heroic poetry the epic devices used to satirize must appear foolish in themselves.

What both Europeans embody is a highly refined form of opportunism, and they become involved with a group of Americans who embody the contrary quality of discipline. This opposition is the subject of *The Europeans,* the central idea that gives the novel its dramatic unity. The terms of this opposition are represented in their abstract essence in a dialogue between Gertrude and Felix. Felix remarks:

> "You don't seem to me to get all the pleasure out of life that you might. You don't seem to me to enjoy. . . . You seem to me very well placed for enjoying. You have money and liberty and what is called in Europe a 'position.' But you take a painful view of life, as one may say. . . ."
>
> "I don't think it's what one does or one doesn't do that promotes

enjoyment" [Felix continues], "It is the general way of looking at life."

"They look at it as a discipline—that's what they do here" [Gertrude replies]. "I have often been told that."

"Well, that's very good. But there is another way," added Felix, smiling: "to look at it as an opportunity."

(pp. 103–105)[8]

The clash of "ways of looking at life" obviously accounts for the make-up of a number of the characters and for their roles in the drama. Thus to Gertrude Mr. Brand represents discipline and Felix represents opportunity. Robert Acton's sense of duty is concentrated in his devotion to his mother, and the Baroness personifies the life of self-gratification he is tentatively inclined to. But James's dramatic representation of the conflict of discipline and opportunity has a more pervasive role in the design of the book. For both opportunism and discipline are many-sided characteristics, particularly when they are regarded as cultural rather than merely personal attributes. The central characters in *The Europeans* together manifest the complexities implicit in these abstract qualities, and the action which engages these characters tests the assumptions about life which impel them.

Felix and his sister express the various meanings latent in the principle of opportunism. In its simplest and most apparent form, their opportunism is a capacity for experiencing pleasure. Felix with his comic imagination finds everything delightful—even muddy roads. Though he may speak of the benefits of a high civilization, he is most often seen as a man fully responsive to the less obvious pleasures of life. His painter's eye is his dominant faculty, and life as he sees it is gayly colored and fundamentally amusing. The Baroness, on the other hand, converts raw experience into traditional forms. Felix delights in the harsh simplicity of the Wentworths' house—"it looks like a magnified Nuremberg toy" (p. 46), he remarks—but the Baroness elaborately decorates the neighboring cottage where she and Felix stay. The accumulated artifices of a traditional culture "make" life. Money, style, and tradition together transform the dreary into the pleasurable.

Both the responsiveness of Felix and the social art of the Baroness are to be held in high regard; each reflects "imagination," which the Wentworths sadly lack. The Europeans introduce the Americans to a way of seeing life and a way of refashioning life, and for doing so they are to be admired. But if their opportunism is a source of happiness and enrichment—for themselves and others—it is at the same time based on selfish motives.

Each is seeking economic gain from the New England relatives, Felix by painting their portraits and Eugenia by marrying one of them. If the Baroness is depressed and Felix is gay in the first chapter, their different moods should not conceal the similarity of their ambitions. Soon however their self-interest blends with a general benevolence. Even the Baroness feels a deep affection for her newly-met kin. The plot of the novel develops from the gentle aggressions of Felix and Eugenia. Each is quickly paired with a New Englander—Felix with Gertrude, the Baroness with Robert Acton. Though we never lose sight of the essential self-interest that governs the two foreigners as they intrigue for fortune and status, their separate operations are viewed sympathetically. Gertrude, after all, needs Felix, who will be the best of husbands for her; nor is there any suggestion of hypocrisy in his expressed love for her.[9] Similarly the Baroness's graces attract Acton, who would certainly profit from marriage to such a woman. Furthermore, if the Baroness is a schemer or adverturess, as some have claimed, she conducts herself with such delicacy that it is Acton, if anyone, who appears crass and self-centered.

The sub-intrigues which the Europeans concurrently undertake also show that their self-interest is in no way incompatible with good will. By the middle of the novel, Felix and Eugenia extend their operations. Felix, who alone sees the obvious affection between Charlotte and Mr. Brand, delicately suggests to Gertrude and to her former suitor that such a match would be a happy one. By directing Mr. Brand's attention to Charlotte, Felix of course eliminates a major obstacle to his own marriage to Gertrude. He additionally profits by asking the obliging Charlotte to plead his own case before her father.

The sub-intrigue engineered by the Baroness is equally a combination of disinterested benevolence and shrewd self-interest. Clifford Wentworth, recently suspended from Harvard for drinking, is a difficult problem for his father. As the scion of the family, he desperately requires reformation. The Baroness, "a woman of finely-mingled motive" (p. 173), undertakes to civilize Clifford, but at the same time she feels that Clifford may be kept in reserve as a potential husband, should her relation with Acton come to nothing. "A prudent archer has always a second bowstring. . . ." (p. 173), she tells herself.

Although the Baroness and Felix seem most suited to experience life in its fullness, they are also shielded from certain dimensions of reality because of their special talents and perceptions. Felix, who is called a child by his sister, has a spontaneity that is refreshing in the chilling atmosphere of New England, but those problems which cannot be viewed in a cheerful light he either flatly ignores or else brushes away with irrelevant jests. His good nature is indeed a tonic to the Wentworths—when they submit to it— but it depends upon a fundamental shallowness of vision. He can successfully disarm Mr. Wentworth and even Mr. Brand by refusing to recognize their distress, but in the significant closing scene with his sister he fails utterly to help her. After an exasperating meeting with Acton, during which she guesses that his reluctance to marry her will eventually lead to her rejection, she guardedly asks Felix to help her. But Felix, the only person capable of influencing Acton to propose, conveniently dodges the veiled message. He does nothing for his sister, choosing to evade a problem in which good humor might prove inadequate. And when he speaks with his sister following her defeat, he can contribute neither advice nor sympathy.

In the end he is nearly as pathetic as Acton in his weak attempt to salvage a hopeless situation by incongruous jollity.[10]

In a different way, the Baroness is also shielded from certain kinds of experience by her devotion to forms. She is not so intolerant of depression as is Felix—and thus she can express a wider range of attitudes and emotions than he—but she is at a loss when feelings are expressed directly, unembellished by conventional graces. It is worth noting that the one person whom she cannot deal with at all is Lizzie Acton, whose "dangerous energy" (p. 132) makes her a natural enemy to the Baroness. Clifford is merely gauche and ill-bred, but Lizzie, who finally "civilizes" Clifford, while the Baroness fails, has an immediate sexual and emotional expression of herself that the Baroness partly envies and partly despises.

The Baroness's artfulness cannot compete with Lizzie's vitality, and to that extent it is a limitation. But her relation with Lizzie is counter-weighted by her relation with Acton's mother, whose directness reveals social ineptness rather than refreshing honesty. Understandably, the Baroness is irritated by the dull tactlessness with which Mrs. Acton, whom she has met only once previously, announces that she is dying and requests Eugenia to remain in the community because "it would be so pleasant for Robert" (p. 233). In the exchange between the two women, art surely shows itself as superior to artlessness. In her ignorance of the rules of conversation, the old woman is unintentionally rude and offensive; the Baroness through intelligence, self-control, and a respect for decorum, prevents the unpleasantness of the situation from coming to the surface. With the single exception of her relation to Lizzie (which is important, because Lizzie defeats her plans with Clifford), the Baroness's artificiality is an expansion, not a repression of herself. Her manner, her conversation, even her clothes and her furnishings fully express her. Robert Acton, on the other hand, most often uses his acquired finesse to conceal his deeper feelings—even from himself. His quasi-worldliness, like his conscience, protects him from reality.

The Baroness has mastered the art of knowing how to be looked at. For her, appearance not only takes on more importance than reality, appearance is reality. She feels it is preferable to carry one's self like a pretty woman than to be a pretty woman. Pathetically and ironically she is regarded by the New Englanders as hardly a person at all, rather a spectacle to be gawked at, or to be paraded before friends and neighbors, like an exotic and unintelligible work of art. Eugenia is crudely rebuked by Acton, who acts as though manners and wit are in themselves sufficient bases of friendship, not requiring the further connection of marriage. Thus his relation to the Baroness remains that of an audience to a theatrical performer. Nor do the Wentworths ever acknowledge the Baroness's existence as a woman:

> They were all standing around [Eugenia], as if they were expecting her
> to acquit herself of this exhibition of some peculiar faculty, some brilliant

talent. Their attitude seemed to imply that she was a kind of conversational mountebank, attired, intellectually, in gauze and spangles.

(p. 63)

The distinguishing qualities of both Felix and Eugenia point simultaneously to the special virtues and special limitations of both the Europeans and the Americans. Eugenia's artistic, self-representation accounts for her own civilized grace, but it is also a measure of her failure to deal with life directly, particularly in its more vigorous aspects. Her grace exposes the severe deficiency of a Mrs. Acton, but it is the reason for her own inferiority to a Lizzie Acton. Correspondingly, Felix can experience a pleasure beyond the capacity of an American, but he cannot recognize the pain which they so exaggerate as an element of life.

But it must be said that there is very little of pain in the novel. Thus the Americans are exposed as quixotic in their fear of a nonexistent evil. Finally what oppresses them is a fear of the unconventional and a fear of pleasure. As representatives of these qualities, the Europeans are harmless. Their suggested faults—their ploting for self-gain, Felix's inability to acknowledge pain, the Baroness's inability to face raw experience—are in no way inimical to the Americans. The Europeans offer only the possibility of happiness to the entire group. If anyone suffers, it is the Baroness, though she is no less admirable than Felix. The reason is simply that Felix's bonhomie proves less difficult for the New World to endure than the Baroness's courtliness.

But Eugenia's failure is not the only unpleasantness in the book. Through symbolism James suggests grave realities underlying the experience of the novel, though the suggestion is too mild to distort the genial tone. Mainly the setting, the dialogue, and the witty narrative voice blend; the discordant notes remain beneath the surface, to be perceived, but not to offset the comic mood.

For instance, James casually develops a complicated symbolism of . youth and age—a rhetorical and scenic set of paradoxes that strengthens the dramatic ironies involved in the conjunction of the two cultures. These ironies are simultaneously frivolous and meaningful. New England, represented in the imagery of both youthful vitality and of death, is at once young and old. The book begins with a view of a dismal graveyard and ends with the death of Mrs. Acton. To the baroness, "Gertrude seemed . . . almost funereal" (p. 54); and to Felix, "there was something almost cadaverous in his uncle's high-featured white face" (p. 52). But if these and other comments reflect something life-denying in the New Englanders, many others reflect their comic youthfulness. Just as Mr. Wentworth regards his eighty-year old house as a "venerable mansion" (p. 47) and as James speaks of Boston as an "ancient city" (p. 1), so not even the Puritan temperament can conceal the youthfulness of the American civilization. The New Englanders are untried and rather timid children. The Wentworth house is not really old, but very fresh; and America is "a comical country" (p. 8).

The Wentworth circle is both young and old—as young and old as the Golden Age. And in a different way, the same paradox applies to the Europeans. In the first chapter the Baroness tells Felix (whose last name is "Young"): "You will never be anything but a child, dear brother."

> "One would suppose that you, madam," answered Felix, laughing, "were a thousand years old."
> "I am—sometimes," said the Baroness.
>
> (p. 21)

Felix's youth—a freedom from suppressions—and the Baroness's antiquity—an absorption in the manners of a very old civilization—help define their combined character. The two are not greatly different, for Felix's childishness differs only in degree from the Baroness's age; both exult in the promises of life. Age is wisdom for the Baroness, but only decay for the Wentworths; youth is gayety for Felix, but only inexperience for the Wentworths.

The Europeans are both younger and older (happier and wiser) than the also young and old (innocent and decayed) Americans, specifically because they are opportunists. And—to compound the paradoxes—their opportunism is characteristic of Americans rather than Europeans, especially as it is also associated with their freedom and their youth. James exploits the reputation of America as the land of opportunity (of course, in other of his works it is rather the land of opportunists, and Europe is the land of opportunity). If the notion of opportunity that motivates the Europeans is not exactly a standard American one, James nevertheless identifies the enterprises of the Europeans with the promises latent in America. At one point Felix thinks, "this was certainly the country of sunsets. There was something in these glorious deeps of fire that quickened his imagination; he always found images and promises in the western sky" (p. 217). Even Eugenia, who is considerably less absorbed in nature than Felix, responds to the promise symbolized by the primitive American scene. Walking through the streets of Boston, "she surrendered herself to a certain tranquil gayety. If she had come to seek her fortune, it seemed to her that her fortune would be easy to find. There was a promise of it in the gorgeous purity of the western sky. . . ." (p. 19)

The suggestion that the Europeans are more archetypically American than the New Englanders is recurrent.[11] It establishes an additional relationship between the sets of characters and thus further refines the shape of the novel. In *The Europeans*, incidents, characters, and places become significant because they correspond to and yet contrast with other incidents, characters, and places. Thus the three prominent houses in the Wentworth neighborhood are each implicit criticisms of each other and of the kind of people who live in them: the Wentworths' is chaste and austere; the Baroness's is lavishly decorated; and Robert Acton's is an awkward compromise between the other two.[12] A less obvious pattern in the novel is formed by the repeated episodes in which lies are told or are commented on. The lie is a regular occasion for moral ambiguity in James; he nearly always employs the lie to differentiate the rigid moralist from the free spirit. To regard the telling of lies as *per se* heinous is to mark one's self as narrow and self-righteous. Thus one of the clearest indications that Gertrude is imaginative is that she tells harmless fibs. A lie is partly responsible for the downfall of Eugenia, though to her (and to our) mind when she lies to Mrs. Acton in her son's presence she is only being courteous. In effect, the Baroness is regarded as a living lie; to the New Englanders she is performing a role rather than living a life. And Felix's flattering portraits of the Wentworth circle are at bottom lies. The New Englanders can regard forms of artfulness only in terms of ethics, because they can express themselves only by a moralistic rhetoric. But the Europeans convert moral questions to aesthetic ones. Thus to Mr. Wentworth Clifford's alcoholism is a moral failing, while to Eugenia and Felix it represents a deficiency in manners.

Gertrude Wentworth is the only New Englander who accepts the offerings of the Europeans. James represents her as a kind of potential Eugenia, with the same tastes and habits though in a cruder, less articulate form. They are the only characters who tell "lies," who respect appearances, and who are described as "restless" and "peculiar."[13] But the main effect of these resemblances is to throw their differences into relief. Thus Gertrude's mistaking the high cultivation of the Europeans for naturalness is evidence that she is at center merely rebellious. The novel implies that one is never so natural—in the sense of giving full expression to the imagination—as when he is endowed with the manners of a rich civilization; but such a perception is certainly beyond the capacity of Gertrude. Gertrude actually fails to respond to the civilizing influences of the Europeans; her main reason for wishing to be like them is to free herself from her "obligations" and "responsibilities"—such as attending church, marrying Mr. Brand, and telling the truth. She has not mastered the tact, the courtesy, and the geniality of Felix; she wants only his freedom. In her various self-assertions she is flippant and inconsiderate. Yet James does not present Gertrude in a harsh light; he simply reveals her as a rather ill-tempered and irritable girl who, in spite of her yearnings, has no real understanding of the life she has determined to lead.

But it is Eugenia rather than Gertrude who is excluded from the harmonious resolution of difficulties at the end. In the language of ancient comedy, Eugenia is what Northrop Frye calls the *pharmakos*—the rascal inimical to the well-being of society who is driven out in the comic resolution. Such an expulsion "appeals to the kind of relief we are expected to feel when we see Jonson's Volpone condemned to the galleys, Shylock stripped of his wealth, or Tartuffe taken off to prison." But the rejection of Eugenia pleases only if *The Europeans* is read as a total approbation of the New Englanders. As the novel stands, however, Eugenia's repudiation is somewhat like those "most terrible ironies known to art" such as "the rejection of Falstaff" and "certain scenes in Chaplin."[14]

In permitting the expulsion of Eugenia, James not only allows himself his only severe judgment of the New Englanders, but he gives a rather harsh turn to the otherwise genial tone of the novel. Eugenia dominates the final chapter, and if her dismissal does not nullify the gayety of the multiple weddings it at least counterbalances the mood of joy with one of unpleasantness. Indeed the seasonal backdrop of the novel is attuned to Eugenia's spirits. Her early gloom is complemented by a late spring snowstorm, but the climate improves and summer arrives as Eugenia's mood lightens; but as Eugenia perceives that Acton will fail her, summer gives way to winter. "Les beaux jours sont passés" (p. 208), the Baroness says, contradicting her brother, and her words reflect both the climactic conditions and her own prospects. Eugenia is rejected not only by Acton, but by Clifford, by Lizzie, and by the Wentworths, and even by her brother, whose jollity in the end is an obvious limitation. Since the Baroness is an imaginative and resourceful woman, she resists mere pity, but there is a sense of loss and a mood of somberness in her departure.[15] We feel that the society which dismisses her is seriously deficient.

The artistic effect of Eugenia's failure is certainly not to tighten the structure and enrich the texture of the novel. Rather the ending extends the small dimensions of the "sketch"—as James sub-titled the novel—into a less restricted and conventional area. It would have been a simple matter for James to arrange the marriage of Acton and Eugenia (as he arranges the benign, yet unconvincing, acquiescence of Mr. Brand to Gertrude's marriage to Felix), but instead of granting his readers the fulfillment of their expectations, James forces them to revise their estimate of the entire affair. James seems unwilling to submit totally to the demands of comedy. He refuses to make the final sacrifices of his artistic freedom to the *a priori* requirements of an artificial form.[16] Though he employs innumerable conventional comic techniques in *The Europeans*, he refuses to employ any for its own sake. Everything in the novel is carefully calculated to develop a central idea—the clash of a life based on responsibility with one based on opportunism—so that even the most mechanical of devices subserve an organic scheme. That there are many such devices may explain why James deprecated the novel. Never again was he to be so reliant upon such contrivances and significantly *The Europeans* is the last novel of its type that James wrote.

Notes

1. See Oscar Cargill, *The Novels of Henry James* (New York, 1961), pp. 67–68. James's admiration for the French dramatists of the 1870's is amply reflected in his essays on the Parisian stage collected in *The Scenic Art*, ed. Allan Wade (New York, 1957). Leon Edel, *The*

*Complete Plays of Henry James* (Philadelphia, 1949), discusses the general influence of the well-made play on James's novels (pp. 34–40).

2. Here and elsewhere in this essay I am indebted to the analysis of comic modes in Northrop Frye, *Anatomy of Criticism* (Princeton, 1957), pp. 43–52, 163–186.

3. The phrase is Professor Frye's, p. 183.

4. It seems probable that James intentionally made the New England scene considerably less urban and cosmopolitan than it actually was. In misrepresenting Boston of the 1840's, James aroused the civic loyalty of Thomas Wentworth Higginson, who reviewed *The Europeans* unfavorably in the *Literary World*, X (Nov. 22, 1879), 383–84. The anachronisms are discussed by Cargill, pp. 62–63, 69.

5. See R. P. Blackmur, "Introduction," *Washington Square* and *The Europeans* (New York, 1959), pp. 5–12.

6. Notably by Edward Sackville-West, "Introduction: *The Europeans* (London, 1952), p. viii; Joseph McG. Bottkal, "Introduction," *The Aspern Papers* and *The Europeans* (Norfolk, Conn., 1950), p. xix; and Osborn Andreas, *Henry James and the Expanding Horizon* (Seattle, 1948), p. 45.

7. For example, by Rebecca West, *Henry James* (New York, 1916), p. 42. Richard Poirier identifies the viewpoint of the Baroness with that of James in *The Comic Sense of Henry James* (New York, 1960), p. 109, and devotes most of his essay on the novel to a demonstration of the admirableness of Eugenia.

8. Page references are to *The Europeans* (Boston, 1873).

9. Also, as F. W. Dupee remarks, Felix "actually rescues the family from possible disruption by this somewhat threatening daughter" (*Henry James* [New York, 1951], p. 103).

10. Thus Felix is rather less than the "person of radical responsibility" he is called by F. R. Leavis, "The Novel as Dramatic Poem (III): 'The Europeans,' " *Scrutiny*, XV (Summer, 1948), 212.

11. See Poirier, pp. 139–40, for further evidences of this irony and for illuminating observations regarding it.

12. See Bowden, pp. 48–50, for a detailed analysis of the symbolic values of the three houses.

13. Here I am summarizing Poirier, pp. 112–16, though, as I suggest subsequently, the differences between Gertrude and Eugenia are as striking as the parallels: the differences are striking precisely because of the parallels.

14. Frye, p. 45.

15. It is typical of James to decrease gradually the comic mood of his novels. *The American, The Spoils of Poynton, The Awkward Age,* and *The Ambassadors,* in particular, are novels in which the casualness and high-spiritedness of the opening chapters give way to tense seriousness.

16. One of James's most recurrent critical principles is his belief that the novelist should remain uninfluenced by external rules and theories and should devise his own restrictions according to his sense of the needs of the novel he is writing. In "The Future of the Novel," for instance, he writes, "[The novel] has the extraordinary advantage . . . that, while capable of giving an impression of the highest perfection and the rarest finish, it moves in luxurious independence of rules and restrictions" (*The Future of the Novel: Essays on the Art of Fiction,* ed. Leon Edel [New York, 1956], p. 36).

# Washington Square: A Study in the Growth of an Inner Self
James W. Gargano*

Except for Richard Poirier, the critics who have written well about Henry James's *Washington Square* have not, for one reason or another, concerned themselves with the special sensibility of the heroine, Catherine Sloper. Cornelia Pulsifer Kelley, for example, ably explores James's indebtedness to Balzac's *Eugènie Grandet:* incidentally, she describes Catherine as possessing "one outstanding and dominant characteristic—her goodness."[1] S. Gorley Putt, almost ignoring Catherine, finds the meaning of James's work in an "enigmatic riddle larger than the book itself," whether or not it is "right to deny another person an experience which one supposes to be harmful."[2] In an otherwise astute and balanced interpretation, Charles T. Samuels surprisingly concludes that James's "narration avoids taking us into the girl's sensibility."[3] F. W. Dupee, J. A. Ward, and Edwin T. Bowden have written persuasively about Catherine and the novel, but they do not focus attention on James's main concern, the process by which she acquires selfhood and inner being.[4]

Poirier's brilliant "dissection" of *Washington Square* concentrates on the comic art with which James presents a subtle and developing view of character.[5] Essentially, Poirier maintains that for nearly half of the novella James scrutinizes Catherine through the ironic eyes of her father: consequently, the early portrait of the girl emphasizes her tractability, dullness, and lack of taste. Poirier further contends that James dissociates himself from Dr. Sloper's fixed point of view as Catherine's consciousness expands.

Though I agree in general with Poirier's reading of the novel, I believe that he ignores Catherine's very early stirrings of life and fails to respond to James's almost clinical precision in recording the wonder of her awakening sensibility. She is, as I hope to demonstrate, an early portrait—without the later nuance and depth-psychology—of the Jamesian protagonist transformed, to her own surprise, by the discovery of selfhood and an inner life. The brilliance of James's work stems from its "science" as well as its vitalism, its methodical analysis as well as its sense of being present at the creation. With rare explicitness, James marks each stage of Catherine's expanding consciousness, almost obtrusively cataloguing her "new" emotions as she experiences them. In addition, he documents, with both excitement and detachment, the relationship between these novel feelings and the emergent interior world where she becomes acquainted with (indeed a fascinated spectator of) her evolving psychic drama. In short, James anatomizes the process by which Catherine's active, secret existence transforms her into an imaginative woman.

However much she may ultimately learn, Catherine is, at the outset of *Washington Square*, a typical Jamesian innocent and a not very promising

*Reprinted with permission from *Studies in Short Fiction* 13, no. 3 (Summer 1976): 355–62.

candidate for psychological growth. Indeed, despite the difference in their ages, she is as nearly a *tabula rasa* as the appealing child-heroine of *What Maisie Knew*. She has affinities, too, with over-trusting Maggie Verver, James's last great heroine. But, like the others, she is waiting to be energized into the susceptibilities and accumulations of a rare nature. In James's fiction, naivete may wear the look of an empty mind, but it is often the ideal preparation for receiving life fully and impressionably. It is not surprising, then, that Catherine will feel more intensely because so far as strong emotions go, she is not only uninitiated but she literally does not know what to expect of them. Her ingenuousness is the key to her genuineness and her sense of seeing, feeling, and judging life for the first time.

In a number of his novels, James dramatizes the first significant act in the developments of an inner life as, paradoxically, the attachment of the self to an extrernal ideal which, while it seems to subordinate the self, awakens and vivifies it. Catherine, obviously, emerges from a sort of dormancy when she meets Townsend. Yet, more importantly, though she moves "outside" herself in loving Townsend, her love becomes a private possession to be concealed, hoarded, and quietly assessed. Interestingly enough, James consistently links the birth of an inner life with a refusal to share one's thoughts and feelings, with dissimulating withdrawal and even positive deceit. Maisie Farange, for example, begins her initiation by savoring "the idea of an inner self or, in other words, of concealment."[6] Catherine, likewise, moves toward maturity by practising disguise and equivocation: no longer straightforward and ingenuously candid, she becomes introverted and acts according to the urgency of secret, personal drives. When for instance, her cousin asks her what she thinks of Townsend and she answers, " 'Oh, nothing particular,' " James attaches importance to this mild duplicity by pointedly observing that she is "dissembling for the first time." Her evasive reply to her father's inquiry as to whether she enjoyed herself at Mrs. Almond's party, where she is introduced to Townsend, leads James to another explicit comment: "For the second time in her life she made an indirect answer: and the beginning of a period of dissimulation is certainly a significant date" (p. 34).

James intends this significant date to signal the origin in Catherine of private, unstereotyped thought and a nascent sense of selfhood. One of the major ironies of *Washington Square* is that the ironic Dr. Sloper fails to glimpse the inner revolution that has taken place in his daughter. Both he and Townsend are blinded by bigotries of self-importance; they cannot see that, in turning inward, the girl has entered a sphere of activity with its own autonomy, beauty, and rewards. She has found a refuge from the external world, an almost Donnean inversion in which the lover achieves extension or aggrandizement. While her father continues to regard her as a listless dunce, her life is filled with warm consolations and novel emotions; anything but a sign of inertness, her reserve has a special dimension and for her, a kind of sanctity. Although she strikes some critics as being merely good, James explicitly states that, in refusing to make a "festival of her secret," she treasures a "consciousness of immense and unexpected favors."

In *Washington Square*, James undertakes the difficult art of making the undemonstrative, psychic unfolding of his heroine arresting. Once Catherine leaves the rut of conventional responses and discovers a "self," he conscientiously labels the life-giving emotions and insights that she experiences for the "first" time. He carefully presents her as "progressing" from rather simple sensations to more and more complex ones. To cite one example: after hearing of Mrs. Penniman's adverturous meeting with Townsend, Catherine "felt angry for the moment"; James adds, in order to fix it as another beginning, that "it was almost the first time she had ever felt angry" (p. 138). Even the insensitive Lavinia observes that "the girl had never had just this dark fixedness in her gaze" (p. 141). Later, when Sloper accuses her of bad taste in wishing to move out of his house, her response is once again new but no longer simple: "for the first time . . . there was a spark of anger in her grief." Still later, at the end of her European trip, she complexly enjoys a kind of elation as she angrily retorts to her father's insistence that Townsend will forsake her: now rather than reacting with a mixture of grief and wrath, she feels "her heart beating with the excitement of having for the first time spoken to him in violence." To the alert reader, which even James's early work requires, these "firsts" constitute important occasions and significant dates in Catherine's learning and psychological ripening.

In addition to endowing his heroine with new feelings, James skillfully traces her developing insight into the ranges and mazes of her own nature. Her early dissimulations and lack of candor establish a habit of inwardness, and James refers to the girl's visions and revisions as if they were discoveries and even epiphanies. At one point, alone with thoughts of her lover, she delights in discovering that "her imagination could exercise itself indefinitely." In attempting to blunt her father's disappointment with her, she makes the "discovery . . . that there was a great deal of excitement in trying to be a good daughter." Almost simultaneously she has "an entirely new feeling" which reveals remarkable powers of introspection and imagination. Seeing herself as both actor and analyst, she pores over her internal drama as if it were a fresh marvel: "She watched herself as she would have watched another person, and wondered what she would do. It was as if this other person, who was both herself and not herself, had suddenly sprung into being, inspiring her with a natural curiosity as to the performance of untested functions" (p. 122). It is hard to write off as dull a young woman with such vivid "contact" with her own development; I am sure that James intended the dullness to be ascribed to the bright people around her who never even glimpse her hidden abysses.

What may distract some readers from the recognition of Catherine's mounting sense of herself is, perhaps, the egregiousness and pertinacity of her misplaced love. Yet, James makes the delusion testify not to her stupidity but to her capacity for wonder, the unreserve of her faith in the possibilities of existence. Admittedly too imprudent and sincere to believe in traps, she is deceived by a masquerade of kindness and affection, but her innocent fanaticism—irrespective of the worthiness or unworthiness of its object or its possible consequences in a predatory society—is a rich expenditure and therefore an attestation of spiritual wealth. I believe that James, for all his ironic realism, wishes the final plenitude of Catherine's character to be measured by the very excess of idealized love that she lavishes on others. No matter how wrong she may be, in contrast to her, Morris Townsend and Dr. Sloper are afflicted with impoverished and cramped souls; they are prudential, calculating, and narrow. They count on a substantial return for investing their affection. It is appalling that Townsend cannot see why she would naturally and generously prefer to be with him in New York than accompany her father to Europe. In exclaiming to himself, " 'Gracious Heaven, what a dull woman!' " he resembles Dr. Sloper, who, in the presence of a beautifully expanding nature, obtusely thinks, " 'She is about as intelligent as a bundle of shawls.' "

Clearly, James realistically associates Catherine's maturing with a transcendentalizing imagination that remakes reality out of strange "soul stuff." This kind of imagination is a creative inner answer to intellectual and psychic undernourishment; it seems preeminently the "gift" of the young, of artists, or culture-starved Americans. Lavish and idealistic, it is a way of seeing that exercises a remarkable tyranny over its victim, who is galvanized, deepened, and yet strangely hoodwinked by it. It prompts Christopher Newman to transform Madame de Cintré into a moon-borne Madonna, Isabel Archer to inflate Osmond's merits, Lambert Strether to turn Madame de Vionnet into a creature of pure ideality, and Milly Theale to find in Densher a sort of sacred fount. Catherine's imagination, too, becomes rhapsodic in the creation of beautiful figments. Once she sees Townsend as having "features like young men in pictures," once she thinks that "he looked like a statue," once she casts him in the role of "a young knight in a poem," she has constructed an ideal which she possesses (and which possesses her) with consuming tenacity. Inevitably, this ideal becomes the paramount value of her life, and other attachments, no matter how strong, must somehow accommodate themselves to it.

Evidently, Catherine's imagination, springing from the faith and poetry of her own nature, works at the profoundest levels of her being and utterly metamorphoses her. It is not, therefore, to be confused with the melodramatic romanticism (which James also calls imagination) of Mrs. Penniman. It has nothing to do with that lady's breathless interest in clandestine trysts, elopements, and beautiful sentiments. In fact, James's burlesque of Mrs. Penniman is a calculated irony: the very antithesis of Catherine's, her species of imagination is a caricature of reality and has no source in felt experience. To exaggerate a bit, it might be said that Aunt Lavinia's fantasies derive from the melodrama of the popular theater and that her niece's idealizations come down humanized from a lofty Platonic sphere. In any case, Lavinia never changes while Catherine achieves her most impressive development when she returns to earth from her high fantasies and learns the truth of the human condition.

Finally, James conceives of the imagination as a constructive force, what might be called the sixth sense of the enriched consciousness. It works with almost mystical intuitiveness and arrives at the wholeness of truth. It is, essentially, a highly charged perception which fuses scattered and transient insights into coherence and meaning. The imagination cannot make its synthesis, however, until it has, in a manner of speaking, collected the necessary data. In other words, the consciousness must take in and assimilate clues that, by some indefinable process, establish a relationship among themselves. Then at the "right" moment, a look, word, or gesture will spontaneously cause the fusion preparing in the subconscious to come to the surface and proclaim itself. Often, these imaginative moments, which abound in James's works, have the quality of revelations or epiphanies. In *Washington Square*, there is, of course, no such epiphanic vision as Isabel Archer arrives at in the famous forty-second chapter of *The Portrait of a Lady*, no revelatory, seeing look as in "The Aspern Papers," no such clarifying "horror" as Strether encounters in the pastoral loveliness of France, and no such leap of the beast as Marcher turns away from in "The Beast in the Jungle." Nevertheless, in an unusual instance of integrated perception, Catherine fearfully glimpses the whole truth about her relation with Townsend: "A sudden fear had come over her: it was like the solid conjunction of a dozen disembodied doubts, and her imagination, at a single bound, had traversed an enormous distance" (p. 238).

This passage and others like it show that Catherine must be numbered among those imaginative Jamesian protagonists doomed to feel ardently, suffer, know, judge, and still endure. After a series of preparatory discoveries, she makes the ultimate and painful discovery—that she has spent her idealism on a hollow, loveless, and predatory world. Yet her own strange words testify that something of value survives her suffering: "it made a great change in my life" (p. 289). The change, precipitated by the confluence of hope, conflict, and trauma, leaves her with an inner self that helps her to bear her demonic knowledge with a measure of grace.

Catherine, thus, is a character who, almost a void at the outset, is only fully created at the end of *Washington Square*. The events of the novel adumbrate the process by which she acquires sensations, develops self-awareness, and comes to imaginative life. Her slow psychological evolution demonstrates "how" she learns as well as "what" she learns; the route she travels (the process) and the knowledge she gains merge and become one. It is difficult, if not impossible, to separate the dancer from the dance. Yet, it is convenient to trace Catherine's movement toward "identity" in the judgments she is forced to make of her aunt, father, and lover. As she judges each person, she suffers a loss but is more herself, loses a support but builds a more personal strength. Of course, like a person in the first stages of learning, she begins to emancipate herself from domestic fetishes with a severe judgment of Mrs. Penniman: "Her aunt seemed to her aggressive and foolish, and to see it so clearly—to judge Mrs. Penniman so positively—made her old and grave" (p. 144).

Naturally, Catherine does not come to a definitive judgment of her father as easily as she sees through her aunt's meddling, romantic personality. Though the process is more complex and protracted, however, it more vividly illustrates her steady progress toward the liberty of individuality. The first serious crisis between father and daughter, which follows upon her suggestion that she move out of "his" house (as she has already done psychologically), ends with a rebellion against his high-handed authority. Entering a more liberated phase of consciousness, "she had an idea . . . that now she was absolved from penance and might do what she chose" (p. 185). In the next phase of her development, during her stay in Europe, Catherine travels with her father but lives exclusively in her mind and imagination. Indeed, it is the impenetrability of her private life that frightens Dr. Sloper and gives her, for the first time, dominance over him. His struggle to coerce her return to her old orbit reaches a high point of frustration when, in the Alps, he practically threatens to abandon her—a gratuitous threat since he has already been abandoned by her. As her parent becomes more sinister and correspondingly helpless, she grows measurably freer and surer of herself. For example, the night before she embarks for New York she refuses to be nettled by his ironic comment that she will soon "go off" with Townsend. Her eyes fully open, she can now attribute to her old idol a "rather gross way of putting things." This candid criticism reveals that Catherine's transformation is so complete that she is ready to understand and explain, without rancor, her father's contempt for her. And she does so with an accuracy, imagination, and generosity that James would only put in the mouth of a character of impressive sensibility: "It's because he is so fond of my mother, whom we lost so long ago. She was beautiful, and very, very brilliant: he is always thinking of her. I am not at all like her. . . . Of course it isn't my fault; but neither is it his fault. All I mean is, it's true" (p. 312). The compassionate impersonality of "All I mean is, it's true" reveals a character that has successfully faced some very hard facts.

It is significant that Catherine's appraisal of Dr. Sloper should be made to Morris, whom she will be compelled to judge with equal objectivity. She will be *complete* (a word James uses in describing his later characters who attain comprehensive vision) when she has the courage to recognize that he has exploited her best feelings and that she has participated in her own deception. Knowledge comes, however, only after a long struggle during which she will not consciously believe what her subconcious already "knows." In this resistance to an enlightenment that will be a too rude awakening she resembles Isabel Archer, Strether, and Maisie, who also intuit the truth long before they will allow themselves to know it. Catherine's

shock, when it comes, is the elemental shock of the uncompromising be-
liever: "It was almost the last outbreak of passion in her life: at least, she
never indulged in another that the world knew anything about. But this
one was long and terrible" (p. 240). She finally submits to the facts that
Townsend has worn a mask and that the profoundest and most emancipating emotion of her life was devoted to a fraud. When she receives his
"beautiful" but heartless letter, she detects the "bitterness of its meaning
and the hollowness of its tone." Only now in having learned to understand
others as others and not as extensions of herself, can she know her own
identity. She is a kind of process, a growth—a compassionate and resigned
"sum" of all that has happened to her.

In *Washington Square*, as in so many of James's later novels, there is
no question that the protagonist finally commands an all-inclusive vision.
What disturbs many readers, however, is that this vision obviates fresh
starts and new passions. Love, as James construes it, is such an ideal and
full commitment that it exacts the unreserved surrender of the lover's spirit
and imagination. Disillusionment, then, results in a too lofty resignation,
as if love once lost, there's no more loving possible. The wounded lover's
quest, it appears, was only superficially for human love; in reality, it was a
search for the height and fullness to which the lover's nature could attain.
In a sense, Catherine is like Hawthorne's Owen Warland, who incorporates
into himself the vision of perfection he attempts to materialize. Like Owen,
Catherine sees the physical manifestation of her vision destroyed; like
Owen, too, she imagines, achieves, and retains something greater than she
has lost. At the end of the novel, Morris Townsend can, like Owen's glittering butterfly, be crushed and cast aside in the fulfillment of his purpose. It
may seem, then, that loss is the real goal for which James's central characters are secretly striving, that they engage life only to see that it falls below
their lofty expectations and that mastery and transcendence (as so often in
Emily Dickinson's poems) are gained by renunciation. Of course, the effect
of this transcendence is curiously to belittle the very quest and struggle
which made it possible. James's heroes and heroines finally reach a summit
where love between man and woman can remain only as a memory of an
earlier, stormier, and grosser incarnation.

For some readers, obviously, the ending of the Jamesian novel of renunciation denies more than it grants and thus seems depressing rather
than genuinely tragic. In *Washington Square*, the emphasis on Catherine's
spinsterishness and mechanical life suggests that her later years will be a
vigil for death. Since her last act in the novel is to pick up her "morsel of
fancy work . . . for life as it were" (p. 291), the wages of wisdom appear to
be of dubious value. There is no Maria Gostry, as in *The Ambassadors*, to
assure her, as Lambert Strether is assured that renunciation is another
word for imagination and unselfish "action." Instead, she endures, as if in
a haunted house, with her scatterbrained aunt for a companion. I must confess that the dreary tone of the conclusion of the novel tends to water down

the impression of Catherine's fulfillment. Still, it should not detract too much from the import and structural intention pervading the scene of Catherine's last meeting with Townsend: clearly, in the presence her still-conniving and unchanged former lover, she reveals how much she has developed and matured. It is Townsend (and his aide, Mrs. Penniman) who wishes to take up the silly melodrama of long ago because the emotions of that time were for him essentially frivolous and without transforming power. By the depth of her feelings and comprehensiveness of her imagination, Catherine has recreated herself into a being that neither Townsend nor Mrs. Penniman, the eternal fools of the earth, (nor, for that matter, the "shrewd" and uncomprehending Dr. Sloper) could understand. When she says goodbye to Townsend, she may seem to be entering a tomb but, in reality she is "free" in the same way that Isabel Archer is when she returns to the prospect of a long stretch of life with the sterile Osmond. Her change, as she herself recognizes, has taken place in the innermost part of her being, where, in Emily Dickinson's words, "the meanings are."

## Notes

1. *The Early Development of Henry James* (Urbana, 1965), p. 278.

2. *Henry James: A Reader's Guide* (Ithaca, New York, 1956), p. 50.

3. *The Ambiguity of Henry James* (Urbana, 1971), p. 146.

4. F. W. Dupee, *Henry James* (New York, 1951); Edwin T. Bowden, *The Themes of Henry James* (New Haven, 1956); J. A. Ward, *The Imagination of Disaster* (Lincoln, Nebraska, 1961), p. 31.

5. *The Comic Sense of Henry James* (New York, 1967), p. 15.

6. *Washington Square* (New York, 1967), p. 31. All subsequent page references to *Washington Square* are to this edition and will be included in parentheses in the text.

# The High Brutality of Good Intentions

William H. Gass*

"The great question as to a poet or a novelist is, How does he feel about life? What, in the last analysis, is his philosophy?"

—Henry James

"Art," Yeats wrote in his essay on "The Thinking of the Body," "bids us touch and taste and hear and see the world, and shrinks from what Blake calls mathematic form, from every abstract thing, from all that is of the brain only, from all that is not a fountain jetting from the entire hopes, memories, and sensations of the body." Yet the world that we are permit-

*Reprinted from *Accent* 18 (Winter 1958):62–71, by permission of the author.

ted to touch and taste and hear and see in art, in Yeats's art as much as in any other, is not a world of pure Becoming, with the abstractions removed to a place safe only for philosophers; it is a world invested out of the ordinary with formal natures, with types and typicals, by abstractions and purest principles; invested to a degree which, in comparison with the real, renders it at times grotesque and always abnormal. It is charged with Being. Touching it provides a shock.

The advantage the creator of fiction has over the moral philosopher is that the writer is concerned with the exhibition of objects, thoughts, feelings and actions where they are free from the puzzling disorders of the real and the need to come to conclusions about them. He is subject only to those calculated disorders which are the result of his refusal, in the fact of the actual complexities of any well-chosen "case," to take a stand. The moral philosopher is expected to take a stand. He is expected to pronounce upon the principles of value. The writer of fiction, in so far as he is interested in morals, rather than, for instance, metaphysics, can satisfy himself and the requirements of his art by the exposure of moral principle in the act, an exposure more telling than life because it is, although concrete, concrete in no real way—stripped of the irrelevant, the accidental, the incomplete—every bit of paste and hair and string part of the intrinsic nature of the article. However the moral philosopher comes by his conclusions, he does not generally suppose (unless he is also a theologian) that the world is ordered by them or that the coming together of feelings and intents or the issuance of acts or the flow of consequences, which constitute the moral facts, was designed simply in order to display them.

It is the particular achievement of Henry James that he was able to transform the moral color of his personal vision into the hues of his famous figure in the carpet; that he found a form for his awareness of moral issues, an awareness that was so pervasive it invaded furniture and walls and ornamental gardens and perched upon the shoulders of his people a dove for spirit, beating its wings with the violence of all Protestant history; so that of this feeling, of the moving wing itself, he could make a style. This endeavor was both aided and hindered by the fact that, for James, art and morality were so closely twined, and by the fact that no theory of either art or morality had footing unless, previous to it, the terrible difficulties of vision and knowledge, of personal construction and actual fact, of, in short, the relation of reality to appearance had been thoroughly overcome. James's style is a result of his effort to master, at the level of his craft, these difficulties, and his effort, quite apart from any measure of its actual success with these things, brought to the form of the novel in English an order of art never even, before him, envisioned by it.

Both Henry James and his brother were consumed by a form of The Moral Passion. Both struggled to find in the plural world of practice a vantage for spirit. But William was fatally enmeshed in the commercial. How well he speaks for the best in his age. He pursues the saint; he probes the spiritual disorders of the soul; he commiserates with the world-weary and encourages the strong; he investigates the nature of God, His relation to the world, His code; he defends the possible immortality of the soul and the right to believe: and does all so skillfully, with a nature so sensitive, temperate and generous, that it is deeply disappointing to discover, as one soon must, that the lenses of his mind are monetary, his open hand is open for the coin, and that the more he struggles to understand, appreciate, and rise, the more instead he misses, debases, and destroys.

> In the religion of the once-born the world is a sort of rectilinear or one-storied affair, whose accounts are kept in one denomination, whose parts have just the values which naturally they appear to have, and of which a simple algebraic sum of pluses and minuses will give the total worth. Happiness and religious peace consist in living on the plus side of the account. In the religion of the twice-born, on the other hand, the world is a double-storied mystery. Peace cannot be reached by the simple addition of pluses and elimination of minuses from life. Natural good is not simply insufficient in amount and transient, there lurks a falsity in its very being. Cancelled as it all is by death if not by earlier enemies, it gives no final balance, and can never be the thing intended for our lasting worship.[1]

Even when William, in a passage not obviously composed with the book-keeper's pen, makes a literary allusion, as here:

> Like the single drops which sparkle in the sun as they are flung far ahead of the advancing edge of a wave-crest or of a flood, they show the way and are forerunners. The world is not yet with them, so they often seem in the midst of the world's affairs to be preposterous. . . .[2]

it turns out to be a covert reference to "getting and spending."

Henry James was certainly aware that one is always on the market, but as he grew as an artist he grew as a moralist and his use of the commercial matrix of analogy[3] became markedly satirical or ironic and his investigation of the human trade more self-conscious and profound until in nearly all the works of his maturity his theme is the evil of human manipulation, a theme best summarized by the second formulation of Kant's categorical imperative:

> So act as to treat humanity, whether in thine own person or in that of any other, in every case as an end withal, never as a means only.

Nothing further from pragmatism can be imagined, and if we first entertain the aphorism that though William was the superior thinker, Henry had the superior thought, we may be led to consider the final effect of their rivalry,[4] for the novels and stories of Henry James constitute the most searching criticism available of the pragmatic ideal of the proper treatment and ultimate worth of man. That this criticism was embodied in Henry James's style, William James was one of the first to recognize. "Your methods and my ideals seem the reverse, the one of the other," he wrote to Henry in a letter complaining about the "interminable elaboration" of *The Golden Bowl*. Couldn't we have, he asks, a "book with no twilight or mustiness in the plot, with great vigour and decisiveness in the action, no fencing in the dialogue, no psychological commentaries, and absolute straightness in the style?"[5] Henry would rather have gone, he replies, to a dishonored grave.

*The Portrait of a Lady* is James's first fully exposed case of human manipulation; his first full-dress investigation, at the level of what Plato called "right opinion," of what it means to be a consumer of persons, and of what it means to be a person consumed. The population of James's fictional society is composed, as populations commonly are, of purchasers and their purchases, of the handlers and the handled, of the users and the used. Sometimes actual objects, like Mrs. Gereth's spoils, are involved in the transaction, but their involvement is symbolic of a buying and a being sold which is on the level of human worth (where the quality of the product is measured in terms of its responsiveness to the purchaser's "finest feelings," and its ability to sound the buyer's taste discreetly aloud), and it is for this reason that James never chooses to center his interest upon objects which can, by use, be visibly consumed. In nearly all of the later novels and stories, it is a human being, not an object, it is first Isabel Archer, then Pansy, who is the spoil, and it by no means true that only the "villains" fall upon her and try to carry her off; nor is it easy to discover just who the villains really are.

Kant's imperative governs by its absence—as the hollow center. It is not that some characters, the "good" people, are busy being the moral legislators of mankind and that the others, the "bad" people, are committed to a crass and shallow pragmatism or a trifling estheticism; for were that the case *The Portrait* would be just another skillful novel of manners and James would be distinctly visible, outside the work, nodding or shaking his head at the behavior of the animals in his moral fable. He would have managed no advance in the art of English fiction. James's examination of the methods of human consumption goes too deep. He is concerned with all of the ways in which men may be reduced to the status of objects and because James pursues his subject so diligently, satisfying himself only when he has unravelled every thread, and because he is so intent on avoiding in himself what he has revealed as evil in his characters and exemplifying rather what he praises in Hawthorne who, he says, "never intermeddled,"[6] the moral problem of *The Portrait* becomes an esthetic problem, a problem of form, the scope and course of the action, the nature of the characters, the content of dialogue, the shape and dress of setting, the points-of-view, the figures of speech, the very turn and tumble of the sentences themselves directed by the problem's looked-for-solution, and there is consequently no suggestion that one should choose up sides or take to heart his criticism of a certain society nor any invitation to discuss the moral motivations of his characters as if they were surrogates for the real.

The moral problem, moreover, merges with the esthetic. It is possible to be an artist, James sees, in more than paint and language, and in *The Portrait*, as it is so often in his other work, Isabel Archer becomes the un-worked medium through which, like benevolent Svengali, the shapers and admirers of beautifully brought out persons express their artistry and them-selves. The result is very often lovely, but is invariably sad. James has the feeling, furthermore, and it is a distinctly magical feeling, that the novelist takes possession of his subject through his words; that the artist is a puppe-teer; his works are the works of a god. He constantly endeavors to shift the obligation and the blame, if there be any, to another; his reflector, his reverberator, his sensitive gong. In *The Portrait* James begins his move-ment toward the theory of the point-of-view. The phrase itself occurs inces-santly. Its acceptance as a canon of method means the loss of a single, uni-versally objective reality. He is committed, henceforth, to a standpoint philosophy, and it would seem, then, that the best world would be that observed from the most sensitive, catholic, yet discriminating standpoint. In this way, the esthetic problem reaches out to the metaphysical. This marvelous observer: what is it he observes? Does he see the world as it really is, palpitating with delicious signs of the internal, or does he merely fling out the self-capturing net? James struggles with this question most ob-viously in *The Sacred Fount* but it is always before him. So many of his characters are "perceptive." They understand the value of the unmolded clay. They feel they know, as artists, what will be best for their human me-dium. They will *take up* the young lady (for so it usually is). They will *bring her out*. They will *do for* her; *make something* of her. She will be *beautiful* and *fine*, in short, she will inspire *interest, amusement,* and *wonder*. And their pursuit of the ideally refractive medium parallels perfectly Henry James's own, except he is aware that his selected lens dare not be perfect else he will have embodied a god again, and far more obnoxious must this god seem in the body of a character than he did in the nib of the author's pen; but more than this, James knows, as his creations so often do not, that this manipulation is the essence, the ultimate germ, of the evil the whole of his work condemns, and it is nowhere more brutal than when fronted by the kindest regard and backed by a benevolent will.

*The Portrait of a Lady*, for one who is familiar with James, opens on rich sounds. None of his major motifs is missing. The talk at tea provides us with five, the composition of the company constitutes a sixth, and his treatment of the setting satisfies the full and holy seven. The talk moves in a desultory fashion ("desultory" is the repetitive word) in joking tones ("That's a sort of joke" is the repetitive phrase) from health and illness, and the ambiguity of its value, to boredom, considered as a kind of sickness, and the ambiguity of its production.[7] Wealth is suggested as a cause of boredom, then marriage is proposed as a cure. The elder Touchett warns Lord Warburton not to fall in love with his niece, a young lady recently captured by his wife to be exhibited abroad. The questions about her are:

has she money? is she interesting? The jokes are: is she marriageable? is she engaged? Isabel is the fifth thing, then—the young, spirited material. Lord Warburton is English, of course, while the Touchetts are Americans. Isabel's coming will sharpen the contrast, dramatize the confrontation. Lastly, James dwells lovingly on the ancient red brick house, emphasizing its esthetic appeal, its traditions, its status as a work of art. In describing the grounds he indicates, too, what an American man of money may do: fall in love with a history not his own and allow it, slowly, to civilize him, draw him into Europe. Lord Warburton is said to be bored. It is suggested that he is trying to fall in love. Ralph is described as cynical, without belief, a condition ascribed to his illness by his father. "He seems to feel as if he had never had a chance." But the best of the ladies will save us, the elder Touchett says, a remark made improbable by his own lack of success.

The structure of the talk of this astonishing first chapter foreshadows everything. All jests turn earnest, and in them, as in the aimless pattern of the jesters' leisure, lies plain the essential evil, for the evil cannot be blinked even though it may not be so immediately irritating to the eye as the evil of Madame Merle or Gilbert Osmond. There is in Isabel herself a certain willingness to be employed, a desire to be taken up and fancied, if only because that very enslavement, on other terms, makes her more free. She refuses Warburton, not because he seeks his own salvation in her, his cure by "interest," but rather because marriage to him would not satisfy her greed for experience, her freedom to see and feel and do. Neither Warburton nor Goodwood appeals as a person to Isabel's vanity. She is a great subject. She will make a great portrait. She knows it. Nevertheless Isabel's ambitions are at first naive and inarticulate. It is Ralph who sees the chance, in her, for the really fine thing; who sees in her his own chance, too, the chance at life denied him. It is Ralph, finally, who empowers her flight and in doing so draws the attention of the hunters.

Ralph and Osmond represent two types of the artist. Osmond regards Isabel as an opportunity to create a work which will flatter himself and be the best testimony to his taste. Her intelligence is a silver plate he will help with fruits to decorate his table. Her talk will be for him "a sort of served dessert." He will rap her with his knuckle. She will ring. As Osmond's wife, Isabel recognizes that she is a piece of property; her mind is attached to his like a small garden-plot to a deer park. But Ralph obeys the strictures *The Art of Fiction* was later to lay down. He works rather with the medium itself and respects the given. His desire is to exhibit it, make it whole, re-fulgent, round. He wants, in short, to make an image or to see one made— a portrait. He demands of the work only that it be "interesting." He effaces himself. The "case" is his concern. *The Portrait's* crucial scene, in this re-gard, is that between Ralph and his dying father. Ralph cannot love Isabel. His illness prevents him. He feels it would be wrong. Nevertheless, he takes, he says, "a great interest" in his cousin although he has no real in-fluence over her.

"But I should like to do something for her . . . I should like to put a little wind in her sails . . . I should like to put it into her power to do some of the things she wants. She wants to see the world for instance. I should like to put money in her purse."

The language is unmistakable. It is the language of Iago. Ralph wants her rich.

"I call people rich when they're able to meet the requirements of their imagination. Isabel has a great deal of imagination."

With money she will not have to marry for it. Money will make her free. It is a curious faith. Mr. Touchett says, "You speak as if it were for your mere amusement," and Ralph replies, "So it is a good deal." Mr. Touchett's objections are serenely met. Isabel will be extravagant but she will come to her senses in time. And, Ralph says,

" . . . it would be very painful to me to think of her coming to the consciousness of a lot of wants she should be unable to satisfy. . . ."
"Well, I don't know . . . I don't think I enter into your spirit. It seems to me immoral."
"Immoral, dear daddy?"
"Well, I don't know that it's right to make everything so easy for a person."[8]
"It surely depends upon the person. When the person's good, your making things easy is all to the credit of virtue. To facilitate the execution of good impulses, what can be a nobler act? . . ."
"Isabel's a sweet young thing; but do you think she's so good as that?"
"She's as good as her best opportunities. . . ."
"Doesn't it occur to you that a young lady with sixty thousand pounds may fall a victim to the fortune-hunters?"
"She'll hardly fall a victim to more than one."
"Well, one's too many."
"Decidedly. That's a risk, and it has entered into my calculation. I think it's appreciable, but I think it's small, and I'm prepared to take it. . . ."
"But I don't see what good you're to get of it. . . ."
"I shall get just the good I said a few moments ago I wished to put into Isabel's reach—that of having met the requirements of my imagination. . . ."

The differences between Gilbert Osmond and Ralph Touchett are vast, but they are also thin.

Isabel Archer is thus free to try her wings. She is thrown upon the world. She becomes the friend of Madame Merle, "the great round world herself"; polished, perfect, beautiful without a fault, mysterious, exciting, treacherous, repellent, and at bottom, like Isabel, identically betrayed; like Isabel again, seeking out of her own ruin to protect Pansy, the new subject, "the blank page," from that same round world that is herself. It is irony of the profoundest sort that "good" and "evil" in their paths should pass so closely. The dark ambitions of Serena Merle are lightened by a pathetic bulb, and it is only those whose eyes are fascinated and convinced by surface who can put their confident finger on the "really good." Ralph Touchett, and we are not meant to miss the appropriateness of his name, has not only failed to respect Isabel Archer as an end, he has failed to calculate correctly the qualities of his object. Isabel is a sweet, young thing. She is not yet, at any rate, as good as her best opportunities. The sensitive eye was at the acute point blind. Ralph has unwittingly put his bird in a cage. In a later interview, Isabel tells him she has given up all desire for a general view of life. Now she prefers corners. It is a corner she's been driven to. Time after time the "better" people curse the future they wish to save with their bequests. Longdon of *The Awkward Age* and Milly Theale of *The Wings of the Dove* come immediately to mind. Time after time the better artists fail because their point-of-view is ultimately only theirs, and because they have brought the esthetic relation too grandly, too completely into life.

In the portrait of Fleda Vetch of *The Spoils of Poynton* James has rendered an ideally considerate soul. Fleda, a person of modest means and background, possesses nevertheless the true sense of beauty. She is drawn by her friend Mrs. Gereth into the full exercise of that sense and to an appreciation of the ripe contemplative life which otherwise might have been denied her. Yet Fleda so little awards the palm to mere cleverness or sensibility that she falls in love with the slow, confused, and indecisive Owen Gereth. Fleda furthermore separates her moral and her esthetic ideals. Not only does she refuse to manipulate others, she refuses, herself, to be manipulated. The moral lines she feels are delicate. She takes all into her hands. Everyone has absolute worth. Scruples beset and surround her and not even Mrs. Gereth's righteousness, the warmth of her remembered wrongs, can melt them through. The impatience which James generates in the reader and expresses through Mrs. Gereth is the impatience, precisely, of his brother: for Fleda to act, to break from the net of scruple and seize the chance. It would be for the good of the good. It would save the spoils, save Owen, save Mrs. Gereth, save love for herself; but Fleda Vetch understands, as few people in Henry James ever do, the high brutality of such good intentions. She cannot accept happiness on the condition of moral compromise, for that would be to betray the ground on which, ideally, happiness ought to rest. Indeed it would betray happiness itself, and love, and the people and their possessions that have precipitated that problem and suggested the attractive and fatal price.

It is not simply in the organization of character, dialogue, and action that Henry James reveals The Moral Passion, nor is it reflected further only in his treatment of surroundings[9] but it represents itself and its ideal in the increasing scrupulosity of the style: precision of definition, respect for nuance, tone, the multiplying presence of enveloping metaphors, the winding around the tender center of ritual lines, like the approach of the devout and worshipful to the altar, these circumlocutions at once protecting the subject and slowing the advance so that the mere utility of the core is despaired of and it is valued solely in the contemplative sight. The value of life lies ultimately in the experienced quality of it, in the integrity of the given not in the usefulness of the taken. Henry James does not peer through experience to the future, through this future to the future futures, endlessly down the infinite tube. He does not find in today only what is needful for tomorrow. His aim is rather to appreciate and to respect the things of his experience and to set them, finally, free.

## Notes

1. William James, *The Varieties of Religious Experience*, Modern Library, New York, p. 163. God does a wholesale not a retail business, p. 484. The world is a banking house, p. 120. Catholic confession is a method of periodically auditing and squaring accounts, p. 126. Examples could be multiplied endlessly, not only in *The Varieties* but in all his work. In *The Varieties* alone consult pages: 28, 38, 39, 133, 134, 135, 138, 330, 331, 333, 340, 347, 429fn, 481, 482.

2. Ibid., p. 450.

3. Mark Schorer's expression, "Fiction and the Matrix of Analogy," *The Kenyon Review*, XI, No. 4 (1949). The commercial metaphor pervades James's work and has been remarked so frequently that it scarcely requires documentation.

4. Leon Edel develops this theme in the first volume of his biography, *Henry James: The Untried Years*, 1843–1870.

5. Quoted by R. B. Perry, *The Thought and Character of William James*, 2 vols., Boston (1935), Vol. I, p. 424.

6. *The American Essays of Henry James*, ed. by Leon Edel, Vintage, New York (1956), "Nathaniel Hawthorne," p. 23.

7. Illness, in James's novels, either signifies the beautiful thing (the Minny Temple theme) or it provides the excuse for spectatorship and withdrawal, the opportunity to develop the esthetic sense (the Henry James theme).

8. A remark characteristic of the self-made man. In the first chapter, Mr. Touchett attributes Warburton's "boredom" to idleness. "You wouldn't be bored if you had something to do; but all you young men are too idle. You think too much of your pleasure. You're too fastidious, and too idolent, and too rich." Caspar Goodwood is the industrious suitor.

9. When, for instance, in *The Portrait* Gilbert Osmond proposed to Isabel, the furnishings of the room in which their talk takes place seem to Osmond himself "ugly to distress" and "the false colours, the sham splendour . . . like vulgar, bragging, lying talk"—an obvious commentary by the setting on the action.

# [*The Portrait of a Lady*]                              Leon Edel*

## II

*The Portrait of a Lady* was the third of Henry James's large studies of the American abroad and twice as long as either of its predecessors. In *Roderick Hudson* he had posed the case of the artist, the limitations of his American background, and the frustration of his creative energy from the moment it was confronted by passion. In *The American* he had pictured an ambitious businessman, bent on civilizing himself, proud enough to know his worth, and arrogant enough to think that the best of Europe was none too good for him. *The Portrait* was envisaged as a kind of feminine version of *The American*, and James began with the thought that his Isabel Archer would be a female Christopher Newman. Indeed this may be why he named her Isabel; there is a certain logic in moving from Christopher to the Queen who sent him faring across the ocean. And Isabel Archer deems herself good enough to be a queen; she embodies a notion not unlike that of Isabella of Boston, whose motto was *C'est mon plaisir*.

In Isabel Archer, Henry wished to draw "the character and aspect of a particular engaging young woman," and to show her in the act of "affronting her destiny." Like her male predecessors she goes abroad a thorough provincial, with her "meagre knowledge, her inflated ideals, her confidence at once innocent and dogmatic, her temper at once exacting and indulgent." A person who is dogmatic and exacting on the strength of meagre knowledge can only be characterized as presumptuous; and there is presumption in Isabel, for all the delicacy of her feeling; presumption suggests also a strong measure of egotism. James presents her to us as a young romantic with high notions of what life will bring her; and also as one who tends to see herself in a strong dramatic light. She pays the penalty of giving "undue encouragement to the faculty of seeing without judging"; she takes things for granted on scanty evidence. The author confesses that she was "probably very liable to the sin of self-esteem; she often surveyed with complacency the field of her own nature." He speaks of her "mixture of curiosity and fastidiousness, of vivacity and indifference, her determination to see, to try, to know, her combination of the desultory flame-like spirit and the eager and personal creature of her conditions." And he adds: "She treated herself to the occasions of homage."

The allusion to her "flame-like spirit" suggests that Isabel images Henry's long-dead cousin Minny Temple, for he was to describe her in the same way. He was to confess that he had actually thought of Minny, in creating the eager imagination and the intellectual shortcomings of his heroine. But Minny, as he pointed out to Grace Norton, had been "incom-

*From *Henry James: The Conquest of London 1870–1881*, vol. 2, by Leon Edel, pp. 421–34.
© 1962 by Leon Edel. Reprinted by permission of Harper & Row, Publishers, Inc.

plete." Death had deprived her of the trials—and the joys—of maturity. Henry, as artist, could imagine and "complete" that which had been left undone. Nevertheless, if Isabel has something of Henry's cousin in her make-up, she has much of Henry himself. He endows her, at any rate, with the background of his own Albany childhood, and as in *Washington Square* he interpolates a section wholly autobiographical, depicting his grand-mother's house, the Dutch school from which he himself had fled in rebel-lion (as Isabel does), the "capital peach trees," which he had always sam-pled and always remembered. The scene is re-evoked years later in the autobiographies.

The most Jamesian of Henry's heroines is thus closely linked by her background and early life to her creator. And when Henry sends Isabel to Europe and makes her into an heiress, he places her in a predicament somewhat analogous to his own. Henry was hardly an "heir"; but his pen had won him a measure of the freedom which others possess through wealth. In posing the questions: what would Isabel do with her new-found privileges? where would she turn? how behave? he was seeking answers for himself as well as for her. The questions are asked in the novel by Ralph Touchett, Isabel's cousin, a sensitive invalid who has silently transferred his inheritance to her. He knows he has not long to live; and he wishes to see how Isabel's large nature will profit by endowment. If this is a sign of his love for her, and the sole way in which he can be symbolically united to her, it is also Ralph's way of living vicariously in Isabel's life and participat-ing in whatever fate her temperament may reserve for her. He, too, has a substantial fund of egotism.

Like her early predecessor in *Watch and Ward,* Isabel presently finds herself with three suitors. The first is a young man of very respectable for-tune and family, from the United States, who has pursued her abroad. His name is Casper Goodwood. He is an individual who has a "disagreeably strong push, a kind of hardness of presence, in his way of rising before her." He insists "with his whole weight and force." He is in short monoto-nously masculine; and if Isabel finds his sheer sexual force attractive it is also terrifying. Passion or sex, as with Roderick, is not freedom. She rejects Goodwood several times during the novel and flees from him at the end when she finds his kiss to be like "white lightning." When "darkness re-turned she was free."

The second suitor is less dull and much less terrifying. He is a British Lord named Warburton, a fine upstanding liberal, without too much imagi-nation, one of the types Henry has met at his club or in country houses, fortunate heir of a position in a hierarchial society and the substantial means by which to sustain it. He inspires a different kind of fear in Isabel. "What she felt was that a territorial, a political, a social magnate had con-ceived the design of drawing her into the system in which he rather invidi-ously lived and moved. A certain instinct, not imperious, but persuasive, told her to resist—murmured to her that virtually she had a system and an

orbit of her own." Social position in a word was also not freedom; moreover, social position in a hierarchical society represented a strong threat to
a woman powerful enough and egotistical enough to believe that she has
"an orbit of her own."

Isabel is romantic and young. "I'm very fond of my liberty" she says
early in the book, and she says also, "I wish to choose my fate," quite as if
the ultimate choice were hers. If we see this as containing a measure of the
egotism of youth, we must recognize that in her case it has its ingenuous
charm. Nevertheless Henrietta Stackpole, an energetic and rather meddle-
some newspaper-woman, recognizes it for what it is—for she is endowed
with not a little egotism herself. She reminds Isabel: "You can't always
please yourself; you must sometimes please other people."

At this stage Henry's heroine is still full of her hopes and dreams.
Asked to define success—a matter of some interest to her author—she replies that it is to see "some dream of one's youth come true." And asked
to define her idea of happiness she offers a vision of a journey into the unknown—"A swift carriage, of a dark night, rattling with four horses over
roads that one can't see." The concept is largely that of a girl who reads
novels. However the young lady from America does not really mean what
she says. She tries very hard to see, at every turn, the roads before her—
and in broad daylight. She is supremely cautious in action, for one so daring in her fancy. And what she discovers is that even in daylight on a clear
highway, it is possible to take a wrong turning.

### III

Isabel's wrong turning occurs without her knowledge, when she meets
a woman of a certain age who is worldly-wise and accomplished, the last
word in refinement, an American expatriate of long standing, who has absorbed Europe into her being and bestrides the Continent with that appearance of freedom and insouciance to which Isabel aspires. The charm
she exhibits, the deep attraction Isabel feels for her, are founded in part on
the girl's inexperience of people and her inability to recognize the treacher-
ies of life. The woman's name is Madame Merle. The *merle* is a blackbird.
Serena Merle introduces Isabel to another American expatriate, who lives
in a thick-walled villa in Florence on Bellosguardo, with his young daughter. At this point Henry places in his novel his early vision of Francis Boot
and Lizzie, recorded in his travel sketch of 1877, when he had mused on
the "tranquil, contented life" of the father and daughter, and the exquisite
beauty that was part of their daily existence. He had spoken of Frank and
Lizzie as "figures in an ancient, noble landscape," and Gilbert Osmond and
his daughter Pansy are such figures. Pansy, though pictured at a younger
age than Henry had ever known Lizzie, is re-imagined as having the same
cultivated qualities of the *jeune fille*, the *achieved* manners of an old civilization. Osmond, however, bears no resemblance to Boot, who was an

open, generous, näive and easy-laughing amateur of life. Osmond's sinister character derives from other sources, and in all critical speculation as to who was his "original," the principal original has been overlooked. To discover him we must compare him first with Catherine Sloper's father in *Washington Square*. He has the same intelligence and the same piercing sarcasm. As a father, Osmond is capable of the same coldness to his daughter's feelings. But he is an infinitely more malign father, and his will to power is infinitely greater than Dr. Sloper's self-aggrandizement in the Square.

"There were two or three people in the world I envied," Osmond tells Isabel shortly after meeting her, "—the Emperor of Russia, for instance and the Sultan of Turkey! There were even moments when I envied the Pope of Rome—for the consideration he enjoys." Nothing less than the Tsar of all the Russias, and the man who could claim to be holier than all others. We grant Osmond his fine irony, as he says this, but we must nevertheless recognize what it expresses. Since he cannot be Tsar or Sultan or Pope, Osmond has consoled himself with being "simply the most fastidious young gentleman living." By now he is no longer young; he is confirmed, however, in his own private domain of power, as the perfect collector of bric-a-brac and *objets d'art*, and a subtle manipulator of persons as well as things. Pansy has been made into one of those objects: and Isabel is to be added to the collection. Strange as it may seem, Osmond clearly expresses one side of Henry James—the hidden side—not as malignant as that of his creation, but nevertheless that of the individual who abjures power by clothing it in meekness and deceptive docility. In this sense, Henry is the "original" of his villain. Osmond is what Henry might, under some circumstances, have become. He is what Henry could be on occasion when snobbery prevailed over humanity, and arrogance and egotism over his urbanity and his benign view of the human comedy. Perhaps the most accurate way of describing this identification with Osmond would be to say that in creating him Henry put into him his highest ambition and drive to power—the grandiose way in which he confronted his own destiny—while at the same time recognizing in his villain the dangers to which such inner absolutism might expose him. In the hands of a limited being, like Osmond, the drive to power ended in dilettantism and petty rages. In Henry's hands the same drive had given him unbounded creativity.

Isabel and Osmond are then, for all their differences, two sides of the same coin, two studies in egotism—and a kind of egotism which belonged to their author. For Isabel, generous high-minded creature though she is, in pursuit of an abstraction she calls "freedom," insists self-centeredly (in spite of grim warnings from all her friends) that she has found it in Osmond. She sees "a quiet, clever, sensitive, distinguished man . . . a lovely studious life in a lovely land . . . a care for beauty and perfection." He is the "elegant complicated medal struck off for a special occasion" and she feels it to be her occasion. Has she not always felt she was rather "the special thing" herself—a subject of her personal homage? And now, possessed of her wealth, it is as if she could combine her own power with the quiet existence of this individual and his exquisite flower-like daughter. When she marries him she believes that it is she who brings powerful elements into the union: "she would launch his boat for him; she would be his providence." This is indeed an exalted notion of her role, and it suggests the role she assigned to Osmond. Thinking back on this later, she wonders at the "kind of maternal strain" she had possessed in her passion; she believes that her money had been her burden. But this is rationalized after the fact. Isabel and Osmond had been attracted to one another because each saw in the other a mirror-image of self. The two had experienced an irresistible need for each other and in the end they cannot suffer each other. Power may be attracted to power, but it cannot endure it. Each insists on supremacy. Osmond tries to bend Isabel to his will. She cannot be bent. Her kind of power refuses to be subjugated: it exerts its own kind of subjugation. His, more devious, returns perpetually to the assault. The impasse is complete.

Henry had written into this work two aspects of himself: there was his legitimate aspiration to freedom, and his covert drive to power hidden behind his compliance, docility, and industry. In the largest sense, egotism and power are the real subjects of *The Portrait of a Lady*, concealed behind a mask of free will and determinism. How was one to possess the power and arrogance of one's genius and still be on good terms with oneself and the world? How was one to establish relationships with people when one felt—and knew—one was superior to them? Yet how avoid loneliness and isolation? Above all, how enjoy one's freedom and not make mistakes in the exercise of it? Ralph watches Isabel make her mistakes: and it is he who in the end delivers the uncomfortable verdict that she has been "ground in the very mill of the conventional." Ralph thereby accepts Isabel at her own evaluation; he believes, as she did, that she was worthy of something more than the conventional. And beyond the unhappiness of Isabel's marriage lies the revelation that she has been the victim of a carefully-laid plot: that Madame Merle had been the mistress of Osmond; Pansy is their child; and the marriage had been arranged by the wily "blackbird" to endow Pansy with Isabel's fortune.

It is possible in this light to see that Isabel's rejection of Goodwood and Warburton went beyond the mere sense that they threatened her freedom. They would have inhibited her freedom to exercise her power. Goodwood would have imposed his masculinity and the power of his passion; Warburton would have involved Isabel in a society where the determinants of power had been fixed long before. She had looked upon one aspect of herself in Osmond and had fallen in love with it. He had done the same in looking at her. The other image, that of Osmond's selfishness and his "demonic imagination," belong in all probability to Henry's "buried life," some part of which he concealed even from himself, but which emerged from the depths in the writing of this character.

In *The Portrait of a Lady* there is a kind of continuous endowment of the characters with aspects of their author and the questions arising in his life even as he was writing the book—as if he were putting on different hats and different neckties and looking at himself in a series of mirrors. Curiously enough this observation was made long before the biographical knowledge we possess today enables us to identify this process of character infiltration. James Herbert Morse, writing in the *Century Magazine* a year after the publication of the novel observed that there was in nearly every personage of *The Portrait* "an observable infusion of the author's personality." He went on:

> The men and women are almost equally quick-witted, curt and sharp. While each has a certain amount of individuality, the sharpness is one of the elements in common, preventing a complete differentiation. It is not wit alone, and repartee, but a sub-acid quality which sets the persons to criticising each other. One does not like to call it snarling. Mr. James is too much of a gentleman to admit snarling among ladies and gentlemen; and yet every leading person in the book does, in a polite way, enter frequently into a form of personal criticism of somebody else.

Since Morse wrote these lines we have come to understand the technique by which James sought to cover up what he was doing; his method of using shifting angles of vision so as to make us feel the way in which people see one another. We see Osmond through the eyes of all the principal characters, and this dramatizes even more Isabel's blindness to his faults during the period when she is debating whether she will marry him. Morse was right, however, in feeling that in a certain sense the various speakers in the novel were "engaged in the business of helping the author develop his characters." On the level of technique, this was one of James's brilliant devices: and later he was even to boast that he created artificial characters for this purpose and managed to endow them with the attributes of life. For biography, however, this method has the unusual effect of throwing a personal shadow behind the impersonal puppets projected and fashioned by the artist's imagination. "We cannot escape the conviction," said Morse, "that he has at least so far written himself into his books that a shrewd critic could reconstruct him from them." And he went on to be the shrewd critic: "The person thus fashioned would be one of fine intellectual powers, incapable of meannesses; of fastidious tastes, and of limited sympathies; a man, in short, of passions refined away by the intellect."

This needs amendment today. The visage of the writer reflected in *The Portrait* is rather that of a man of large sympathies and powerful passions, which are in some degree inhibited, and which are struggling to be set free, indeed which are using all kinds of indirection to find some liberating channel. And it is in the relationship between Isabel and Osmond that we can best observe this at work.

In the end one feels that Isabel's disillusionment, the damage to her self-esteem and the crushing effect of her experience, reside in the shock she receives that so large a nature should have been capable of so great a mistake; and in her realization that instead of being able to maneuver her environment, as her freedom allowed, she had been maneuvered by it. Christopher Newman had had a similar shock, in the Faubourg St. Germain. But he could write it off as the corruption and deceit of the French nobility. The deeper illusion here resides in the fact that Serena Merle and Gilbert Osmond are Americans, and the implications are that as expatriates, long divorced from their native soil, they also have been corrupted: they conceal a world of evil unknown to Isabel. America had ill prepared her for this. The American and the Americana, in Henry's two novels, represented—in the larger picture—the New World's concept of its own liberties, the admixture of freedom and of power contained in America's emerging philosophy, and in the doctrines of pragmatism of which Henry's brother William was to be a founder. In drawing his novel from the hidden forces of his own experience into the palpable world of his study and observation, Henry James had touched upon certain fundamental aspects of the American character.

## IV

When he had sent off his early instalments, Henry received certain worried letters from Howells. The editor suggested that Isabel was being over-analyzed; and that the figure of the American newspaperwoman, Henrietta Stackpole, was overdrawn. "In defense of the former fault," Henry replied, "I will say that I intended to make a young woman about whom there should be a great deal to tell and as to whom such telling should be interesting; and also that I think she is analysed once for all in the early part of the book and doesn't turn herself inside out quite so much afterwards." This, in the end, was not to be true; Henry was to consider the book's finest passage to be Isabel's self-analysis after she perceives the relationship between Madame Merle and Gilbert Osmond. As for Miss Stackpole, Henry told Howells that she was not "I think really exaggerated—but 99 readers out of a 100 will think her so: which amounts to the same thing. She is the result of an impression made upon me by a variety of encounters and acquaintances made during the last few years; an impression which I had often said to myself would not be exaggerated." Henry however added that perhaps it was an impression which "the home-staying American" would not receive as vividly as the expatriate. "It is over here that it offers itself in its utmost relief."

It is possible to discover one "original" for Miss Stackpole in Henry's letters. Shortly after he had moved to London, William sent to him a young woman from Cambridge, a Miss Hillard (probably the Katherine Hillard who edited her mother's journal and later an abridgement of Madame Blavatsky's doctrines). Writing to William on June 28, 1877, Henry says: "I have got to go and see your—excuse me but I must say—accursed friend Miss Hillard, who has turned up here and writes me a note every three days, appointing an interview. I do what I can; but she will certainly tell you that I neglect her horribly. Do you admire her particularly? She is, I suppose, a very honorable specimen of her type; but the type—the literary spinster, sailing-into-your-intimacy-American-hotel-piazza type—doesn't bear somehow the mellow light of the old world, Miss H. announced her arrival here to me by writing to ask me to take her to the Grosvenor Gallery and Rembrandt etchings and then go out and dine with her—at Hammersmith miles away!—at the Conways'! And this a maid whom I had never seen!" Henry then interrupted this letter to call on Miss Hillard and on returning added: "I have in the interval of my two sentences driven over to the remote region of Paddington and back, at an expense of three shillings, to see Miss H. whom I did not find. But she will nevertheless deem that I have neglected her."

On the back of this letter, in William's hand, are the following words: "Do you notice the demoniac way in which he speaks of the sweet Miss Hillard?" Decidedly Miss H. had impressed the brothers quite differently. In a letter a few days later Henry added to the chronicle of his adventures with Miss H. "I did what I could further about Miss Hillard, who has left London: called again upon her and saw her, and went to a party at the Boughtons' in order to meet her." He added: "She is a good girl: her faults are that she is herself too adhesive, too interrogative and too epistolary. I have received (I think) seven notes and letters from her, for two or three that I have written her." The final mention of her occurs in a letter some weeks later, when Henry says to his mother of William: "His silence has led me to fear that he is 'mad' at what I wrote touching poor dear Miss Hillard; if so I take it all back."

If he took it back, he nevertheless had found his type. And Henrietta Stackpole, her forthrightness, good humor, meddlesomeness, and hundred-per-cent Americanism, in the *Portrait* was to be but the first of a number of characterizations of the gossipy American journalist abroad. Miss Stackpole is able to say all the things Goodwood, in his supreme inarticulateness, does not utter. She is completely characterized in an interchange between Isabel and Ralph: "She's a kind of emanation of the great democracy—of the continent, the country, the nation," Isabel says. And Ralph replies: "She does smell of the Future—it almost knocks one down."

## V

A great deal has been made of the resemblance of *The Portrait of a Lady* to *Daniel Deronda*. As *Roderick* had been Henry's conception of the novel Hawthorne might have written about Rome, so *The Portrait* was Henry's way of making of Isabel Archer the personality he felt George Eliot should have made of Gwendolen Harleth. His description of Gwendolen, in his dialogue on the Eliot novel, can be applied to Isabel. Henry had written that she "is a perfect picture of youthfulness—its eagerness, its presumption, its preoccupation with itself, its vanity and silliness, its sense of its own absoluteness. "But," he added, "she is extremely intelligent and clever, and therefore tragedy *can* have a hold upon her." And again: "The universe forcing itself with a slow, inexorable pressure into a narrow, complacent, and yet after all extremely sensitive mind, and making it ache with the pain of the process—that is Gwendolen's story." It is Isabel's as well. She is indeed the victim of her own complacent temperament, and the real determinism of the novel is psychological determinism. If *The Portrait of a Lady* can be related to George Eliot's novel (and the character of Grandcourt related to Osmond), the work Henry wrote is still pure James, and the distillation of his own experience, his fierce will to freedom as an artist, his hidden fear of his drive to power, his awareness that, no matter how careful one may be, one can still be betrayed by one's own egotism.

Over and above its substance *The Portrait of a Lady* established itself by degrees, as one of the best written novels of its age. In a prose of high style, with a narrative unsurpassed for its rhythmic development, with a mastery of character and of all the threads of his complicated story, Henry had created a novel that could be placed among the supreme works of the century. It introduced into a Europe that was reading Turgenev and Flaubert, and would soon be reading Tolstoy, a distinctly American heroine.

Her portrait hangs in the great gallery of the world's fiction. We can see Isabel as we saw her when she first stepped into the garden of the Touchetts, at Gardencourt; her clasped hands are in repose, they rest in the lap of her black dress. She looks at us with her light gray eyes, and her face, framed by its black hair, possesses a distinctive American beauty. She holds her head high; she possesses a great pride, and there is something arrogant in her steady gaze. The gallery in which Henry placed her was remarkable. On its walls were the paintings of many other women who, like Isabel, had never literally "lived." All of them were tissued out of the minds of their authors, mere figments of the literary imagination, creatures of the printed word. And yet they all had taken on a life of their own— Becky Sharp, or Dorothea Brooke, the Lady of the Camellias or Jane Eyre, Anna Karenina or Emma Bovary. It was as if they had really lived. And Isabel Archer, who partakes of this reality, and who actually seems to have resided in Albany, and ultimately in a palace in Rome, retains her uniqueness among her European sisters. Theirs had been largely dramas of love, often of physical passion. Isabel's had been a drama of suppressed passion, passion converted into high ideals and driven by a need for power that reckoned little with the world's harsh realities.

The painting is exquisite. Every touch of the artist's brush has been lovingly applied to his subject who though not a daughter of the Puritans, has something of their rigidity in her bearing and not a little of their hardness of surface. She looks down at us always in the freshness of her youth—and the strength of her innocence and her egotism.

## Introduction to *The Bostonians*                       Irving Howe*

In the year 1886 Henry James, by then a writer of acknowledged rank, published two lavishly composed novels, *The Bostonians* and *The Princess Casamassima*. Taken together they mark a distinct phase in his career, for not only do they constitute an impressive portion of the work he accomplished during his "middle period"—that high plateau of creativeness which begins with *The Portrait of a Lady* and ends with *The Awkward Age*—but they also share a community of subject matter and literary method that sets them somewhat apart from the bulk of James's fiction.

Both novels deal ambitiously, though also rather furtively, with the public world, with the fluid contours of society and the tempting dangers of politics. Rich and supple in style, they are written with an assurance which suggests a master's growing awareness that, come what may and be his fortune what it will, he *is* a master. In both novels James negotiates that risky transition from public to private experience which is the sure sign of a writer sensitive to the nature of society and convinced, however little he may say so, that it has a reality of its own which cannot be grasped simply by observing its members individually. And in both novels no distinction can finally be made between public and private experience, so that the deformations of the one soon become the deformations of the other. Yet James does not rest there, for he knows that the private deformations will react upon the public, causing those tragedies, absurdities and spent heroisms with which the novels are filled.

Neither the reviewers nor the public were very friendly to the two books when they first appeared. Today it is a little hard to understand why, since quite apart from any deeper or more recondite significance that may be assigned to these novels, one supposes they would have delighted readers simply through their surface vivacity, *The Princess Casamassima* by its boldness in seizing upon European anarchism for its locale, *The Bostonians* by its marvellously dry wit in satirizing New England society.

The explanation for their failure is to be found—if one can be found at all—in the quality of American culture during the 1880's. Wit and the talent it implies for self-criticism were not greatly cherished in the America of seventy years ago; an age of complacence, as we have reason to know,

*From *The Bostonians*, by Henry James. © 1956 by Random House, Inc. Reprinted by permission of Random House, Inc.

prefers that its writers avoid the satiric and astringent. *The Bostonians* wounded the self-regard of earnest middle-class readers, for it took a dim view of the New England reforming tradition which, by then, had been comfortably aligned with the national appetite for self-congratulation. In a tone of biting cleverness that must have bewildered many of his readers, James had called into question the persistent fondness of Americans for thinking of themselves as the salt of the earth—the newest salt and the best salt. Nor has time softened the force of his attack. If *The Bostonians* is read with a full awareness, which means a readiness to admit that it jars many of our fondest opinions, it becomes clear that the book is a deep-going and, thereby, radical criticism of American life.

The public failure of *The Bostonians* and *The Princess Casamassima* hurt and bewildered James. Nor was he so vain as to pretend indifference. "I have entered upon evil days," he wrote to William Dean Howells in 1888, "I am still staggering a good deal under the mysterious and (to me) inexplicable damage wrought—apparently—upon my situation by my last two novels. . . ."

To some extent this disappointment may have hastened his turn from the social novel, which meant, as he knew, to forego his earlier ambition to become the American Balzac. But for all his surface tenderness, James was not the man to be deflected from his path because reviewers were obtuse and readers apathetic. What decided him in abandoning the public themes of these two novels (he wrote to his brother) was his "sense of knowing terribly little about the kind of life I have attempted to describe." Though essentially true for *The Princess Casamassima*, this was not at all true for *The Bostonians*—which may help explain why the first is an absorbing failure and the second a masterpiece. Nonetheless, James's remark contains a shrewd self-criticism, for despite lucky hits and clever guesses he lacked that passionate absorption in the worlds of business and politics which a social novelist must have.

## II

Yet it would be a mistake to suppose that these novels constitute a mere sport in James' career. Both in the writing of nineteenth-century America and in James' own novels one can see the slow growth of a literary tradition that will reach a climax in *The Bostonians*. Those areas of native experience which an American Balzac would have had to exhaust, James had already begun to outline in his early novels. Especially noteworthy as a forerunner of *The Bostonians* is that brilliant short novel *The Europeans*, in which James struck the "New England tone" at its fine thin best, a New England tone he brought into ambiguous but finally triumphant relation with the more sumptuous tones of Europe. New England is the setting of both novels, but in *The Europeans* it is notable for its moral refinement while in *The Bostonians* it has declined into a mean and eccentric shabbiness. Between the "worlds" of the two novels there falls the shadow of the Civil War.

The roots of *The Bostonians* extend, of course, beyond James' own work. A heavy line of intellectual and literary influence can be traced from Hawthorne to James, visibly so in *The Bostonians*, deeply buried but still to be felt in such novels as *The Golden Bowl*. Both writers face problems that clearly place them as sensitive Americans living in the nineteenth century. In Hawthorne the moral sense has been largely detached from its earlier context of orthodox faith, but it has found little else in which to thrive, certainly no buoying social vision—which may explain why Hawthorne turned to allegory, the one literary mode in which it might seem possible to sustain the moral sense as an independent force. In James the moral sense is at least as acute and troublesome as in Hawthorne, but James has learned how to embody and test it through portrayals of social manners and relations. Yet the themes of the two writers are quite similar. Both are obsessed by the problem of integrity: how, they repeatedly ask, can a human being, involved as he must be in limiting and treacherous social relationships, yet maintain something of his personal uniqueness? The great sin in Hawthorne's novels, which is the presumption of taking into one's hands the destiny of another person, is also the great sin in James' novels. Both writers are concerned with the emergence and survival of personality, and both see this problem as particularly difficult in a culture where the idea, not to mention the fact, of experience is morally suspect. No portrait of Hawthorne, wrote James, "is at all exact which fails to insist upon the constant struggle which must have gone on between his shyness and his desire to know something of life; between what may be called his evasive and inquisitive tendencies." This sentence is one of the most important ever written about American literature, and not least because it is as true for James as for Hawthorne.

When Hawthorne came to write *The Blithedale Romance*, a novel that is in many ways a forerunner of *The Bostonians*, he tried to relate the problem of experience to the idealistic and sentimental reformers who had swarmed over New England in the decades before the Civil War. James' complaint that the book lacked the wounding edge of satire, that it let "the author's fellow-communists . . . off so easily," is accurate yet hardly to the point, for James failed to see that no matter what Hawthorne said about his fellow-colonists at Brook Farm they held for him the attraction of abundant and savored experience. The sexually magnificent Zenobia and even the fanatical reformer Hollingsworth are the figures in *The Blithedale Romance* through whom the blood of life pulses, while the "positive" characters are prim, dry, bleached.

Hawthorne looked upon the enthusiasm, if not the ideas, of the reformers as a temptation, and temptations can seldom serve as the object of satire. James, however, had taken a step beyond temptation; his reformers no longer have the capacity for a large irregular experience, they have declined into eccentric chatter. When he wrote that *The Blithedale Romance* was too mild he was not really telling us very much about the book; he was anticipating the assumptions from which *The Bostonians* would later be written.

But in another criticism of *The Blithedale Romance* James was far more acute:

> As the action advances in *The Blithedale Romance* we get too much out of reality . . . I should have liked to see the story concern itself more with the little community in which its earlier scenes are laid. . . .

This seems exactly right—yet, one may wonder, isn't it also true for *The Bostonians*, a novel in which the first 150 pages treat brilliantly of the world of Boston reform and the remainder narrows down to a personal struggle between Olive Chancellor, the bitter feminist, and Basil Ransom, the Southern conservative? I hope to show that it is not true. For James, whether knowingly or not, had found a way of avoiding the weakness that had beset Hawthorne when he tried to deal with an American political theme and would beset most other American novelists when they confronted American politics. In almost every nineteenth-century American novel which touches, no matter how gingerly, on the life of politics, one comes up against the despairing cry: *It is too late, there is no place for the sensitive and thoughtful man, perhaps there never was.*

This cry is heard most sharply in Henry Adams' *Democracy*, a novel published seven years before *The Bostonians;* it is heard, even if dimly and muffled in *The Blithedale Romance.* James, who had fewer hopes or illusions than most American writers, shared in this feeling, yet he found a way of avoiding its literary price; he found a way of avoiding that surrender to the "evasive tendency," that withdrawal from the urgencies of the subject matter, which occurs about midways through so many American novels dealing with the life of politics.

### III

James generally started a novel with a clear sketch in mind of his essential themes and structure. In a notebook entry for 1883 he wrote concerning the relationship of Olive Chancellor and Verena Tarrant that it "should be a study of one of those friendships between women which are so common in New England." After remarking that the idea for the book had been suggested to him by Daudet's *Évangéliste*, he goes on to say:

> If I could only do something with that pictorial quality. At any rate, the subject is very national, very typical. I wished to write a very American tale, a tale very characteristic of our social conditions, and I asked myself what was the most salient and peculiar point in our social life. The answer was: the situation of women, the decline of the sentiment of sex, the agitation on their behalf.

What is more, the device through which James generally works out a disciplined relation to his material—the strict confinement of a novel's "point of view" to one or two observing characters—does not seem to interest him very much in *The Bostonians*. Judged by narrowly "Jamesian" standards, *The Bostonians* might even be said to suffer from an undisciplined pictorial looseness. But if so, we have every reason to be grateful. Much of its charm, even some of its wit, comes from James' affectionate rendering of places and scenes. The elegance of Olive Chancellor's drawing room, the dinginess of the Cambridge street in which the Tarrants live, the glimmering mildness of Cape Cod in the summer—these are among the permanent values of the book. The musty mumbling circle of reformers meeting, and sagging, in Miss Birdseye's rooms, the wonderful and gently satirized Miss Birdseye as she summons the heroic past of Abolitionism, the moment when Ransom and Verena stand gravely before the scroll of the dead in Memorial Hall, the brutal clash between Ransom and Olive at Verena's New York debut—these scenes, etched with a dry sharp clarity, stay fresh and alive in one's mind.

But even in terms of strict loyalty to his theme, James was entirely right in turning to the pictorial method. The dramatic concentration that is gained from seeing an action through the eyes of one or two sensitive observers is sometimes possible in *The Bostonians*, and then the camera narrows down to the blighted vision of Olive Chancellor or Basil Ransom. But such a narrowing is not always desirable. For *The Bostonians* as conceived, and its first 150 pages as written, it is essential that we gain a sense of the larger workings and rhythms of society, which in most of James' novels, confined as they are to private dramas, he can afford to skimp. One of the ways, for example, in which James suggests that the glories of Abolitionism and the Boston reform movements are a thing of the past is by showing us the slowly accumulating seediness of the city itself as it stumbles into the factory age:

> [From Olive Chancellor's window one could see] a few chimneys and steeples, straight, sordid tubes of factories and engine shops, or spare, heavenward finger of the New England meeting house. There was something inexorable in the poverty of the scene, shameful in the meanness of its details, which gave a collective impression of boards and tins and frozen earth, sheds and rotting piles, railway-lines striding flat across a thoroughfare of puddles . . . loose fences, vacant lots, mounds of refuse, yards bestrewn with iron pipes, telegraph poles and bare wooden backs of places.

Apart from such superb descriptive passages, James' yielding to the pictorial impulse makes possible a treatment of character that sets *The Bostonians* apart from most of his other novels. James' excessive identification with the weakness and deprivations of his more vulnerable characters— which mars such books as *Roderick Hudson*, *The Portrait of a Lady* and *The Princess Casamassima*—is here no problem at all. There are no "poor shabby gentlemen" in *The Bostonians* over whom James can quiver and softly moan, no brave American girls trapped in the moral pits of Europe. The luxury of renunciation, one of the few to which James was ever susceptible, does not tempt him in *The Bostonians*, for the characters of this novel do try to live by their desires. In *The Bostonians* James keeps his distance, often a quite cool and hostile distance, from almost all of his characters; he is not, in any damaging sense, involved with their destinies.

But James' concern with the pictorial does something even more remarkable for *The Bostonians*. It allows him a free and happy release of aggressive feelings such as he seldom ventures in his other novels: he needn't, in *The Bostonians*, "consider" his characters too tenderly, they are fair game, at times mere objects of satire—and it would be sanctimonious to deny that James finds a distinct pleasure, or that we share it, in swooping down on the frauds and quacks of Boston. When we first meet Olive Chancellor, we are told that a smile playing about her lips "might have been likened to a thin ray of moonlight resting upon the walls of a prison." Selah Tarrant, mesmerist father of Verena, "looked like the priest of a religion that was passing through the stage of miracles"; Matthias Pardon, the poisonous reporter, "regarded the mission of mankind upon earth as a perpetual evolution of telegrams." In such sentences, and in the passages from which they are drawn, the prose races forward with a spontaneous sharpness and thrust, it breathes an assurance that permits James to risk, and control, the broadest touches of burlesque.

The qualities I have related to James' striving for pictorial effects are central to the book, and all of them contribute to its underlying tone or attitude. *The Bostonians* is infused with skepticism, not only in regard to New England reformers but also to the claims and pretensions of American society as a whole. The idea of social reform is treated less with hostility—for it isn't ideas as such that form his main target—than with cool and ironic misgivings. This may be offensive to our liberal or radical pieties, but there, as James might say, it is. Nor is the offense to conservative pieties any the less, for it is precisely the conservative mood of the book that brings it into a certain conflict with conservative doctrine.

James' skepticism is that of a man who is living, and knows he is living, in the backwash of a great historical moment. It is the skepticism of a man who in his own life has known something about the reformers of yesterday (many of them friends of his father, Henry James, Sr., himself one of the more attractive figures of the Emersonian Age) and who wants little to do with them, except perhaps to honor their memories. Though entirely nonpolitical in the ordinary sense, James had been a warm partisan of the North during the Civil War, and the fact that the years of sacrifice and consecration had been followed by a time in which mediocrity and downright venality dominated national life, had left a scar upon his consciousness. James, to be sure, felt none of the frustration at having been brushed aside by the politics of his time that ate into the heart of Henry Adams, but he understood—or sensed—the nature of the social and moral changes that were brushing aside people like Adams. The bitterness that rises from every page of Adams' *Democracy* is a far more intense emotion than the skepticism of *The Bostonians,* but given the differences in temperament, character and ambition of the two men, they still share many implicit attitudes toward the America of the 1870s and 1880s. Both stand on the margin of American society, estranged from its dominant powers, helpless before the drift toward a world of industry and finance, money and impersonality. Only, Adams grows heartsick watching the death of the earlier America to which he is emotionally pledged, while James finds a kind of solace, to say nothing of a remarkable fulfillment, in the practice of his art.

## IV

*The Bostonians* charts the parallel disarrangement, sometimes verging on a derangement, of public and private, political and sexual life. James was bold enough to see that the two spheres of experience could not be kept apart, and that it would be a fatal error for a novelist if he tried to. He was even bolder in supposing that the ideological obsessions which form so constant a peril for public life will leave their mark, not merely on social behavior, but also on the most intimate areas of private experience.

This boldness of observation is beautifully mirrored in James' prose. Because he is so thoroughly in command of the relation between public and private experience, James can allow himself an epigrammatic swiftness and "hardness" of style that is rare in both his earlier and his later work. For he is writing on the secure assumption that the social surface can be made to yield the necessary clues as to what is happening beneath it—and this may help explain why in *The Bostonians* James is so much less concerned than in his other novels with getting to the "essence" of characters and situations, why he places a higher value on the outer grain and texture of experience. It is for similar reasons that neither Olive Chancellor nor Basil Ransom changes very much in the course of the novel, or that no revelation is made of previously unseen depths in their characters. Both are essentially the same at the end that they were at the beginning, except that one has triumphed and the other has been defeated; and it is precisely to the clash leading to the triumph and the defeat that our main attention is directed. We are concerned here primarily with the terms of their struggle, and concerned on the assumption that, in the hands of a writer like James, this will tell us all we need to know.

In seeing how ideology—the systematized hardening of ideas—can penetrate even the most private areas of experience, James anticipated one of the great insights of psychoanalytic theory: that the price of a complex civilization is often the complex diminution of pleasure. And he understood, as well, that civilization seems to take a malicious delight in exacting this price from those most intent on reforming it. All the major characters in *The Bostonians*—Olive Chancellor, through her need to reject both the masculine and feminine modes of life, Verena Tarrant, through her need to believe in the wisdom of those who make demands on her, Basil Ransom, through his need to proclaim his masculinity as if it were a manifesto—are victims not only of each other but also of themselves. Olive Chancellor is an open enemy of the pleasure principle, because she knows it cannot be reconciled with her peculiar brand of feminism; Verena Tarrant is a befuddled enemy, because she has "bad lecture-blood in her veins"; and even Basil Ransom, the one character ready to invoke the pleasure principle, does not and cannot really live by it.

*The Bostonians*, said James, was to be concerned with "the decline in the sentiment of sex"—a phrase that can be read in at least two ways. One of them would point to the problematic status of women in modern society, the other to the equally problematic relation between pleasure and civilization. Not one of the people in *The Bostonians* has a secure sense—so secure, that is, as to require neither affirmation nor discussion—of what his culture expects from him in his sexual role. All of them are displaced persons, floating vaguely in the large social spaces of America.

What one notices first is the extent to which a breakdown has occurred in the traditional role of women—a role that is more exalted in national legend than in actuality. And while Basil Ransom is ready to talk about the proper place of women, who are for him the solacing and decorative sex, James is far too much a realist to suggest that they can or ever will again assume this place: even Ransom's lady relatives in Mississippi, deprived of their darkies, have been reduced to hard work. If Ransom is expressing James' views at all, it is in a style so deliberately inflated as to carry the heaviest ironic stress. In the hidden depths of the novel there may be some notion of what a harmonious relationship between the sexes should be, but it is not the relationship Ransom advocates and, except for vague intimations of a comely conservatism, it is not a relationship James could easily have specified. Nor was there any reason why he should have. It was enough that he so brilliantly observed the dislocations of sentiment and status which create, in almost all the characters of the novel, a nagging, distinctly "modern" anxiety.

Part of the humor in *The Bostonians*—at times, it must be admitted, a rather hard-spirited humor—comes from James' quickness at seizing upon those large glaring elements of the ridiculous that were inherent in the feminist movement and, for that matter, in the whole feminine effort to find new modes of social conduct. Yet James is fair enough to grant that feminism cannot be understood as if it were a mere sport of the New England mind. That such a movement could hardly avoid neurotic and morbid contaminations seems obvious enough: no social movement can. But this fact would hardly be very interesting if James did not also see feminism as inseparable from the conditions of American culture, as emblematic of a social and moral malaise. James understood that, while his immediate task was to focus on whatever might be strange and eccentric in his subject, his final aim could only be to present a critical vision of American life.

Far from indulging any notions about "eternal" wars between the sexes—Olive Chancellor and Basil Ransom can hardly be said to represent the sexes!—James established his drama in the actualities of late nineteenth-century American life. The form, the tone, the quality of feminism in *The Bostonians* is not to be imagined as existing anywhere and at any time but those specified by James—which is to say that it is part of the vast uprooting of American life which begins after the Civil War and has not yet come to an end.[1]

If, then, *The Bostonians* is concerned with dramatizing a parallel disarrangement of social and sexual life, what are we to make of the underlying view of society or, if you wish, of human behavior from which the book is written?

Part of the answer, I think, has already been suggested. James writes from a conservative skepticism that is more readily understood as a cultural value than as an explicit politics. This conservative skepticism is a remnant of politics, not his own, but that of his family and tradition, which James is perhaps repudiating but more likely shedding. Like many writers who appear after an age in which politics has been important, James registers a certain impatience with the idea or the need for politics. And like the good innocent American that on one side of himself he was to remain throughout his life, James is also registering an uneasy contempt for the very idea of "public life," which for him would always be at odds with private values.

At times this comes rather close to being an esthetic (perhaps even an esthete's) reaction to the life of politics, a judgment of one area of experience in terms of another, which is almost always a dangerous kind of judgment to make. One of the few times that James relaxes his hostility to Olive Chancellor is the moment she draws back from the feminists because they offend, not her moral sense, but her fastidious sensibility. Throughout the book there are occasions in which James seems to be applying small measures to large matters, judging difficult social and moral issues by esthetic criteria a little too neat for the job.

But both his conservative skepticism and his occasional estheticism are secondary to the perception that lies at the heart of the novel: that somehow, for reasons he cannot quite grasp, the proportions and rhythms of life in America have gone askew. In the mass industrial society that was coming into existence toward the end of the nineteenth century, the role of the sexes with regard to one another was no longer clear, the centers of authority and affection had become blurred, the continuity of family culture was threatened, but most important of all: the idea of what it meant to be human had come into question. All that we have since associated with industrial society was moving into sight—call it depersonalization or *anomie*, the sapping of individuality or the loss of tradition. James could not quite meet this problem through a frontal attack, but in *The Bostonians* he approached it in his own way. He did not specify the social coordinates, the fundamental causes, of the problem, but he dramatized and elaborated it with a critical sharpness that no American novelist has yet surpassed. Basil Ransom, the recalcitrant Southerner, was a convenient device for marshalling the possibilities of opposition to things as they were: he appealed to James' sense of complaint and his sense of humor; but it went no further, James' irony spared him no less than it spared anyone else in *The Bostonians*.

V

For a writer who is often said to shy away from physical experience, James, in *The Bostonians*, seems remarkably aware of the female body. It is an awareness that comes into play somewhat negatively, since he is presenting a singularly unattractive group of women; but his acute and witty apprehension of their sexlessness or their sexual distortions would be quite impossible if he did not have in reserve a sense of the possibilities of human sexuality.

Mrs. Luna's "hair was in clusters of curls, like bunches of grapes; her tight bodice seemed to crack with vivacity." Verena Tarrant, predictably, has "a flat young chest" and Miss Birdseye "no more outline than a bundle of hay." Dr. Prance is "spare, dry, hard, . . . If she had been a boy she would have borne some relation to a girl, whereas Dr. Prance appeared to bear none whatever." Olive Chancellor's appearance is deliberately left vague, except for the clue given our sense of catastrophe when we learn, upon her first meeting with Ransom, of "the vague compassion which [her] figure excited in his mind."

Not only do these descriptions quiver with a life of their own, they also point to the social relations and complications that James is trying to illuminate. The disarrangements of society, as sometimes the obsessions of politics, are embodied in the often deformed and grotesque sexual lives of the characters, and particularly the women.

Mrs. Luna, that bound and bulging female, claims to command the traditional resources of her sex, but the claim is so preposterous as to become a subject for comic by-play. She seems always to have just emerged from the armory of her boudoir, wielding the weapons of sexual calculation with so absurd a belief in their power that they quite obliterate her personal sex. ("Mrs. Luna was drawing on her gloves; Ransom had never seen any that were so long; they reminded him of stockings, and he wondered how she managed without garters at the elbows.") Yet she is at least as far as any woman in the novel from the norm of womanliness James seems to have intended, for her sexuality has turned rancid, it has been corrupted into a strategy for social acquisition.

For all the moral and psychological differences between them, Mrs. Luna and Olive Chancellor occupy symmetrical points of distance from their society: it is hardly an accident that James imagined them as sisters who despise one another. Olive Chancellor regards the sexual impulse as an enemy of her purpose, Mrs. Luna employs it as a convenience of her ego. In Olive the sexual impulse has been starved by her radical fanaticism, in Mrs. Luna it has been debased by her conservative parasitism. Olive feels nothing but aggression toward society, Mrs. Luna wishes merely to appropriate its comforts. Nonetheless, Olive's rejection of the feminine role and Mrs. Luna's exploitation of it have many elements in common. Both are self-betrayed in their life as women, the one through the grandeur of ideology and the other through the paltriness of vanity. Neither really "belongs" anywhere, Olive keeping a finicky distance from the reformers with whose cause she identifies, Mrs. Luna being unable to break into the elegant social circles to which she aspires. And in both women the waste of sexual power is paralleled by a social malaise that seeps into their very souls, leaving one of them embittered and the other petulant.

Except for the still impressionable Verena, all the women in the novel seem, by intent, off-center and abnormal, lacking in womanliness or femininity. Dr. Prance, for example, represents an extreme possibility of feminism; she is a comic grotesque, rather likable for her blunt common sense but also frightening in her disciplined incapacity for emotion. She is a *reductio*, though hardly *ad absurdum*, of feminism, a warning of what it could become if driven to its extreme. For she has done what Olive Chancellor would like to do but cannot quite manage: she has totally denied her life as a woman. This, James seems to be saying, is how you may yet prance, dear ladies—like the good and terrible Mary Prance.

But James was too shrewd an observer, and too skilled a novelist, to set off against this grim specter of feminism an ideal or idealized figure of feminine loveliness. Verena Tarrant has little but her promise, and her promise consists of little but her malleability. If all the other characters are seen in their activity, she alone is treated in terms of her "essence," so that no matter how much her outer, social being has been tarnished by the quackery of Boston there remains a pure feminine center, available to none but Basil Ransom.

If James meant Verena as the one "positive" moral force, the one figure toward whom our response should be more sympathetic than ironic, he failed; for she is unable—she simply is not interesting enough—to assume so crucial a role. But if she is intended mainly as a charming creature over whose imperilled innocence a violent battle of ideologies is being fought, he brilliantly succeeded. For seen in this way Verena need exert no active power, she need only be more attractive and receptive than the other women—which, in the circumstances, is not very difficult.

Still, James is not given to romantic idealizations in *The Bostonians* and even toward Verena, one of its few attractive figures, he can show a healthy disrespect. In a chilling passage toward the end of the novel, he proves himself quite aware that even at its most apparently innocent the feminine character can have a biting malice of its own and an aggressiveness that is almost as great a threat to male assurance as the open assaults of the feminists. When Verena asks Ransom, "Why don't you write out your ideas?", James remarks with a stress that is unmistakable: "This touched again upon the matter of his failure; it was curious how she couldn't keep off it, hit it every time." And this, we may surmise, will be Verena's role in the future; to "hit it off every time" her all too normal contribution to the felicities of domestic life in America.[2]

But it is through Olive Chancellor that James registers the full and terrible price that is paid by a first-rate intelligence as it is ravaged by social disorder and psychological obsession. Her condition is analyzed with so fine a touch that for a time it almost seems true, as some critics have argued, that she is merely the sum of her symptoms. Finally, however, it is not at all true, for precisely the ruthlessness in James' treatment of Olive, his refusal, except perhaps at the very end, to offer her a shred of sympathy, drives him to the most intense dramatization of her predicament. Were he sympathetic to Olive, James could risk a number of literary short cuts, but being hostile he must, for persuasion's sake, depict and penetrate and comment with a particular fullness.

Conceiving of herself as a St. Theresa of Beacon Hill, Olive is afflicted with a yearning for martyrdom that can find no satisfactory release, if only because she cannot bear to acknowledge the private and contaminated sources of this yearning. Her rejection of femininity goes far beyond a distaste for the traditional status of women: it is part of her fundamental impatience with the elementary conditions of human life. ("It was the usual things of life that filled her with silent rage; which was natural enough inasmuch as, to her vision, almost everything that was usual was iniquitous.") She rejects the idea of "the natural," either as fact or category. Olive's sexual ambiguity, like her social rootlessness, is in part due to her fastidious incapacity for accepting any of the available modes of life. It would be a gross error to see her feminist ideas simply as a rationalization for her private condition, since part of what she says—it might be remembered—happens to be true. Partly her rebellion is against society, but her mistake is to suppose it entirely against society; she does not see—how can she bear to see?—that it is also against herself, and not merely against that which, by accident or luck, is misshapen in herself but against all that is biologically "given" or conditioned in human life.

Olive's lesbianism becomes both cause and emblem of her social incapacity. Though James hardly presents heterosexual relations in any ideal light, he implies that they at least make possible sustained and regular communication between human beings, thereby becoming one of the tacit means by which society is knit together. Olive's lesbianism, however—partly because it is antipathetic to society, partly because it is suppressed—cuts her off from everyone, except for a time Verena, and renders her incapable of genuine communication in either public or private life. Only in light of this fact can one grasp how overwhelming, indeed almost shocking a humiliation James imposes upon her in the final scene where she is forced to placate an audience roaring with impatience to hear her lost and beloved Verena.

Seen from one point of view, Olive is a descendant of Hawthorne's villains—but with this crucial difference, that James realizes she commits the great sin of manipulating human beings not from some sourceless malignity but from her own clearly specified sickness and vulnerability. Actually, she is the most vulnerable figure in the book and toward the end James allows not merely an awareness of how painful her defeat is (for she is never even granted a confrontation, she is simply run away from) but also a sense that in defeat she achieves a gloomy sort of magnificence.

Her symptoms are presented with a remarkable directness: persistent hysteria, a will to power that is inseparable from a will to prostration, an unqualified aggression toward men.[3] Her activities always demand analysis in terms of something other than their apparent meaning. When she talks about politics, we think of sex; when she talks about love, we think of the urge to power; when she talks about history, we think of humiliation. Yet, as James keeps insisting, she is a woman of attainment and rectitude—were she not at least the intellectual equal of Basil Ransom, her defeat would hardly matter. Her fanaticism is a function of a gnarled and impoverished psyche; her destructive will, the means by which ideology is transformed into hysteria. Both as a person in her own right and as the agent of a mean and narrowing culture, she is lost.

## VI

In opposition to this disordered world Basil Ransom stands for—for what? It is a temptation to see him as the representative of masculine strength, traditional order, conservative wit. Thus, one critic:

> Of first-rate intelligence, completely "unreconstructed," holding "unprogressive" ideas of manliness, courage and chivalry, Basil Ransom . . . has a set of civilized principles to fall back upon. . . .

Another critic:

> By choosing a Southerner for his hero, James gained an immediate and immeasurable advantage. . . . When he involved the feminist movement with even a late adumbration of the immense tragic struggle between North and South, he made it plain that his story had to do with a cultural crisis. . . .
>
> James conceived Ransom as if he were the leading, ideal intelligence of the group of gifted men who, a half-century later, were to rise in the South and to muster in its defense whatever force may be available to an intelligent romantic conservatism. . . .
>
> [Ransom] has the courage of the collateral British line of romantic conservatives—he is akin to Yeats, Lawrence and Eliot in that he experi-

ences his cultural fears in the most personal way possible, translating them into sexual fear, the apprehension of the loss of manhood.

These remarks seem to me an instance of how critics can be "taken in" by a character who did not for a moment delude his creator. From the very moment we see him, Basil Ransom—an opinionated provincial ("he had read Comte, he had read everything")—is treated by James with a cool and detached irony. Ransom *does* have a considerable attractiveness, if only because he is trying, by the force of his will, to extricate himself from defeat. But he can lay claim to none but personal powers; his cultural tradition is smashed and no one knows this better than he. It is true that he is free from the small shabbiness of the New England mind in its decline, but neither does he command anything resembling its original power; for him, writes James, vice was "purely a species of special cases of explicable accidents." And while he lays claim to a disenchanted realism, he reveals more than a touch, as James meant he should, of the sentimental and callow. He considered that women "were essentially inferior to men and infinitely tiresome when they refused to accept the lot which men had made for them"— an example, no doubt, of the "civilized principles" upon which he can fall back.

James' tone is unmistakable. Ransom's appearance, he writes, "might have indicated that he was to be a great American statesman; or, on the other hand, [it] might simply prove that he came from Carolina or Alabama." A little later James remarks of Ransom that "he had an immense desire for success," thereby noting that side of the Southern conservative which, if given half the chance, will out-Northern the Northerners. Still later, James writes that Ransom's "scruples were doubtless begotten of a false pride, a sentiment in which there was a thread of moral tinsel, as there was in the Southern idea of chivalry. . . ."

But most remarkable of all is the incident in which Ransom solemnly declares himself ready for both marriage and the future on the extraordinary ground that one of his essays has finally been accepted by "The Rational Review," a journal of which the title sufficiently suggests both its circulation and influence. If nothing else, this would be enough to convince us that Ransom is as naively and thoroughly, if not as unattractively, the victim of a fanatical obsession as Olive Chancellor—this characteristic delusion of the ideologue (the pathos of which is one of the few things that makes poor Ransom endearing) that if only his precious words once appear in print, the world will embrace his wisdom and all will be well.

Were Ransom an "ideal intelligence," the novel would be hopelessly unbalanced. For what possible drama or significance could there be in a clash between so exalted a figure as he would then be and so wretched an antagonist as Olive Chancellor? The truth, I would suggest, is that in his way Ransom is as deeply entangled with his ideology as Olive with hers, and that the clash between styles of culture which is supposed to be reflected in their struggle is actually a rather harsh comedy in which both sides, even if to unequal degrees, are scored off by James.

Nowhere is this truer than in Ransom's presumed "apprehension of the loss of manhood." For while it is a common assumption of our culture that the "biological" is the most profound and fundamental variety of experience, before which all else must seem pale and unreal, it is worth remembering that the biological, or the sense of it, can also become imbued with ideology. In the case of Ransom, his "apprehension of the loss of manhood," in addition to being an authentic personal emotion, is frequently part of his rhetoric of moral and intellectual aggrandizement.

This, indeed, is the great stroke of *The Bostonians*: that everything, even aspects of private experience supposedly inviolable, is shown to be infected with ideology. When Ransom, in his Central Park speech, appeals to Verena to break from Olive, he does so not merely in the name of his personal love but also through the catch-words of politics, and curiously enough one that is closer to New England radicalism than to Southern conservatism: he urges her to stand forth in the name of *personal freedom*. When Olive and Verena listen to Beethoven, "symphonies and fugues only stimulated their convictions, excited their revolutionary passion. . . ."—the very music becomes a medium of ideology. Everything is touched by it, from politics to sex, from music to love.

That being so, we are in a better position to judge the complaint often made about *The Bostonians*, that there is a loss of certainty and brilliance midway through the book. It is true that *The Bostonians* does falter about halfway, but only because James is not quite sure how to manage one of the boldest and most brilliant transitions of his entire work. The first 150 pages of the novel present directly a world of contention and decline: there follows a somewhat hesitant section, set mainly in New York—and then the struggle is resumed, more bitterly, more fiercely, more poisonously, on the face of it a struggle of love but in its depths a struggle of politics.

Ransom wins. Despite all of James's qualifications in regard to Ransom, he grants him certain attractions and powers. Ransom is no poor shabby gentleman watching life glide away; he is a man of energy and will, as hard as Olive and less frenetic. And for James, always a little uneasy before the more direct forms of masculine energy, there is a fascination in seeing this energy exert itself. But the logic of the book itself demands that Ransom win. For if the struggle between Ransom and Olive over Verena is a struggle between competing ideologies over a passive agent of the natural and the human, then it is a struggle between ideologies that are not equally in opposition to the natural and the human. When she is finally driven to her choice, Verena chooses in accordance with those rhythms of life which Olive bluntly violates, but Ransom merely exploits. In a dazzling final sentence James writes that "It is to be feared that with the union, so far from brilliant, into which she was about to enter, these [tears] were not the last she was destined to shed." What James thought of Ransom's pretensions, what he made of the whole affair, how thoroughly he maintained the critical and ironic tone throughout the book, is suggested in this hint that Ransom and Verena, married at last, would live unhappily ever after.

## Notes

1. The disposition to speak of society in metaphors drawn from personal life was to remain with James throughout his life. Some 20 years after *The Bostonians*, he wrote of devastated Richmond:

> The feminization is there just to promote for us some eloquent antithesis; just to make us say that whereas the ancient order was masculine, fierce and mustachioed, the present is at most a sort of sick lioness who has so visibly parted with her teeth and claws that we may patronizingly walk around her.

2. The idea that passive femininity can subdue male energy as aggressive feminism cannot is another link between *The Blithedale Romance* and *The Bostonians*. In Hawthorne's novel the saturnine reformer, Hollingsworth, is finally captured and tamed by Priscilla, a pale New England maiden who, like Verena, has been involved in mesmerist exercises. Toward the Priscilla-Verena figure and all that she stands for Hawthorne betrays a deeper, if more cautious, hostility than James: he had more at stake.

3. It is sometimes asked whether James "really knew" how thoroughly he had drawn a lesbian type. The question is relevant only if we suppose that because people of an earlier age did not use our vocabulary they necessarily understood less than we do.

## *The Princess Casamassima*                              Oscar Cargill*

In his Preface to *The Princess Casamassima* James tells us that "the simplest account" of the origin of this novel is that it "proceeded quite directly . . . from the habit and interest of walking the streets." He goes on to tell how his perambulations suggested to him the creation of "some individual sensitive nature or fine mind," a product of those streets yet capable of profiting from all of the civilization that London afforded—all the "freedom and ease, knowledge and power, money, opportunity and satiety, . . . but . . . with every door of approach shut in his face." In sum, "I arrived so at the history of little Hyacinth Robinson—he sprang up for me out of the London pavement."[1]

The foregoing may, indeed, be "the simplest account" of the origin of the novel, but it is characteristically far from being a full or adequate account. To begin with, Daniel Lerner has pointed out how much *The Princess* owes directly to Ivan Turgenev's *Virgin Soil* (1876).[2]

Lerner is not content with showing the resemblances between the heroes of the two stories and the involvements into which their separate ca-

*Reprinted from *The Novels of Henry James* by Oscar Cargill. © 1961 by Oscar Cargill. Reprinted with permission of Macmillan Publishing Company.

reers are launched; he brings out important and detailed resemblances between the supporting casts in each novel. Each has its "vivid oddities": Fomishka and Fimishka in *Virgin Soil;* Miss Pynsent and Mr. Vetch in *The Princess.* "Turgenev's Snandulia, crippled sister of the revolutionary Paklin, is matched by James's Rosy Muniment, crippled sister of the revolutionary Paul. Both crippled sisters are impoverished, but devoted to . . . the aristocracy." Each novel is provided with a revolutionary leader, "cool, reasonable, balanced, devoted to the cause without excess emotion," who serves as an antithesis or counterpoise to the aesthetic hero. Nezhdanov thinks of his leader, Solomin, in exactly the same terms as Hyacinth, lying on the river bank, thinks of Paul Muniment: " 'He knows what he wants, has confidence in himself, and arouses confidence in others. He has no anxieties and is well balanced! That is the main thing: he has balance, just what is lacking in me.'[3] Hyacinth and Nezhdanov are thus excellent examples of 'fatal Hamletism,' of the constitutional inability to match ideas to action which Turgenev discussed in his famous dichotomy of human natures, *Hamlet and Don Quixote."*

With the three important women in Nezhdanov's life, however, with Mme Sipyagina, Mashurina, and Mariana, James does some fancy juggling of roles and traits to produce the Princess, Lady Aurora, and Millicent Henning. The beauty of Mariana, a lady by birth, is vulgarized and given to the sexually attractive cockney, Miss Henning, while the purity and sincerity of the proletarian conspirator Mashurina are given to Lady Aurora Langrish who, at the same time, is made "big, ugly, and awkward." Sipyagina, according to Lerner, is scaled upward to become the Princess. "The novels are identical even to details. Both aristocratic women are lost to the 'strong, balanced men,' Solomin and Muniment, who treat them in a far different manner than had Nezhdanov and Hyacinth. Solomin and Muniment take the advances of these aristocratic ladies calmly, regard their progressive views skeptically, and announce they might be willing to 'use' them for the cause. The 'young ladies by birth' who are genuinely devoted to the cause, Mariana and Lady Aurora, are also lost to Solomin and Muniment. When Hyacinth loses his last refuge, Millicent Henning, he blows a bullet through his head—as does Nezhdanov."

Lerner's detailed analysis of the dependence of *The Princess Casamassima* on *Virgin Soil,* besides suggesting the aims of Henry James in his novel, controverts the general notion that *The Princess* is a product largely of James's observation[4] and makes it instead his most derivative book. But a derivative book with James is more original than the utterly free invention of another man. Though he had persuaded his friend Thomas Sergeant Perry to translate *Virgin Soil* for Turgenev's sake, he had held it to be "a very slight affair."[5]

James's private judgment of *Virgin Soil* is correct;[6] his use of it, then, was an act of salvage of its "many fine things." But it would not appear that when he launched himself upon his own novel he had any intention of laying his source under any such contribution;[7] his commitment to supply the *Atlantic* with installments, while *The Bostonians* was still in the serialization stage, forced this expedient upon him. His original intention seems to have been to gather the materials for his novel in Zolaesque fashion, with notebook in hand;[8] at least he started out to do this, for on December 12, 1884, he wrote his friend "Tommy" Perry, "I have been all the morning at Millbank prison (horrible place) collecting notes for a fiction scene. You see I am quite the Naturalist. Look out for the same—a year hence."[9] This visit to Millbank furnished the materials, of course, for the prison scene in the novel, admired by William James and Robert Louis Stevenson.[10] Further evidence of his desire to proceed in this way is found in two things: his expressed wish to go to Ireland in order to "see a country in a state of revolution"[11] and the article which he put together on "London" after *The Princess* was finished,[12] out of the residue notes, possibly, for that volume. This rich and impressionistic essay ranges over most of the sprawling city, touching places as disparate as Green Park, the open-air "club of the poor," where "a thousand smutty children are . . . sprawling. . . , and the unemployed lie thick on the grass and cover the benches with a brotherhood of greasy corduroys" to Piccadilly, where "everything shines more or less, from the window panes to the dog collars." But James was forced to abandon the notebook method through pressure on him to produce installments of his novel; he fell back upon the thorough familiarity with London that he had acquired on his morning walks and he found that wholly adequate.[13] He presents a great variety of London settings in his novel and all are astonishingly authentic.[14] Dupee is far from wrong in calling *The Princess* James's "ambitious study in the *vie de Londres*."[15] It is his second great work in the manner of Zola without the latter's salaciousness; it anticipates Zola's *Lourdes* and *Rome* without their tyranny of facts. We may concede that the idea and structure of *The Princess* were borrowed from Turgenev and still hold that the novel is essentially James's own if we will remember that its total enrichment, both in scene and character, came from James's observation and memory.

All of the foregoing makes dubious any great debt to Dickens in the novel, which F. R. Leavis has asserted is complete, in so far as the novel is at all meritorious.[16] This view S. Gorley Putt has also challenged, citing James's distaste for "the grotesque, the fantastic and romantic" treatment of the English lower middle class "of which Dickens . . . is so misleadingly, of which even George Eliot is so devastatingly, full."[17] Putt concedes that the prison visit with Mrs. Bowerbank "may indeed be Dickensian in treatment," but he points out that the germ of it might, nevertheless, have been the childhood visit James had taken to Sing Sing.[18] We have just seen, instead, that the realism of that visit depends more on the notes James deliberately took at Millbank. Despite H. Blair Rouse's query, "Does one ever know and feel that one understands Hyacinth Robinson and his London friends of *The Princess Casamassima* quite as one knows Dickens' folk?"[19]

I am ready to assert that we *do* know Miss Pynsent and Mrs. Bowerbank in quite this way, possibly because they step right out of life as Dickens' people do. Is there anyone in Dickens any more vital than the enticing young cockney Millicent Henning? No one has imparted more of the "fleshly" quality to a woman in fiction than James has given to this child of the London slums. She must have been drawn from life, one would hazard, like Philip Carey's Mildred in *Of Human Bondage.*

Closely related to this issue is the contention that James knew nothing about revolutionaries. "The anarchists belong so decidedly in the realm of comic opera that it would be idle to speculate upon their relations to the death of the hero," A. H. Quinn has written.[20] Yvor Winters thinks that the impressions James gives us of the revolutionary underworld "have little more force or dignity than a small boy under a sheet on Hallowe'en; they repeatedly approach the ludicrous."[21] But one does not have to go back to James's Fourierite father to show that the novelist had an interest in social problems which attracted him to radicalism and acquainted him with different types of radicals at this time. Newton Arvin has cited letters which show that James thought upper-class British society completely corrupt and looked for its overthrow.[22] James had been close to Turgenev when the Russian was writing his own novel based on the anarchism of Bakunin, and Turgenev, with whom Bakunin had resided in Berlin,[23] had doubtless talked with James about the great conspirator. Not only did James know of Bakunin and his exploits through Turgenev, but it may be that he met Prince Kropotkin, a later leader of the anarchists, through the Russian novelist.[24] At any rate, when Kropotkin, after serving a term in a French prison, settled near London in 1886, Mrs. Robert Louis Stevenson, "at the urgent request of Henry James, . . . consented to meet him, and found him to be a most charming person."[25]

But whatever knowledge of anarchists James got in this way, he actively supplemented by purposeful reading. During the six-week journey in Provence which provided the substance for *A Little Tour of France* (1885), James read the radical newspapers.[26] A bomb outrage in Lyons provoked this comment from him:

> Of course there had been arrests and incarcerations, and the *Intransigeant* and the *Rappel* [left-wing papers] were filled with the echoes of the explosion. The tone of these organs is rarely edifying, and it had never been less so than on this occasion. I wondered, as I looked through them, whether I was losing all my radicalism; and then I wondered whether, after all, I had any to lose. Even in so long a wait as that tiresome day at Lyons I failed to settle the question, any more than I made up my mind as to the possible future of the militant democracy, or the ultimate form of a civilization which should have blown up everything else. A few days later, the waters went down at Lyons [there had been a flood], but the democracy has not gone down.[27]

James also glanced over a number of books to improve his knowledge of radicalism. The inventory of his library at his death lists him as possessing Théophile Gautier's *Tableau de siège* (Paris, 1871), an account of the Commune, and J. Zeller's *Les Tribuns et les révolutions en Italie* (Paris, 1874).[28] A casual, disparaging reference to Hyndman indicates that James was aware of Hyndman's radical activities and possibly had read either the latter's "The Dawn of the Revolutionary Epoch" in the *Nineteenth Century* for January, 1881, or his tract, *England for All* (1881).[29] Inveterate reader of George Sand, he had not been repelled by her socialism,[30] but the knowledge of French radicalism which makes Poupin and his wife so plausible in his novel came from his reading of *Jacques Vingtras* "by the Communist, Jules Valtes," which he recommended to T. S. Perry in 1879: "It is odious, but remarkable—I will send it to you."[31] It was the international anarchist movement—"the circle of Bakunin"—as Lerner maintains (and Lionel Trilling after him),[32] that really furnished James with the models for his conspirators.[33] Trilling speculates that the shadowy Hoffendahl might have been synthesized from Bakunin and Johann Most, sent to prison for criminal libel by a British jury for having exulted in the assassination of the Czar; pointing out that anarchism did not so much attract factory workers as members of the skilled trades, Trilling makes an excellent point that James had very appropriately made Hyacinth a bookbinder, since that not only suited his aesthetic temperament but assigned him to a class to which anarchism made a special appeal.[34]

Among the critics knowledgeble on the subject of radicalism . . . James's conspirators are accepted as valid studies.[35] "Paul Muniment . . . is a true revolutionary type," writes Stephen Spender. "He has the egoism, the sense of self-preservation, the cynicism, of a person who identifies himself so completely with a cause that he goes through life objectively guarding himself from all approach."[36] C. Hartley Grattan, who regards *The Princess* as "an astounding, muddled mixture of profound insight, sympathetic understanding, and weird *mis*-understanding," finds Muniment a very satisfactory revolutionist;[37] the drawing of Eustach Poupin is warmly praised by Van Wyck Brooks and Louise Bogan;[38] and S. Gorley Putt goes further, enthusiastically declaring, "his portrait is indeed a luxury, and a splendid example of the young novelist's high spirits."[39] "I am not sure," Pelham Edgar wrote, "that his [James's] most delicate triumph of observation was not achieved in the diffident, dowdy, and wholly delightful Lady Aurora";[40] she seems indeed a flawless setting forth of the gentlewoman of generous heart and blighted hopes who finds herself enlisted for no rational reason in some radical cause. It is one of the fine ironies that the Princess elects to have Lady Aurora, rather than Hyacinth, show her the conditions of the poor. She intuitively chose well. Schinkel, who has elicited no critical commentary, is hardly a nonentity despite the slightness of his drawing—very German, slow, and devoted, he is yet marked off skillfully from

Hyacinth's other radical acquaintance. All in all, James demonstrates not merely his ability to "do" radicals but to select and sharply distinguish types among them.

Of the nonradicals whom Henry James created for this novel Millicent Henning has won universal praise. "She is vulgarity done in the grand manner"[41]—"the big, joyous symbol of the energetic, capable working class, the most vivid to be found in fiction. . . ."[42] She is, in a word, the triumphant proof of the validity of James's assertion of eight years before that he was now so familiar with London and her citizens, that he was himself "a cockney." Millicent is London, both aspiration and reality.

Captain Sholto is Millicent's fate, and it is one of James's most distinctive achievements in the drawing of each of these characters to make us wish that he were not. Miss Bogan couples him with Muniment's sister as a true fool and a snob. He is the sort of man who becomes a rich woman's lapdog and he is obeying the wisdom of his animalism when he follows a disillusioned married woman about, expecting that sometime she will fall to him. But the Princess knows his kind too well. What his role is in relation to the conspirators is deliberately left vague. Dupee is positive that he is "a police spy,"[43] and he is sinisterly capable of that role, but he certainly has no regular connection with the police, for that would too much limit his activities as a pursuer—he is known to the Prince and has followed the Princess from Italy. As for Rose Muniment, although she is "presented on her sick bed as an object of pity, [she] succeeds in filling the reader with a reluctant shame-faced distaste."[44]

The delineation of Amanda Pynsent and Anastasius Vetch and the study of their relations to each other, as well as to Hyacinth, is one of the most happily contrived things in the novel. James ingeniously devises it so that Pinnie strengthens the boy's romanticism, against the grumbling dissent of Mr. Vetch, who, however, ironically supplements her small legacy so that Hyacinth may have the holiday on the Continent that contributes to his confusion and ruin. The lugubrious and heavy-handed turnkey, Mrs. Bowerbank, symbol of the most humane of England's penal institutions, throws a shadow beyond the early chapters where she has her only lines. Cast as a very minor actor and physically the opposite of the powerful Bowerbank, Hyacinth's mother survives the female turnkey as an image in the minds of her son and the reader, there accumulating value, as Michael Swan notes: "The magnificent scene at the beginning of the book, where Miss Pynsent takes the ten-year-old Hyacinth to the Holloway Gaol to visit his dying mother, shows James handling a Dickensian scene of great drama with an assurance he was never to attempt again. . . ."

One feels that no purely sexual promiscuity would have driven Mme Grandoni, the deeply loyal companion to the Princess, away from her mistress, but when Christina combines an infatuation for Paul Muniment with the most fanatical radicalism, involving danger from arrest or even murder, this superb and plain-spoken old lady becomes "solidly disillusioned." Her

previous clandestine meetings with the Prince involve no disloyalty to the
Princess; they are calculated to keep that "morbidly jealous" man from
worsening his case with his wife; they look toward reconciliation.[45] One of
the fine touches in the book occurs when James permits Mme Grandoni to
define Christina to Hyacinth with devastating candor as a "*capricciosa.*"[46]
She likewise defines Hyacinth: "*Poverino!*" But when the Prince is reproved by her for jealousy, for which we know from *Roderick Hudson* as
well as from this novel that he has just cause, however, he may have acted
on the specific occasion when his wife left home, we realize that Mme
Grandoni is managing him with the one end of reconciliation, for *everyone's sake*, in view. We must distinguish her artfulness from her candor.

That to a supreme point Mme Grandoni could remain with the Princess is the finest attestation we have in the novel which bears her name to
the fact that her beauty and charm cover more than dissoluteness. Christina is the only major character that James ever revived from an earlier
work, for it was a conviction with him that if a character were fully expressed it could yield nothing further in a new connection. Though he confesses as a revivalist to a pleasurable indulgence in "going on" with this
woman who had deeply interested him before, other reasons, we may be
sure, moved him more strongly. He cites her availability—she was "an extremely *disponible* figure."[47] A Londoner in her station could not have es-
poused radicalism without a notoriety that would have marred her appeal
to Hyacinth; possessed of great means from her still infatuated husband but
separated from him and in a foreign country, she can plausibly conduct herself as the novelist wishes. James needed her, however, more for Hyacinth's development, as he admits, than he needed to show further the fatal
quality of her vanity and beauty.[48] "She was to serve for his experience in
quite another and more leading sense than any in which he was to serve
for hers." After this, James admits to only one concern, namely, that she
be consistent, and having "travelled far" from what she was when we first
knew her as Christina Light, that she should sense nothing "banal" in herself in reaching down into the life of the little London bookbinder. She is
"world weary" and she needs "to feel freshly about something or other—it
might scarcely matter what. . . ."[49]

Though Christina is brought forward from *Roderick Hudson,* James
does little in *The Princess Casamassima* to acquaint the reader with her
previous history. There is no mention, for example, of the unfortunate
sculptor from "Northampton, Mass.," who cast himself off a precipice after
losing his head over her, presumptively because there have been other infatuated men to displace his memory. But her tolerance for Captain Sholto,
despite her contempt for him, indicates either a numbed indifference or a
decayed taste. But even to appreciate this, one must know more of the
Princess' past than James allows us in her new connection. Miss Bogan's
perceptive critical study makes more allowance for this past, and for the
previous novel, than do other examinations. She produces, for example, a

parallelism in the origins of the Princess and of the bookbinder which other critics have failed to notice. . . .[50]

Dupee misses the lingering *quality* in the Princess, testified to no more than by her recognition of something finer and more courageous in her young friend. It is a value, however, which she herself temporarily denies for a connection with the more deeply involved, more calculating, and more masculine Muniment. Dupee rehearses accurately all the various exhibitions of her meretriciousness, ending with that scene in which Paul Muniment lets her down, telling her bluntly that only her money (now cut off) has been useful to the cause and predicting that she will return to her husband. " 'Ah, Paul Muniment,' she says, 'you *are* a first-rate man!' and she bursts into tears. And we see her at last as a rather futile woman whose surrender of her feminine and aristocratic status has left her with nothing but an insatiable appetite for adventure and for men." But this just is not so. Her exclamation of involuntary admiration for Muniment does not come upon her personal rejection by him but upon his declaration that he will not intrude himself between Hyacinth and the latter's assignment, though both recognize that its execution may bring disaster to their mutual friend.[51] It is her recognition of his hardness, not merely to herself, but toward Hyacinth as well, engendered by his revolutionary discipline. But *after* she has recognized the necessity of such a discipline for a revolutionist, she implicitly repudiates it by going to Hyacinth. Though she had said to Muniment that she would replace their young friend herself as a more effective instrument in a terrorist mission, this is not her reason for going. Something that Rowland Mallet had awakened in her long before has stirred again. Is it not credible that she has drawn a parallel between the finer sensibility of Hyacinth and the talent of Roderick Hudson, to both of which she may seem to herself to have been destructive, or if not, is she not to draw it after covering the body of the poor suicide with her own? The act is as symbolical as it is emotional, and James counterpoints it by having Schinkel, picking up the revolver, wish that it might have been used on its designated object. In his brief relation with her, Hyacinth has had all his sensibilities awakened by the Princess, but does he not reciprocate by reminding her of her duty to the forms, if nothing else?[52] Is she to continue as a revolutionist? Or the facile vanquisher of men? James did not name his novel *The Princess Casamassima* because *The Bookbinder* or *The Revolutionist* would have been weak titles and *Hyacinth Robinson* slightly absurd, but because the novel belongs not wholly to Hyacinth but equally to the Princess. She has now been, in James's meaningful phrase, "completely recorded."[53]

Yet James was right in stressing that if he could obtain the "appearance of consistency" with Hyacinth he could remain at ease about Christina.[54] The task he undertook with the little bookbinder was much more involved than that which engaged him with the Princess. It called for the creation of a central intelligence, denied direct access to all the fine things it could most appreciate and thus motivated to radical resentment, yet capable of "a lively inward revolution" arraying it eventually on the side of the preservation of order, because order preserves the things admired.[55] That James failed in the task he set himself has been asserted with a great deal of vigor by a number of critics, beginning with Van Wyck Brooks, who held that social envy was improperly attributed to Hyacinth: "In real life the last thing that would have occurred to a young man in Hyacinth's position would have been to 'roam and wander and yearn. . . .' he would have gone to Australia or vanished into the slums, or continued with the utmost indifference at his trade of binding books."[56] Waiving altogether the question of whether the average London bookbinder would have behaved as Mr. Brooks says he would, one finds an easy rejoinder in the care that James takes to make Hyacinth a *conditioned,* special figure. No one adored the gentry more than Miss Pynsent to whom he was entrusted, and none made more of the fact than she that Hyacinth was the son of a noble lord. The boy is steeped in her romanticism (of which no critic has made anything, though James's treatment suggests the current Flaubertism) and piled on that was the indoctrination of his radical friends and, later, the whole influence of the Princess.[57]

Pelham Edgar attacks James's creation at another point: the change that occurs in the boy as he comes to have some experience of the world of valued possessions:

> . . . The provision that he [James] makes for this violent transition is wholly insufficient, and the inadequacy of his explanation diminishes our sympathy with Hyacinth to such a point that his tragic predicament leaves us cold. Much is made of the ascendancy over his mind of Paul Muniment, and much, too, is made of his dual nature, in which centuries of luxury and poverty combine without blending. . . . If the enchantress of Medley [the Princess] had determined to bewitch him with luxury and beauty, we might concede some weight to the hereditary impulse. Her influence, however, is laid wholly in the other scale.[58]

Without Pelham Edgar's analysis, Stephen Spender's purely Marxian observation, "Hyacinth, with his strong leaning towards the upper classes, and yet his feeling that he is somehow committed to the cause of the workers, might today become a Socialist Prime Minister [Ramsay MacDonald], who, at the height of his power, would dismay his followers by too frankly going over to the other side,"[59] amounts to the same sort of stricture.

Insisting that Hyacinth is not "the little snob" that he has been made out to be, Louise Bogan sketched originally the line of refutation followed by those who dissent from the Pelham Edgar-Stephen Spender point of view. James made the boy essentially "an artist, a clear, sensitive intelligence, filled with the imagination 'which will always give him the clue about everything.' James endowed him, indeed, with the finest qualities of his own talent; and this is what is meant when James says that Hyacinth had watched London 'very much as I had watched it.' Hyacinth is, like James, 'a person on whom nothing is lost. . . .' James wanted a cool and undistorting mirror to shine between the dark and violent world of the disinherited on the one hand and on the preposterous world of privilege on the other. . . . James kept Hyacinth detached to the end."[60] Neither the revolutionist nor the man of sensibility triumphs according to this view. To Elizabeth Stevenson, Hyacinth is adequately explained as a person of sensitivity and intelligence who, desiring to realize his full nature, *to be himself*, discovers he is the victim of a triple betrayal. "His friend Paul is no friend, his Princess is false. . . . Both betrayed him, and in the end they betrayed him together. . . . At this point he is called upon for the fulfillment of his vow. Hyacinth finds that not only others have betrayed him, he has betrayed himself. His sympathies and beliefs are not his to give. He almost necessarily kills himself."[61] This listing of betrayals is not complete without including Hyacinth's final discovery of the disloyalty of Milicent Henning— if he betrayed himself, he was also betrayed not only by his chief revolutionary friends, but by his class, as represented by Miss Henning. . . .

But perhaps we have not yet realized all that James meant to convey by Hyacinth and his tragedy. Lionel Trilling has groped for something more by trying to resolve Hyacinth's story into that of the general myth of "The Young Man from the Provinces."[62] James gives us a clear hint, however, for looking in another direction when, in his Preface, he compares Hyacinth's awareness of his situation to the awareness of Hamlet and Lear, who, like him, are surrounded by the blind and the stupid, ministering to their fate.[63] To F. W. Dupee, James's prefatorial comparison of his hero to Shakespeare's protagonists is an "unfortunate" juxtaposition: " . . . Surely Hyacinth travels far to learn what he could have read any day in the *Times:* that radicals are envious."[64] Waiving for the moment the question of whether all that Hyacinth learned may be summed up as facilely as Mr. Dupee epitomizes it . . . we might question whether it was fatuity that led James, meticulous in all things, to juxtapose his poor hero against so awesome a creation as Hamlet. Our questioning might carry us a step further: Do we not assume too much veneration of Hamlet when we call the juxtaposition "unfortunate?"

There is a European attitude, both critical and creative, extending from Voltaire to Jules Laforgue,which does not at all correspond with the Anglo-American reverence for the Danish prince. Hamlet, in this European view, is permanently adolescent and too much given to reflection. James's master, Ivan Turgenev, made two notable *titled* contributions to this view or *tradition:* one creative, in "The Hamlet of the Shtchigri District," and the other critical, in *Hamlet and Don Quixote: An Essay.*[65] In the fiction, the Hamlet who is portrayed is a sort of Russian Prufrock, an assigned bedfellow to the narrator at an all-bachelor party in the country, whom he keeps awake with his own devastating self-analysis until a neighboring guest demands through the partition that he be permitted to sleep.

The Shtchigri District Hamlet lost his father, was dominated by his mother, studied German philosophy abroad, returned to be an eternal bore with his "reflections," took refuge in a pallid wife who so little responded to him that he contemplated hanging himself in his barn, but is left only with garrulous self-pity when the girl fades out of life. To an English or American reader, Prufrock's "I am not Prince Hamlet, nor was meant to be" would seem a proper summary of Turgenev's "caricature"; but to a European reader, Prufrock himself would seem a type of Hamlet and a legitimate descendant of Turgenev's poor creature, or at least of his fictional nephew, Dostoevski's Raskolnikov. In his critical essay, *Hamlet and Don Quixote,* Turgenev bestows more dignity on his conception of Hamlet: he becomes one of the "twin anti-types of human nature, the two poles of the axletree on which that nature turns." Don Quixote, the other type, is the personification of faith; "Hamlet is, beyond all else, analysis and egoism, skepticism personified. . . . He has no faith in himself, yet is a coxcomb; he knows not what he desires, his life lacks a goal, yet, for all that, he loves life. . . . The Hamlets of this world profit the masses not at all. . . . Don Quixote, on the other hand, despite his age, isolation, and poverty, undertakes to redress all the evils in the world. Hamlet, although he disbelieves in good, does not believe in evil. Evil and deceit are his inveterate enemies. His skepticism is not indifference."

Although these two titled pieces demonstrate Turgenev's deep interest in Hamlet, they are not his only use of the Shakespearean hero. P. Kropotkin believed that Turgenev "himself belonged to a great extent to the Hamlets" and that he made Bazaroff of *Fathers and Sons* in his own and Hamlet's image.[66] But if Turgenev loved Hamlet, he admired Don Quixote and men of action. "Did you know Myshkin?" he asked Prince Kropotkin in 1878, naming a famous revolutionist. "*That* was a man; not the slightest trace of Hamletism."[67] Probably thinking of this conflict in Turgenev's soul between his love for the Hamlets and his admiration for the Don Quixotes, so like his attitudes toward Nezhdanov and Solomin in *Virgin Soil,* Professor Daniel Lerner makes his almost casual observation that Nezhdanov is an illustration of "fatal Hamletism"—and Hyacinth Robinson is, too! . . .[68]

Not merely in his Preface to *The Princess Casamassima* does James refer to the relative awareness of Hamlet and of Hyacinth to their respective plights. In his Preface to *The Tragic Muse,* right after naming *The Princess Casamassima* again, in discussing how a dramatist may not present "a usurping consciousness" the way a novelist can, he observes, "the prodigious consciousness of Hamlet, the most rapacious and most crowded, . . . only takes its turn with that of the other agents of the story, no matter how occasional these may be"[69]—thereby again demonstrating how the consciousness of Hamlet is associated with that of Hyacinth in his mind, only here by way of contrast, for that of Hyacinth is "a usurping consciousness" and the point of view maintained throughout the book. It is, however, a dominated consciousness, rather than a dominating consciousness, for

James is studying not the effect of Hyacinth on a revolutionary conspiracy, but the effect of a conspiracy on a man who is all sensibility. His story is the story of the man of feeling who is the inevitable dupe of extreme enterprises to benefit mankind.

Hyacinth "is not Prince Hamlet, nor was meant to be," but James's whole treatment of him is marvelously enriched by reference to details in the Hamlet story, or rather, to the *two* Hamlet stories, for James apparently had both Turgenev's and Shakespeare's in mind.[70] In following Turgenev, he made Hyacinth seem pitiable and small, the little bookbinder caught up by the princess and betrayed by her and the man of action of the story, its Solomin and Don Quixote, Paul Muniment. Too many reflections press in upon Hyacinth and floor him. But if James makes him pitiable and small, he also endows him with an acute perceptiveness, which makes him, like Shakespeare's protagonist, a tragic figure. One can best get an estimate of Hyacinth's comparative worth by asking whether it would be equally moving to see either Paul Muniment or Hyacinth's Princess die. With an eye on Shakespeare's Hamlet, Henry James sought to create a more engulfing sea of troubles than that which in the end swamped the Elizabethan hero, for it is the sea of troubles that floods the consciousness of each protagonist and is the logic of their actions. It may be temerity to suggest that James wished to improve on Shakespeare's logic.[71] Hamlet debates suicide, but is accidentally slain by a poisoned sword. He drives Ophelia to madness and thereby qualifies the pity we must feel for him; the wanton slaying of Polonius does not too much affect him and so again he is diminished. The fatalism of *Hamlet* is not so much of situation as it is of pure caprice. In watching the play, I think, we are captivated as much by Hamlet's capacity to do harm as we are by his moral problem.

Because he is influenced by Shakespeare, James, who elsewhere is a champion of free will, introduces an element of fate into *The Princess Casamassima.* "The initial tragic error of Hyacinth Robinson . . . is conceived as a free choice made in ignorance of the essential knowledge which would have prevented it."[72] He pledges himself to commit an act of wanton violence before he knows what it will entail; like Hamlet, he has a binding sense of honor, a loyalty to a code, that makes it imperative, short of death, to carry out his pledge. If the reader assumes that Hamlet's mother's filthiness makes Hamlet see all women as depraved and that this accounts wholly for his treatment of Ophelia (and I know of no reader who has done this), there would be a consistency in Hamlet and his violent death would be indicated as inevitable. Seeing something like this, however, James involved not only Muniment and the Princess in Hyacinth's destruction but also Millicent Henning. She is not a dangling object like Ophelia; but after being betrayed by the Princess and Muniment, Hyacinth turns to the cockney girl—only to find her with Captain Sholto. But James does something with Shakespeare's idea of madness, or rather, the *suggestion* of madness: the Princess has the mad idea of substituting for Hyacinth; one supposes that she is purged of this kind of madness by her rejection by Muniment and by Hyacinth's death. The tragic irony of the Princess' tardy display of feeling for Hyacinth is that it comes too late to save him from complete disillusionment with womankind and with life.[73] Yet on his death-dealing mission a double specter must have arisen in his consciousness: that of his murdered father and his father's murderess. To escape the dreadful destiny of following precisely in his poor mother's footsteps, thereby demonstrating the utter rule of tainted blood, Hyacinth elects the only other choice left open to him, self-destruction. James has selected what is apparently his most predestined character to exhibit freedom of the will.

It has been charged that James lacks ideas in his novel.[74] That is probably because Hyacinth does not windily debate his situation—because he only *feels* it. He has no Shakespearean rhetoric. But what, in spite of his muddlement, must have been his thoughts on human loyalty? On impulsive enlistment in causes? On the gift of sensibility without the wherewithal to exercise it? On destiny? James's silences in this novel are as deliberate and as portentous as his revelations—and more inescapable. His chief triumph, however, is artistic: the assembly of an extraordinarily varied and vivid cast of characters, in some respects the most varied and vivid in all his novels, and their plausible involvement with one another with telling effect upon the focal figures, the Princess and Hyacinth Robinson, each of whom becomes a measure in the end of the other's worth and of the folly of the enterprise which put them to the test. And the cast is not dwarfed by a backdrop that is all of London.

## Notes

1. *The Art of the Novel*, ed. R. P. Blackmur (New York, 1934), pp. 59–61. The order of quotation is mine. *The Princess Casamassima* was serialized in the *Atlantic*, Sept., 1885– Oct., 1886; it was published by Macmillan in 3 vols., on Oct. 22, 1886. I follow the text of the London edition.

2. "The Influence of Turgenev on Henry James," *Slavonic and East European Rev.*, XX (Dec., 1941), 46–51. I take great satisfaction in Lerner's article, for it was the product of a suggestion of mine (carried out beyond my happiest expectation), made in a graduate seminar, that some student investigate the relations of *The Princess* to *Virgin Soil*.

3. Turgenev, *Virgin Soil* (London, 1911), p. 168 (Lerner's note).

4. F. W. Dupee, *Henry James* (New York, 1951), p. 153; Stephen Spender, *The Destructive Element* (Philadelphia, 1953), p. 44; Carl Van Doren, *The American Novel* (New York, 1921), p. 204, etc.

5. James to Perry, Apr. 18, 1887. Virginia Harlow, *Thomas Sergeant Perry* (Durham, N.C., 1950), p. 48; see also Harlow, pp. 293, 294, 296. For the Turgenev letter to which James refers, see Jean Seznec, "Lettres de Tourguéneff à Henry James," *Comparative Literature*, I (Summer 1949), 202. Perry's translation was in the Leisure Hour Series (Boston, 1877).

6. *The Novels of Turgenev*, VI and VII, *Virgin Soil*, tr. Constance Garnett, 2 vols. (New York, 1920).

7. If he had intended to borrow from the start as much as he eventually did, he would hardly have confided to his notebook, "I have never yet become engaged in a novel in which, after I had begun to write and send off my MS., the details had remained so vague." *The Notebooks of Henry James*, ed. F. O. Matthiessen and K. B. Murdock (New York, 1947), p. 68.

8. At this period James's admiration for Zola was high. (James to Perry, Nov. 2, 1879, Harlow, p. 304).

9. Harlow, p. 319.

10. *The Letters of William James*, ed. by his son Henry James (Boston, 1920), I, 250; *Letters to His Family and Friends*, ed. Sidney Colvin (New York, 1918), I, 435.

11. James to Perry, Jan. 24, 1886, Harlow, p. 320. I have often wondered if James's intention at one time was to write on the Irish affair.

12. *Century Magazine*, (Dec., 1888), 219–239.

13. F. O. Matthiessen (*Henry James: The Major Phase*, New York, 1944, p. 4) cities his habit of morning walks in Venice "looking at pictures, street life, &c, till noon." There is reason to suppose that he continued the habit in London. Forrest Reid compares the slum scenes favorably with those in Gissing. *The Eighteen-Eighties*, ed. Walter De La Mare (Cambridge, England, 1930), p. 249.

14. Clinton Oliver, "Henry James as a Social Critic," *Antioch Rev.*, VII (Summer, 1947), 251. . . . Alexander Cowie, *The Rise of the American Novel* (New York, 1948), p. 716.

15. *Henry James*, p. 153.

16. *The Great Tradition* (New York, 1950), p. 172. Messrs. Matthiessen and Murdock (The Notebooks, p. 69), lumping *The Princess* with *The Bostonians*, write, "These two novels constitute James's attempt to handle the Dickensian type of social novel." Spender, p. 44: "a book in the broad English tradition of Dickens and Thackeray." Elisabeth L. Cary (*The Novels of Henry James*, New York, 1905, p. 104) speaks of "a momentary inclination toward the art of Dickens."

17. "A Henry James Jubilee, I," *Cornhill*, No. 969 (Winter, 1946), 189. The quotation is from a letter to H. G. Wells, Nov. 19, 1905. *The Letters of Henry James*, ed. Percy Lubbock (New York, 1920), II, 40.

18. Ibid., p. 193. Putt cites Ch. xiii of *A Small Boy and Others*.

19. "Charles Dickens and Henry James: Two Approaches to the Art of Fiction," *Nineteenth-Century Fiction*, V (Sept., 1950), 154.

20. *American Fiction* (New York, 1936), p. 290.

21. *Maule's Curse* (Norfolk, Conn., 1938), p. 205. . . . (Van Doren, pp. 203–204). See Carr, n. 23 below.

22. "Henry James and the Almighty Dollar," *Hound & Horn*, 7 (April-June, 1934), 434–443.

23. John Rae, *Contemporary Socialism* (New York, 1884), p. 271; for what were generally accepted as Bakunin's views at this time, see pp. 271–300. For Bakunin's relations with Turgenev in 1840–42, see also E. H. Carr, *Michael Bakunin* (London, 1937), pp. 93–104. Relying on Carr, p. 317, M. S. Wilkins points out that the Princess Obolensky, who later retired to Casamicciola, was a focal figure in Bakunin's organization in Naples in 1864, and suggests James knew both of the Princess and her place of retirement. "A Note on *The Princess Casamassima*," *Nineteenth-Century Fiction*, XII (June, 1957), 88.

24. Turgenev met Kropotkin in Paris in 1878, the year after James took up residence in London. See P. Kropotkin, *Memoirs of a Revolutionist* (Boston, 1899), pp. 203–209. But James saw and corresponded with Turgenev after that (Seznec, pp. 203–209).

25. Nellie Van de Grift Sanchez, *The Life of Mrs. Robert Louis Stevenson* (New York, 1920), p. 121. I owe this citation to Professor Leon Edel. That James continued to have some

association with Kropotkin is an inference that can be drawn from his acquaintance with Edward and Constance Garnett (the latter, the translator of Turgenev) and their Russian circle. See David Garnett, *The Golden Echo* (New York, 1954), *passim*.

26. *A Little Tour* (Boston, 1885), p. 237. Probably too little has been made, in relation to *The Princess*, of James's trip to this area of social ferment that later produced Felix Gras's *The Reds of the Midi* (1896). Kropotkin was imprisoned at this time in Lyons.

27. *Ibid.*, pp. 238—239. At Carcassonne, James met a voluble "fierce little Jacobin" and commented in this fashion: "Such a personage helps one to understand the red radicalism of France, the revolutions, the barricades, the sinister passion for theories. . . . it is yet untouched by the desire which one finds in the Englishman, in proportion as he rises in the world, to approximate the figure of a gentleman" (p. 151).

28. I owe this information also to Professor Edel.

29. See H. M. Hyndman, *The Record of an Adventurous Life* (New York, 1911), pp. 206–207, 228–230. See also n. 22, above. James's attitude toward Hyndman (a Marxist) might have been determined, of course, by his connections with Bakunin and Kropotkin.

30. Henry James, *French Poets and Novelists*, London, 1878, p. 221.

31. Harlow, p. 304. Not *Valtes* (an error in transcription), but Jules Vallès, whose three-part novel, L'Enfant, Le Bachelier, L'Insurge (Paris, 1923–1924), originally published in 1879, 1881, and 1886, is closely autobiographical, being based on the author's long revolutionary career, beginning with the revolution of 1848 and culminating in the Commune.

32. "Introduction," *The Princess Casamassima* (New York, 1948), I, xviii-xxv.

33. George Woodcock, in "Henry James and the Conspirators"—*Sewanee Rev.*, LX (Spring, 1952), 219–229—properly denying that *The Princess* is evidence of "an authentic radicalism" on James's part, attacks the anarchist case as stated by Trilling and contends that "the international organization of conspirators in *The Princess Casamassima*, with its highly rigid form in fact resembles that of such more or less authoritarian groups as the Italian Carbonari or the Blanquists of France."

34. On Nov. 25, 1883, James noted, "I have just sent about 100 vols. (mostly French) to the binders" (Harlow, p. 314). Edel, who called my attention to this, points out that this visit occurred just two months before James wrote his first letter to Aldrich offering *The Princess* as a serial for 1885. If James carried his books to or from the printers, he may have got well acquainted with the persons in Hyacinth's craft.

35. A notable exception is Granville Hicks: "[His] thesis forced him to deal not only with ideas he did not grasp but also with types of character he did not understand" (*The Great Tradition*, New York, 1935, p. 114). We must remember, however, that when Hicks made this judgment he was an avowed Communist and not likely to have been pleased with the portraits.

36. *The Destructive Element*, p. 44. Elizabeth Stevenson goes further (*The Crooked Corridor*, p. 18): "one of the most effective revolutionary figures in English literature."

37. *The Three Jameses: A Family of Minds* (New York, 1925), pp. 269–271; so, too, does S. Gorley Putt, "A Henry James Jubilee, I," *Cornhill*, No. 969 (Winter, 1946), 196.

38. *The Pilgrimage of Henry James*, p. 101; "James on a Revolutionary Theme," *Nation*, CXLIV (April 23, 1938), 472.

39. *Cornhill*, No. 969, p. 196.

40. *Henry James, Man and Author* (New York, 1927), p. 283. It was an amusing touch when Mme Grandoni calls her "Lydia Languish" immediately after Hyacinth has given her correct name. James wished this absurd comparison. *The Princess*, II, 22.

41. Edgar, p. 272.

42. Cary, p. 136.

43. *Henry James*, p. 159. I note that in his paperback revision (1956) Dupee has

dropped this suggestion. Michael Swan is more effective because more vague in his epitome: "Captain Sholto does not move in a society so different from the one he was born into from any political interest; he is an adverturer in the widest sense of the term, . . . a fellow traveler in the thing for some fun" (*Henry James*, London, 1952, p. 69). Frederick Highland writes me (Mar. 4, 1956) on "the extraordinary prophetic quality of the book . . . in the creation of two authentic twentieth-century personality types in Christina and Captain Sholto, . . . the 'bitch-heroine,' beautiful, restless, and destructive; and . . . the trench-coated desperado of our day."

44. Putt, p. 197. Trilling (p. xliii) has a most illuminating passage on Miss Muniment.

45. Bogan, p. 474. Dupee, p. 159: "Divided between her affection for the Princess and her obligations to the Prince, Mme Grandoni . . . is a touching case of mental suffering and the most tragic figure in the book."

46. *The Princess*, II, 102. The preceding quotation is from Swan, pp. 66–67.

47. *The Art of the Novel*, p. 73.

48. He had evidently been fired by the idea of doing something better with the role that Mme Sipyagina plays in *Virgin Soil*.

49. *The Art of the Novel*, p. 74.

50. *Henry James*, pp. 159–160; Bogan, pp. 473–474.

51. *The Princess*, III, 229.

52. Hyacinth is really serviceable to the Princess only finally—it is *beyond* the book that his influence most counts; her disillusionment with radicalism is contributed to partially by Muniment, we must remember.

53. After speculating in his Preface on "the obscure law" by which certain characters "revive" for the novelist to haunt "his house of art," James asks, "Why should the Princess of the climax of Roderick Hudson still have made her desire felt, unless in fact to testify that she had not been—for what she was—completely recorded?" (The Art of the Novel, p. 73). How can one go along with Professor Baker (*History of the English Novel*, 10 vols., London, 1938, IX, 257): "seen through the eyes of the disillusioned plotter Hyacinth Robinson . . . she remains to the last a beautiful mystery"? Or, with H. S. Canby (*Turn East, Turn West*, Boston, 1951, p. 181). . . . M. E. Grenander's very fine study ("Henry James's 'Capricciosa'," PMLA, LXXV [June, 1960], 309–319 is marred, it seems to me, by being too harsh toward the Princess, though valuable for noting changes in her.

54. *The Art of the Novel*, p. 75. There is an excellent discussion of Hyacinth as "a center of consciousness" in Alwyn Berland, "Henry James," *Univ. of Kansas City Review*, xvii (Winter, 1950), 102–105. See also John Henry Raleigh, "H. J.: The Poetics of Empiricism," PMLA (Mar. 1, 1951), 115.

55. *Ibid.*, 60–61, 69–73.

56. *The Pilgrimage of Henry James*, pp. 82–83. Brooks, of course, maintains the motivation is James's and falsely assigned to Hyacinth. But why should the little bookbinder have no portion of the sensibility of his creator? Henry James was, after all, the grandson of an Irish immigrant, a thing too often overlooked.

57. Granville Hicks's idea (p. 114) that James made Hyacinth plausible by making him special is sound, though it does not follow that James "defeated his fundamental intention." It depends, doesn't it, on what one regards as his intention?

58. *Henry James, Man and Author*, pp. 277–278.

59. *The Destructive Element*, p. 44.

60. Bogan, p. 474. Clinton Oliver (pp. 252–256) bears down even harder on the autobiographical character of Hyacinth's perceptivity.

61. *The Crooked Corridor* (New York, 1949), p. 67.

62. Intro., pp. ix–xv. Exemplars of the type include Julien Sorel of *The Red and the*

*Black,* James Gatz of *The Great Gatsby,* Rastignac of Père Goriot, etc. This sort of generalized connection seems to me less fruitful than the general resemblance which Edmund Wilson notices between Hyacinth and Frédéric Moreau of *L'Education sentimentale,* "The Ambiguity of Henry James," *Hound & Horn,* VII (April-June, 1934), 399–401.

63. *The Art of Fiction,* p. 62.

64. *Henry James,* p. 157.

65. *A Sportsman's Sketches,* tr. Constance Garnett (London, 1916), II, 106–145; *Hamlet and Don Quixote: An Essay,* tr. Robert Nichols (London, 1930), 31 pp.

66. *Ideals and Realities in Russian Literature* (New York, 1905), pp. 105–107.

67. *Memoirs of a Revolutionist* (Boston, 1899), pp. 411–414.

68. See above p. 148.

69. *The Art of the Novel,* p. 90.

70. Was it not natural that he should think of getting aid from Shakespeare since, as Lerner and I have shown, he had made use of another great dramatist, Sophocles, in *The Bostonians?* See "Henry James at the Grecian Urn," PMLA, LXVI (June, 1951), 316–331.

71. "We find *no* fault with Mr. Henry James's *The Princess Casamassima;* it is a great novel. . . . the drama works simply and naturally; *the cause and effects are logically related;* the theme is made literature without ceasing to be life." W. D. Howells, "Editor's Study," Harper's, LXXIV (April, 1887), 829. (Italics ours.) (Called to my attention by Professor William Gibson.) Contrast: "one of the worst books [no reasons given] by a good writer that I have ever read," Frank Swinnerton, *The Georgian Scene* (New York, 1934), p. 28.

72. Winters, pp. 176–177. Compare Isabel Archer's choice.

73. Detecting, as he thinks, misogyny in *the Princess,* as well as "the pendulum swing of life between satiation and ennui," determinism, and pessimism, and relying on three allusions to the German philosopher by Christina and Hyacinth (*The Princess* [2 vols., London, 1908], II, 48, 59, 142—Firebaugh's note), Joseph Firebaugh is led to call the book "A Schopenhauerian Novel" in an article with that title in *Nineteenth-Century Fiction,* XIII (Dec., 1958), 177–197. But the final act of the Princess, to say nothing of the self-sacrifices of Miss Pynsent and Aurora, and Hyacinth's desperate revolt against heredity, erase misogyny, determinism, and pessimism and make the epithet inapplicable to the novel as a whole.

74. I doubt if more artistic ideas were ever exploited in a novel; Mr. Dupee seems to mean "assigned opinions." Howells, contrasting *The Princess* with W. H. Mallock's *The Old Order Changes,* in the admirable review cited in note 71, takes Mallock to task for this very thing.

# Miriam as the English Rachel: Gérôme's Portrait of the Tragic Muse

Adeline R. Tintner*

James was careful, when he revised *The Tragic Muse,* to make sure that volume one ended with the scene in the greenroom of the Théâtre Français.[1] There in the central scene of the novel Miriam makes her choice for the career of an actress rather than the wife of an ambassador, a proposition offered her by Peter Sherringham who is passionately in love with her.

*This essay was written specifically for this volume and is published here for the first time by permission of the author.

Jean-Leon Gérôme (1824–1904), *Rachel*, La Comédie Française, Paris.
*Photo: Bibliothèque Nationale.*

For when the novel was first published in two volumes in 1890, volume one did not end with this scene but with a chapter following it that concerned Nick Dormer and Julia Dallow. It is only in the revised version of the New York Edition that the scene becomes the vivid climax with which volume one closes. Miriam's story is the main interest for the reader, for Nick Dormer's problems become dramatically viable only after he paints Miriam as The Tragic Muse and Julia creates difficulties only when, after finding Miriam in Nick's studio, she mistakenly thinks there is some personal bond between them.

Miriam chooses the stage because of two strong influences operating on her in that scene. The first and chief is the effect on her as she stands before it of the portrait of Rachel as The Tragic Muse by Jean-Léon Gérôme (1828–1904), which hangs in the greenroom of the theater and with which she immediately identifies at the beginning of the scene as well as at its end. The other influence is her interview with a now living, leading actress, Mademoiselle Voisin, who represents for Miriam the Comic Muse and presents possibilities other than tragedy for her in the theater. The two avenues of expression, through the impressive portrait of France's greatest *Tragédienne* and through the manner of a great contemporary *comédienne* convince Miriam of what her choice should be. As the scene opens and closes with the presence of Dashwood, Miriam's future manager and husband, her life present and future is here encapsulated, and so is the dramatic ending for volume one.

James was quite aware of the impact of the greenroom scene, because he himself had, only a month before the first chapter of *The Tragic Muse* had begun to appear in the *Atlantic Monthly*, been privileged for the first time to enter the sacrosanct foyer of the Théâtre Français. We read in his *Notebooks* for 2 February 1889, "How much I must put into. . . . Sherringham's visit to the Comédie Française—my impression of Bartet, in her *loge*, the other day in Paris" (NB, 92). This distinguished *comédienne* of the Théâtre Français lends herself to the portrait of Mademoiselle Voisin whom Miriam so admires.

James had been under the spell of the French theater since 1876 during his year in Paris, during which time he had written a long piece on the Théâtre Français; which he had frequented almost nightly. As to how the traditions of the theater were kept "I never found out—by sitting in the stalls: and very soon I ceased to care to know. One may be very fond of the stage and yet care little for the green-room" (SC, 75). So he consoled himself for not being able to enter the sanctuary of the actors themselves. There also he felt the magic of a great actress he had never seen perform, but whose legendary fame Mrs. Kemble had as a witness reported to the young author. "Even if I had never seen Rachel, it was something of a consolation to think that those very footlights had illumined her finest moments and that the echoes of her mighty voice were sleeping in that dingy dome" (SC, 75). One can imagine, then, how the Gérôme likeness of

Rachel must have affected James who was in the last days of 1888 in the process of creating a novel in which the portrait as the highest form of pictorial art is extolled. He never mentioned his impression of the Gérôme in his *Notebooks* because he didn't have to. It operated as one of his technical narrative secrets to be revealed in its fictive demonstration.

Commissioned by Rachel's sister Sarah just after the death of the actress in 1858 at the age of thirty-seven, Gérôme's portrait was finished in 1859 and exhibited at the Salon of that year. It was sold in 1861 to the Théâtre Français for 20,000 francs. Signed by the artist, it is a large life-size picture somewhat over seven feet in length and over four feet in width.[2] Gerome relied not only on his own memories of the actress but also on photographs by Nadar. In it Rachel wears an orange-red gown, with the background of the picture a greenish color, appropriate to the color associated with jealousy, one of the attributes of Melpomene, the muse of tragedy.[3] In fact, the snakes of jealousy can be seen held by the Etruscan God of Fear in the upper right hand corner of the picture. On the column next to the pedestal on which Rachel stands are the names of the tragedies by Racine in which Rachel excelled, of which *Phèdre* is the topmost one. Obliquely back of the actress a stonelike colonnade suggests both architectural forms and the curtain of the theater. It is backed by a kind of double of itself which can be partially seen in the rear of the picture, a repetition clearly presented to emphasize the ambiguity of its function as well as its clarity as a representation of classical order.

In Rachel's hand held against her body is a wand pertaining to her powers as one of the nine muses and her head is crowned with the traditional ivy wreath of Melpomene. The column to Rachel's left and our right is a rigid architectural member of the Ionic order, suggesting the type of memorial column in the Greek funerary tradition. The ambiguous architectonic character of the curtain or colonnade is complemented by the body of Rachel which is, in the emphasis Gérôme has given to the arms conceived as columns themselves, the more relaxed of the three columnar forms. Her brooding head and her glowering eyes are the only source of emotional projection, aside from the tragic mask on the plinth against which Rachel leans. The garment, the head fillet and the sandals are strictly within the canons of traditional Greek costume.

The dignity and coolness of the portrait, in spite of the rich coloration of the robe, are a visual declaration of the discipline and classical formality of Rachel's acting technique, which Madame Carré will insist on in Miriam's training throughout volume one during the period in which she is striving to become the English Rachel.

This solid concrete testimony of Rachel's existence should have contributed to James's awareness of the "melancholy" he felt because so few words remained of "the fleeting achievement of the actor—the reduction of his work to the mere name or echo—the irrevocable, the inaudible, the lost," thoughts he expressed in a letter written within a year after his novel was published.[4] The impact of the portrait helps Miriam to decide about her career, and her impression of the living and contemporary *comédienne* is presented in terms which emphasize the classical coldness and the impersonality of Rachel's artistry.

James had been well prepared to write a novel in which the spirit of Rachel would dominate and direct the whole first half of the novel, the section devoted to the evolution of crude material into trained excellence in performance. His chief source was Mrs. Fanny Kemble of the famous acting family who had seen Rachel in *Marie Stuart* by Schiller as well as in other triumphs, in London and elsewhere. She could easily be persuaded to describe "some splendid figure of the past, such as Rachel, whom she still considered the greatest dramatic genius she had ever seen except Kean, 'and he,' she said, 'was not greater,' ending: 'Rachel excelled Ristori as much in tenderness as she did in power, and as for any comparison between Rachel and her successor on the French stage, Mademoiselle Sarah Bernhardt, I do not admit any such for a moment.' "[5] Mrs. Proctor, Barry Cornwall's widow, another old friend of James, who also talked about Rachel whom she had seen on her famous tour to England, was another venerable link to a vanished past.

As James was familiar with the critical writings of Théophile Gautier, he must have been well aware of the feeling, well expressed by the author of many *Salons*, that Rachel "was born antique, and her pale flesh seemed made of Greek marble." She "was cold as were the ancients, who thought the exaggerated manifestation of sorrow. . . . indecent." Gautier's apostrophe to the Gérôme portrait must have whetted the appetite of the young James who had not the authority to ascend to the *foyer des artistes* himself: "This portrait," Gautier wrote, shows "where Rachel waits like a pythoness in the portico of a temple, drunk with fumes from the Estruscan God of Fear, and leaning with daring grace against a pedestal of her triumph in the foyer of Rachel's theatre, the Français."[6]

James had seen and had also written on Gérôme's paintings of the East in his articles on art in the 1870s, noting especially what he called the "cold literalness" of Gérôme's work. When in 1872 commenting on the famous *Combat de Coqs* he observed that "the room and accessories are as smartly antique as Gérôme alone could have made them," and that the whole thing was "painted with incomparable precision and skill." From his comment that there is "a total lack of . . . sentimental redundancy or emotional byplay," one sees how Gérôme was the ideal portraitist of an actress like Rachel whose lack of sentimentality in her version of classical tragedy has already been mentioned (PE, 51). The "cold literalness" of Gérôme in the Neo-grec phase in which Rachel was painted would suit the rendering of the actress's special talents. James clarified his judgment of Gérôme in the following way: "His pictures are for art very much what the novels of M. Gustave Flaubert are for literature," but he adds, "only decidedly inferior" (EAE, 1038).

Legends and memories of the Jewish Rachel Félix appeared in literature (even in Charlotte Brontë's *Villette*) so that James knew enough about
her life and appearance to create a heroine built in her image. Like Rachel,
Miriam Rooth is descended from Jews on her father's side with a certain
amount of suspicion cast upon her *soi-disant* aristocratic Gentile mother.
Although made more respectable than "the divine street-child" who with
her sisters "sang on the streets for coppers,"[7] her father is made an antique
dealer as well as a banker, becoming thus a translation of Jacob Félix,
Rachel's father, a peddler who sold trinkets. Rachel's extreme poverty is
translated into the shabby gentility of Mrs. Rooth's life in cheap European
boarding houses, made bearable by the free light and warmth of café life.
Rachel who was known to have studied *Phèdre* for eleven years[8] is the
model for Miriam's endless hours of study. "By careful training" Rachel's
voice "originally hard and harsh had become flexible and melodious."[9] So
Miriam's becomes tamed by Madame Carré's training. Like Rachel's in her
various portraits Miriam's "low forehead overhung her eyes; the eyes themselves in shadow, stared, splendid and cold. . . . she looked austere and
terrible." In fact, she resembles so much the dead French actress as Gérôme painted her that it "drew from Sherringham a stifled cry." He tells
Nick, "you must paint her just like that. . . . As the Tragic Muse" (TM,
1:103–4). Her eyes are "tragic," (TM, 1:110); she is "the dark-browed girl"
(TM1:112), and she is "pale and fatal" (TM, 1:115).

When Miriam tells Peter, "I want to be the English Rachel" (TM,
1:204–5), he says since she's Jewish she's "sufficiently of Rachel's tribe."
She answers, "I don't care if I'm of her tribe artistically. I'm of the family
of artists—*je me fiche* of any other! I'm in the same style as that woman—
I know it!" Peter responds, "You speak as if you had seen her," because
she so identifies with Rachel. Like her model who was almost illiterate,
Miriam "never read what he [Peter] gave her," but at the Louvre "in the
presence of famous pictures and statues she had remarkable flashes of perception" (TM, 1:226). This is to prepare us for the acuteness of Miriam's
reaction when she sees Gérôme's portrait. It is a question of "les grands
esprits se rencontrent!" a meeting of like personalities which James must
have felt was such a success in this novel that he repeated it in a varied
form in *The Wings of the Dove* when Milly sees herself in the Bronzino
portrait (WD, 1:223).

All these resemblances between James's heroine and Rachel in racial
inheritance, personal habits, family background and appearance which are
scattered throughout the first volume of *The Tragic Muse* are given their
rationale in the greenroom scene, and James carefully constructed it to
make all of Miriam's decisions take place dramatically in the physical actuality of Rachel's painted form. As Nick will find out in volume two, the great
portraits, distinguished from events, alone remain. It is "the beauty of the
great pictures" that "had known nothing of death or change" that lasts, for
"the tragic centuries had only sweetened their freshness. The same faces,

the same figures looked out at different worlds, knowing so many secrets the particular world didn't," even though "every kind of greatness had risen and passed away . . ." (TM, 2:391).

How does James convert his feeling for and knowledge about Rachel into the climax of volume one when Miriam chooses to become the English Rachel? In Chapter 2, the first of the two chapters devoted to the green-room, Peter decides to spend "an hour in the *foyer des artistes* of the great theatre," and does it through the offices of Mademoiselle Voisin, the talented *comédienne*. The importance of this hour to Miriam is indicated by James's comparing her to a "young warrior arrested by the glimpse of the battle-field" (TM, 1:353). Acutely sensitive to the environment she notices "the high decorum which had begun at the threshold—a sense of majesty in the place." The atmosphere was "the tone of an institution, a temple." Miriam is affected. "I feel them here, all, the great artists I shall never see." She becomes aware of the Gérôme portrait of Rachel over the fireplace. "Think of Rachel—look at her grand portrait there! and how she stood on these very boards and trailed over them the robes of Hermione and Phèdre" (TM, 1:355).

But it is in Chapter 21, the last of volume one, that the portrait takes over the imagination of Miriam, as it had that of James. There is a passionate scene between Peter and Miriam who accuses him of hating her and her associates. "Yes, at bottom, below your little cold taste, you *hate* us!" At this point Peter asks her to come away with him. With the "cold light still in her face" she is astounded that he wants her "to give it up" (TM, 1:261). He begs her to give up the stage as she stands within the magic circle of its reality. The adjective "cold" has been added twice in the New York Edition to emphasize the classicism exuded by the atmosphere. At this point

> She quitted her companion and stood looking at Gérôme's fine portrait of the pale Rachel invested with the antique attributes of tragedy. Peter . . . watched his friend a little, turning his eyes from her to the vivid image of the dead actress and thinking how little she suffered by the juxtaposition
>
> (TM, 1:362).

Here we are prepared for the complete identification of Miriam with Rachel. She then asks whether "that's what your cousin [Nick Dormer] had in mind" when he "offered to paint my portrait." Peter reminds her that he himself "put him up to it." She responds, "Was he thinking of this?" referring to the portrait over the fireplace. Peter's answer is important to the reader. "I doubt if he has ever seen it. I dare say *I* was." We now know surely that it was Gérôme's picture that Peter was thinking of when he urged Nick to paint Miriam as The Tragic Muse. They next discuss Nick's ability to paint, at which point Miriam "looked once more at Gérôme's picture" (TM, 1:363).

So far in chapter 20 there had been only one reference to the portrait by name. With the arrival of Mademoiselle Voisin the attention shifts from the picture to her, but the attention paid to the *comédienne* is always in terms of the impression that the portrait of Rachel has made on the two spectators and on the reader. Miriam gets the feeling of the living actress's style: "the impression of style, of refinement, of the long continuity of a tradition." She appears more as a "princess than a *cabotine*." In fact, she appears like "the charming wife of a secretary of state," which ties her to Miriam in her refinement (TM, 1:368). This figure renders metaphorically one of the elements of the choice Miriam must make in this chapter and it makes its point with irony since it is applied to an actress who could not be, because of the social chasm, what she suggests.

When in chapter 21 Miriam rejoins Peter in the foyer where they are by themselves, Miriam "moved back to the chimney-piece, from above which the cold portrait of Rachel looked down," the fourth time it is referred to, at which point Peter asks her again to "give it up and live with *me*. . . . and I'll marry you tomorrow." She mockingly answers, "This is a happy time to ask it! . . . And this is a good place!" He answers that, on the contrary, it is exactly why he does ask it; "it's a place to make one choose—it puts it all before one."

"To make *you* choose, you mean, I'm much obliged, but that's not my choice. . . ."

"You shall be anything you like except this."

"Except what I most want to be? I *am* much obliged" (TM, 1:369). We are to be visually aware that the two lovers are under the portrait of Rachel. The scene is treated as if it were a play, enacted not on stage, but in the foyer of the theater. Peter asks her, "Haven't you any gratitude?" to which she answers, "Gratitude for kindly removing the blest cup from my lips? I want to be what *she* is—I want it more than ever." He answers, "Ah what she is." This "she" is not Rachel, although it is all said under her picture. It is the living actress, Mademoiselle Voisin. But her effect is described as close to that of the Gérôme painting. "She's strange, she's mysterious. . . . She has a hard polish, an inimitable surface." Still discussing the life of Mademoiselle Voisin, Miriam "remained looking at the portrait of Rachel," the sixth mention (TM, 1:371). She continues to ask questions about the social status of Mlle. Voisin, for she wants to find out what kind of a social life is open to an actress like her. She learns that although not received by ladies she "lives in the world of art," as Rachel had before her. For Miriam that settles the question: her choice has been made. "Everything's done—I feel it tonight" (TM, 1:373). Since Peter won't "share" her life, she suggests that they "always be friends" (TM, 1:373), at which point Dashwood enters the scene and chapter, book and volume are over.

Surely the reader must be aware of the overemphasized role that the portrait of Rachel plays in this scene made up of chapters 20 and 21. Rachel's name and her presence are mentioned six times, after the one pre-

figurative mention in the preceding chapter 19. Miriam seems to be consulting the portrait of Rachel at which she looks four times to help her
make her decision. The interrelation between Miriam and the masterpiece
of art is here more clearly stated than in any other novel James ever wrote
in which he uses as a piece of strategy such an interrelation. That it should
take place in the novel in which the importance of a commitment to art is
the issue at stake is not accidental. Form here fits function absolutely.

And it was the form of the novel James took great pride in. In 1890
after the book came out James wrote to Grace Norton that he had tried so
hard to make it a success "that if it hadn't been it would have been failure
indeed" (HJL, 2:296). He thanks William for seeing "so much good" in it.
He had indicated to Robert Louis Stevenson in 1890 that he wanted him
especially to read it because he was the only "Anglo-Saxon capable of perceiving—though he may care for little else in it—how well it is written"
(HRS, 27). He also had written to Stevenson, "I have lately finished the
longest and most careful novel I have ever written" (HRS, 183). The care
is reflected in the way the Rachel element dominates the form of volume
one. Even after he had written his preface in 1908 from which almost all
critics of the book have taken his word for it that the book was not the success he had planned it to be, James gave indications that he still thought
the book good. As late as 1913 James thought of *The Tragic Muse* as one
of his five best novels, putting it into the more "advanced" list of the two
he sent to the young Stark Young as a guide to reading his fiction (HJL,
4:683).

Once the crucial role of the painting of Rachel has been established
the reader can go back and see how the entire volume has prepared both
Miriam and the reader for her great scene of decision-making, a scene
which builds up in scene 19 just before we get to the greenroom. In it we
are again in Madame Carré's rooms and Miriam is practicing her lines, only
now she is no longer a raw recruit; she has become an accomplished actress
trained in Rachel's "cold" tradition. When Peter entered "she had no emotion" in seeing him again for "the cold passion of art had perched on her
banner." The coldness of art will be repeated in the next scene when
Rachel's portrait is described (TM, 1:355). That "art is icy" was one of
James's long held opinions (HJL, 3:87). Miriam is "now the finished statue
lifted from the ground to its pedestal," a prefiguration of the way in which
Rachel stands on her pedestal in the Gérôme portrait.

After Miriam as Camille recites a few lines from Corneille's *Horace*,
one of Rachel's great roles, Madame Carré realizes her greatness and now
wants her to stay in France. "I'll teach you Phèdre," she promises her, offering her Rachel's greatest vehicle, by which she meant that Miriam
should stay on in Paris and actually become Rachel's successor. But Miriam's goal is to be the *English* Rachel. She wishes to apply the example of
Rachel to Shakespeare's tragedies, not to Racine's. About her own performance of Constance in *King John* Miriam said, "I didn't miss a vibration of

my voice, a fold of my robe," thus testifying to her achieved resemblance to Rachel whose magic was rooted in her extraordinary voice and in her classical robes remembered in the portrait. Miriam's final triumph as Juliet is probably a combination of the achievement of Rachel with that of Mrs. Kemble who as a young actress was known for her extraordinary Juliet. This use of Mrs. Kemble as a model will reveal itself in volume two, where Miriam truly becomes the English Rachel.

In this chapter the facade of the Madeleine is brought in as an example of "the falsely classical," reenforcing the way it had been introduced earlier when Julia Dallow who had no feeling for art sat opposite the neoclassical church with Nick. No, Miriam should not want to look like "the portico of the Madeleine when it's draped for a funeral" (TM, 1:346). Madame Carré says this because she thinks that Miriam is "pure tragedy" or she's "nothing," and the neoclassical Madeleine produces from a funeral held on its premises only a travesty of tragedy. At this declaration by her teacher Miriam breaks out with "one of the speeches of Racine's Phaedra." Basil Dashwood then predicts: "You'll be the English Rachel" (TM, 1:346). Madame Carré believes "an English Rachel" is a contradiction in terms, but her objection has the function of emphasizing further Rachel's influence, preparing the reader for the next chapter where the Gérôme portrait of the actress will dominate the scene.

But even before that Rachel has been planted in the novel as Miriam's role-model through a similarity in her looks and her background. Early in chapter 4 where Miriam is described and where her Jewish blood is remarked on, Peter says, "It is as good as Rachel Félix," well-known for her Jewish origins. After that we get another concentration of Rachel associations made in regard to Miriam in chapter 7. Miriam is speaking before Madame Carré and is described very much as Rachel appears in her portrait. Rachel had been described as having "great deep-set eyes," and Queen Victoria had reported that she was "striking-looking"[10] Like her Miriam is given a "strange strong tragic beauty." Clothed in a "dress which fell in straight folds" like that worn by Rachel in the Gérôme portrait, she is seen by Peter "as an incarnation the vividness of which drew from [him] a stifled cry." For it is as Rachel that he sees her. "You must paint her just like that," he tells Nick, "As the Tragic Muse." We learn later in the greenroom scene that Peter was indeed thinking of the Gérôme portrait when he made this remark.

Toward the end of chapter 7 the name of Rachel comes up again when Madame Carré claims that for the actress natural gifts were not as important as hard work. Peter cites "the great Rachel as a player whose natural endowment was rich," but Madame Carré claims it was her drudgery that gave success to that endowment. Rachel's name occurs here four times in rapid succession, which makes a total of a dozen times that Rachel is mentioned in volume one. These allusions to Rachel's attributes and Peter's awareness of Miriam's resemblance to Gérôme's portrait clearly build up to

Miriam's confrontation with that portrait. At that point her model and her life-goal coalesce.

In volume two there is only one mention of Rachel, for now Miriam has finally become not only the English Rachel, but herself. Like Rachel, she has taken on the single appelative: one calls her Miriam, Peter declares, "as one says 'Rachel' of her great predecessor" (TM, 1:297). For Miriam has now developed into an original modern British actress. Volume two concentrates on the creation of a portrait of "the modern personage." A new Tragic Muse by Nick Dormer, an English painter, is going to be a contemporary version of the theme in a very different picture from the French Gérôme picture of Rachel. The master to whom Nick will owe something is Sir Joshua Reynolds (whose Tragic Muse was a portrait of Mrs. Siddons, the great English actress who is mentioned once in the novel) even though the name of Sir Joshua is only inserted in the New York Edition when Gabriel Nash makes a joke about Nick finally becoming president of the Royal Academy. "You'll become another Sir Joshua, a mere P. R. A.!" (TM, 2:194). Yet there is no resemblance between Miriam's pose and that of Mrs. Siddons.

In his preface, James states that it was Miriam who gave him his "lucky title" as well as his "precious unity" and as a link to Nick's tale she "*is* central to analysis . . . a centre in virtue of the fact that the whole thing has visibly, from the first, to get itself done in dramatic, or at least in scenic conditions" (FOP, 1112). How important it is that the scene here is mounted within the interior of the theater where Rachel acted is emphasized by James's directions to Coburn, the photographer who made the frontispieces for the New York edition. He was instructed to use a photograph of the colonnaded facade of the Théâtre Français for volume one of *The Tragic Muse*. "I yearn for some aspect of the Théâtre Français for possible use in *The Tragic Muse* but something of course of the same transfigured nature: some ingenuously hit-upon angle or presentment of its rather majestic big square mass and classic colonnade" (HJL, 4:417). This might explain why Mme. Carré has a name that means "square," a verbal play to emphasize the classical elements of her tutelage and her continuation of the traditions of the Théâtre Français.

Even for volume two (where the parallel with Rachel is no longer maintained because the point has been made and Miriam is now the English Rachel) the frontispiece chosen by James was the gate and classical columns of a house in Saint John's Wood, where Miriam, the rising young actress who has conquered London, now lives. The classical columns pertain to her discipline learned in France and transpose the French theatre with its classical greenroom to Miriam's quarters. Saint John's Wood was a rich locus for James, for as a youth he had heard Mrs. Kemble read from Shakespeare there (EAE, 1078). His close friendship with her and her example undoubtedly reenforced his choice of location. In presenting Miriam as a developed actress James has borrowed from the life of the English actress of distinction he knew best. Mrs. Fanny Kemble was a link to her aunt, Mrs. Siddons, who "had sat to Sir Thomas Lawrence, . . . and Sir Thomas Lawrence was in love with Sir Joshua's Tragic Muse," (EAE, 1074) as James wrote in his memorial essay to Mrs. Kemble three years after *The Tragic Muse* appeared. In contrast to Rachel, Mrs. Kemble had been eminently respectable, and never "savored" of the "shop" (EAE, 1076). It was "the complete absence of any touch of Bohemianism in her personal situation" that made her for James, "a very original figure in the history of the stage" (EAE, 1071), and Miriam's respectability established for her by her mother derives from Mrs. Kemble's example. Just as she had been "a tremendous success as Juliet in 1829" when only nineteen years old, so Miriam triumphs as Juliet as volume two ends (EAE, 1075).

In the second volume of *The Tragic Muse* the great scenes take place in Nick's studio where the painter repeats the situation of Sir Joshua's painting of the portrait of Mrs. Siddons as The Tragic Muse by painting Miriam as The Tragic Muse. In this sense the English Rachel lives to sit for her portrait as Mrs. Siddons had, whereas the French *tragédienne* had had to be reconstructed by Gérôme after her death. Nick makes two versions of her portrait, in a sense imitating the two versions of Sir Joshua's Tragic Muse.[11] Volume 2 is a tribute to London as volume 1 is to Paris and ends with the curtain falling on an English stage, an English play and an English actress.

The link that connects the studio scene to the green-room scene is Nick's portrait of Miriam who will join Rachel (her predecessor in a profession distinguished for the temporary character of its presentations) in a perpetuity only made possible by a practitioner of the art of portraiture designed to preserve beauty. Her portraits by Nick Dormer are destined "to prevail and survive and testify" (TM, 2:390), as Gérôme's portrait of Rachel had survived to present the dead actress to the living one. Basil Dashwood in the tradition of Mrs. Siddon's actor-manager husband decides that "the right place for the two portraits" was "the vestibule of the theatre," which he has taken for Miriam "where everyone . . . would see them. . . ." (TM, 2:387). For Miriam's portraits to hang on the walls of the greenroom equivalent of her own theater would be the act of completion of her successful development into the English Rachel; Nick will have conferred on her through the art of portraiture the same kind of immortality that Gérôme conferred on Rachel.

The curtain falls, too, on the problems of the troubled young man, Peter, and his sister, Julia. Miriam's performance of Juliet is so "sublime" that "the great trouble" of Peter's "infatuation" for Miriam is made to subside because of the purifying effect of her great tragic performance. He felt "recalled to the real by . . . the supreme exhibition itself," that of art (TM, 2:438). Julia gets over her unjustified panic about Miriam and finally has herself successfully painted by Nick. The curtain falls on the performance and on the novel which is a bravura performance in itself. It encompasses the arts of the act, the picture, and the word. The last two arts preserve the first.

## Notes

1. The Théâtre Français is also known as the Comédie Française.

2. The picture measures $218 \times 137$ centimeters ($85.75 \times 54$ inches).

3. Gerald M. Ackerman supplied me with these facts from his forthcoming book: *The Life and Works of Jean-Léon Gérôme* (London: Sotheby's/ACR, 1986).

4. Unpublished Henry James Letter, signed and dated 1 October 1891 to Mr. Pemberton thanking him for a copy of a biography of Sothern (author's collection).

5. Margaret Armstrong, *Fanny Kemble: A Passionate Victorian* (New York: Macmillan, 1938), 370.

6. Gérôme: *A Collection of the Works of J. L. Gérôme in One Hundred Photographs*, ed. Edward Strahan, vol. 2 (Samuel L. Hall, 1881). Unpaginated.

7. Joanna Richardson, *Rachel* (London: Max Reinhardt, 1956), 15.

8. Ibid., 60.

9. *Encyclopeadia Brittanica*, 11th edition.

10. Richardson, *Rachel*, 40.

11. The earlier version, signed and dated 1784, is in the Huntington Library, San Marino, California. The replica was painted in 1789 and is in Dulwich College, London. During the Nineteenth Century the Huntington portrait had been in the collection of the Duke of Westminster where it is possible Henry James might have seen it. (Robert R. Wark, *Ten British Pictures* [San Marino: the Huntington Library, 1971], 57).

## Key to Works by Henry James:

| | |
|---|---|
| EAE | *Henry James: Literary Criticism: Essays on Literature; American Writers; English Writers* (New York: The Library of America, 1984). |
| FOP | *Henry James: Literary Criticism; French Writers, Other European Writers, The Prefaces to the New York Edition* (New York: *The Library of America*, 1984). |
| HJL 3 | *Henry James Letters*, ed. Leon Edel. Vol. 3, 1883–1895 (Cambridge: Harvard University Press, 1980). |
| HRS | *Henry James and Robert Louis Stevenson*, ed. Janet Adam Smith (London: Rupert Hart-Davis, 1948). |
| NB | *Notebooks of Henry James*, ed. F. O. Matthiessen and Kenneth B. Murdoch (New York: Oxford University Press, 1947). |
| SA | *The Scenic Art*, ed. Allan Wade (New Bruswick: Rutgers University Press, 1948). |
| TM 1 & 2 | *The Tragic Muse* (New York: Charles Scribner's Sons, 1908). |
| WD 1 | *The Wings of the Dove* (New York: Charles Scribner's Sons, 1909). |

# INDEX

199

**DATE DUE**